*Ṭibb al Qulūb Series - The Medicine of the* [partially covered by label]



# WINNING THE WAR WITHIN

## THE HEART, THE SELF, ANGELS & DEVILS

**Selections from the Works of:**

Ibn Taymiyyah (d. 728 AH رَحِمَهُ ٱللَّهُ), Ibn Qayyim (d. 751 AH رَحِمَهُ ٱللَّهُ)
and Others

**Selected & Compiled by:**

Abū Suhailah 'Umar Quinn

ISBN: 9798852579713 (Paperback)

First printing edition Muḥarram 1445 / July 2023.

Al Ḥasan al Baṣrī (رَحِمَهُ ٱللَّهُ) said:[1]

«حَادِثُوا هَذِهِ الْقُلُوبَ بِذِكْرِ اللَّهِ، فَإِنَّهَا سَرِيعَةُ الدُّثُورِ، وَاقْدَعُوا هَذِهِ الْأَنْفُسَ فَإِنَّهَا طُلَعَةٌ، وَإِنَّمَا تَنْزِعُ إِلَى شَرِّ غَايَةٍ، وَإِنَّكُمْ إِنْ تُطِيعُوهَا فِي كُلِّ مَا تَنْزِعُ إِلَيْهِ، لَا تُبْقِي لَكُمْ شَيْئًا»

"Brighten these hearts with remembrance of Allah, for indeed they quickly tarnish. Restrain these souls, for they are excessively curious and fully inclined towards extreme evil. If you obey them in everything they aspire to, they will leave nothing for you."

---

[1] Reported by Ibn al Mubārak in *al-Zuhd*, Ibn Abīl-Dunyā in *Muḥāsabah al-Nafs*. See, for uncommon words, *Gharīb al Ḥadīth* by Abu 'Ubayd al Qāsim b. Salām and *al Kāmil* by al Mubarrad.

فهرس

# TABLE OF CONTENTS

مقدمة

# INTRODUCTION

بسم الله الرحمن الرحيم

This book is the first in a series about "*Ṭibb al Qulūb*," the *"medicine of the hearts."* This series, Allah willing, aims to collect invaluable selections from the classical writings of the scholars about the subject matter of purifying and rectifying the heart, disciplining and training the self, reforming and refining moral character, and safeguarding the individual and the society from *Shayṭān* and his traps. Imām Ibn al Qayyim (d. 751 AH رحمه الله) was arguably the most prolific to ever write exhaustively on the subject, using the *Qur'ān*, the *Sunnah*, the *tafsīr* transmitted from the *Salaf*, and the insights of generations of scholars preceding him in every field to outline the framework of such topics masterfully and then explain their finer details and complexities. He both simplifies and elaborates in greater detail much of what was taught on such topics by Shaykh al Islām Ibn Taymiyyah (d. 728 AH رحمه الله). May Allah (جل وعلا) shower him with mercy and grant him a spacious abode in the loftiest parts of Paradise.

There is so much to learn about Islām and its branches of knowledge, yet often the purpose of this learning — to rectify the heart — is neglected. Imām Aḥmad b. Ḥanbal (d.

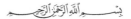

241 AH رَحِمَهُ ٱللَّهُ) was once asked a question by Ibrāhīm b. Ja'far (رَحِمَهُ ٱللَّهُ), to which he famously responded:[2]

"انْظُرْ مَا هُوَ أَصْلَحُ لِقَلْبِكَ فَافْعَلْهُ".

"Look at what is best for your heart and do it."

Everything of knowledge and implementation in the religion is medicine for the hearts and a cure for societal ills. So this subject is the ultimate objective for the seeker of knowledge.

Shaykh al Islām Ibn Taymiyyah (d. 728 AH رَحِمَهُ ٱللَّهُ) said:[3]

"وَالشَّرْعُ طِبُّ الْقُلُوبِ ، وَالْأَنْبِيَاءُ أَطِبَّاءُ الْقُلُوبِ وَالْأَدْيَانِ".

"The religion is the medicine of the hearts and the Prophets (عَلَيْهِمُ ٱلسَّلَامُ) are the doctors for the hearts and religious matters."

Imām Ibn al Qayyim (d. 751 AH رَحِمَهُ ٱللَّهُ) said:[4]

"فَأَمْرَاضُ الْقُلُوبِ أَصْعَبُ مِنْ أَمْرَاضِ الْأَبْدَانِ؛ لِأَنَّ غَايَةَ مَرَضِ الْبَدَنِ أَنْ يُفْضِيَ بِصَاحِبِهِ إِلَى الْمَوْتِ، وَأَمَّا مَرَضُ الْقَلْبِ فَيُفْضِي بِصَاحِبِهِ إِلَى الشَّقَاءِ الْأَبَدِيِّ، وَلَا شِفَاءَ لِهَذَا الْمَرَضِ إِلَّا بِالْعِلْمِ.

"The diseases of the hearts are more difficult than the diseases of the bodies. This is because the ultimate consequence of a bodily illness is death, whereas the illness of the heart leads its possessor to eternal misery. There is no cure for this disease except through knowledge.

وَلِهَذَا سَمَّى اللَّهُ تَعَالَى كِتَابَهُ شِفَاءً لِأَمْرَاضِ الصُّدُورِ، قَالَ تَعَالَى:

---

[2] Ṭabaqāt al Ḥanābilah (1/237).

[3] *Majmū' al Fatāwā* (34/210).

[4] *Miftāḥ Dār al-Sa'ādah* (1/306-307) the 87th virtue of knowledge.

For this reason, Allah has called His book a healing for the diseases of the chests. He (سُبْحَانَهُ وَتَعَالَىٰ) says:[5]

﴿ يَاأَيُّهَا النَّاسُ قَدْ جَاءَتْكُم مَّوْعِظَةٌ مِّن رَّبِّكُمْ وَشِفَاءٌ لِّمَا فِي الصُّدُورِ وَهُدًى وَرَحْمَةٌ لِّلْمُؤْمِنِينَ ﴾

**"O mankind, there has come to you an admonition from your Lord and healing for what is in the breasts and guidance and mercy for the believers"**

وَلِهَذَا السَّبَبِ نِسْبَةُ الْعُلَمَاءِ إِلَى الْقُلُوبِ كَنِسْبَةِ الْأَطِبَّاءِ إِلَى الْأَبْدَانِ، وَمَا يُقَالُ لِلْعُلَمَاءِ: «أَطِبَّاءُ الْقُلُوبِ» فَهُوَ لِقَدْرٍ مَا جَامِعٍ بَيْنَهُمَا، وَإِلَّا فَالْأَمْرُ أَعْظَمُ مِنْ ذَلِكَ؛ فَإِنَّ كَثِيرًا مِنَ الْأُمَمِ يَسْتَغْنُونَ عَنِ الْأَطِبَّاءِ، وَلَا يُوجَدُ الْأَطِبَّاءُ إِلَّا فِي الْيَسِيرِ مِنَ الْبِلَادِ،

Due to this, the relation of scholars to the hearts is like the relation of doctors to the bodies. And when the scholars are referred to as "doctors of the hearts," it is because there is some common ground between them. However, the matter is even greater than that. Indeed, many nations can do without doctors, and doctors are only found in a few regions.

وَقَدْ يَعِيشُ الرَّجُلُ عُمْرَهُ أَوْ بُرْهَةً مِنْهُ لَا يَحْتَاجُ إِلَى طَبِيبٍ، وَأَمَّا الْعُلَمَاءُ بِاللَّهِ وَأَمْرِهِ فَهُمْ حَيَاةُ الْوُجُودِ وَرُوحُهُ، وَلَا يُسْتَغْنَى عَنْهُمْ طَرْفَةَ عَيْنٍ.

A person may live their entire life or a significant portion without needing a doctor. But as for the scholars who possess knowledge of Allah and His commandments, they are the life and soul of existence, and one cannot do without them even for a moment.

فَحَاجَةُ الْقَلْبِ إِلَى الْعِلْمِ لَيْسَتْ كَالْحَاجَةِ إِلَى التَّنَفُّسِ فِي الْهَوَاءِ، بَلْ أَعْظَمُ."

The heart's need for knowledge is not like the need of breathing for air; rather it is greater."

---

[5] Yūnus (10): 57.

Administering the medicine of the hearts was the mission and message of the Prophets and Messengers (عَلَيْهِمُ السَّلَامُ). Ibn al Qayyim (رَحِمَهُ ٱللَّهُ) wrote:[6]

"فَأَمَّا طِبُّ الْقُلُوبِ، فَمُسَلَّمٌ إِلَى الرُّسُلِ - صَلَوَاتُ اللَّهِ وَسَلَامُهُ عَلَيْهِمْ-، وَلَا سَبِيلَ إِلَى حُصُولِهِ إِلَّا مِنْ جِهَتِهِمْ وَعَلَى أَيْدِيهِمْ،

"As for the medicine of the hearts, it is entrusted to the prophets (عَلَيْهِمُ السَّلَامُ) and there is no way to achieve it except through them and by their hands.

فَإِنَّ صَلَاحَ الْقُلُوبِ أَنْ تَكُونَ عَارِفَةً بِرَبِّهَا، وَفَاطِرِهَا، وَبِأَسْمَائِهِ، وَصِفَاتِهِ، وَأَفْعَالِهِ، وَأَحْكَامِهِ، وَأَنْ تَكُونَ مُؤْثِرَةً لِمَرْضَاتِهِ وَمَحَابِّهِ، مُتَجَنِّبَةً لِمَنَاهِيهِ وَمَسَاخِطِهِ، وَلَا صِحَّةَ لَهَا وَلَا حَيَاةَ الْبَتَّةَ إِلَّا بِذَلِكَ، وَلَا سَبِيلَ إِلَى تَلَقِّيهِ إِلَّا مِنْ جِهَةِ الرُّسُلِ (عَلَيْهِمُ السَّلَامُ)،

Indeed, the rectitude of the heart is to know its Lord and Creator, His names, His attributes, His actions, and His rulings, and to prioritize His pleasure and love, avoiding His prohibitions and disapprovals. There is no health or life for it at all except through this, and there is no way to receive this except from the direction of the prophets.

وَمَا يُظَنُّ مِنْ حُصُولِ صِحَّةِ الْقَلْبِ بِدُونِ اتِّبَاعِهِمْ، فَغَلَطٌ مِمَّنْ يَظُنُّ ذَلِكَ، وَإِنَّمَا ذَلِكَ حَيَاةُ نَفْسِهِ الْبَهِيمِيَّةِ الشَّهْوَانِيَّةِ، وَصِحَّتُهَا وَقُوَّتُهَا، وَحَيَاةُ قَلْبِهِ وَصِحَّتُهُ، وَقُوَّتُهُ عَنْ ذَلِكَ بِمَعْزِلٍ، وَمَنْ لَمْ يُمَيِّزْ بَيْنَ هَذَا وَهَذَا فَلْيَبْكِ عَلَى حَيَاةِ قَلْبِهِ، فَإِنَّهُ مِنَ الْأَمْوَاتِ، وَعَلَى نُورِهِ، فَإِنَّهُ مُنْغَمِسٌ فِي بِحَارِ الظُّلُمَاتِ".

Presuming a healthy heart can be achieved without following them is a blunder from those who imagine such. That is only the life, health and strength of one's animalistic lustful self. The life of his heart, its health, and its strength are something apart from this.

[6] *Zād al Ma'ād.*

Whoever cannot distinguish between this and that should weep for the life of his heart, for he is among the dead, and for its light, for he is immersed in the seas of darkness."

---

Elsewhere, Ibn al Qayyim (رَحِمَهُ ٱللَّهُ) highlights how any other approach than that of the Prophets is ineffectual and will have the opposite outcome to what was intended. He said:[7]

"وَتَزْكِيَةُ النُّفُوسِ أَصْعَبُ مِنْ عِلاجِ الْأَبْدَانِ وَأَشَدُّ، فَمَنْ زَكَّى نَفْسَهُ بِالرِّيَاضَةِ وَالْمُجَاهَدَةِ وَالْخَلْوَةِ الَّتِي لَمْ يَجِئْ بِهَا الرُّسُلُ فَهُوَ كَالْمَرِيضِ الَّذِي يُعَالِجُ نَفْسَهُ بِرَأْيِهِ دُونَ مَعْرِفَةِ الطَّبِيبِ.

"The purification of souls is more difficult and intense than treating bodily sicknesses. Whoever purifies themselves through a way of self-discipline, striving, and seclusion that is not brought by the messengers is like a patient who treats themselves based on their own opinion without a physician's knowledge.

فَالرُّسُلُ أَطِبَّاءُ الْقُلُوبِ، فَلَا سَبِيلَ إِلَى صَلَاحِهَا وَتَزْكِيَتِهَا إِلَّا عَلَى أَيْدِيهِمْ، وَبِمَحْضِ الِانْقِيَادِ وَالتَّسْلِيمِ لَهُمْ. وَاللَّهُ الْمُسْتَعَانُ".

The messengers are the physicians of the hearts, and there is no way to rectify and purify them except through their guidance and complete submission to them. And Allah is the One ultimately sought for help."

---

Elsewhere, Ibn al Qayyim (رَحِمَهُ ٱللَّهُ) provides a common example of this. He discusses why some of the early *Salaf* cautioned against singing and music, stating that it plants

[7] Madārij al-Sālikīn (3/46).

hypocrisy in the heart; despite this warning many mystics later popularized singing and music as spiritual remedies and a means to experience ecstasy. He says:[8]

"هَذَا مِنْ أَدَلِّ شَيْءٍ عَلَى فِقْهِ الصَّحَابَةِ فِي أَحْوَالِ الْقُلُوبِ وَأَعْمَالِهَا، وَمَعْرِفَتِهِمْ بِأَدْوِيَتِهَا وَأَدْوَائِهَا، وَأَنَّهُمْ هُمْ أَطِبَّاءُ الْقُلُوبِ، دُونَ الْمُنْحَرِفِينَ عَنْ طَرِيقَتِهِمْ، الَّذِينَ دَاوَوْا أَمْرَاضَ الْقُلُوبِ بِأَعْظَمِ أَدْوَائِهَا، فَكَانُوا كَالْمُدَاوِي مِنَ السَّقَمِ بِالسُّمِّ الْقَاتِلِ،

This is from the clearest evidence of the understanding of the Companions (رَضِيَ ٱللَّهُ عَنْهُمْ) regarding the conditions and actions of the hearts and their knowledge of their ailments and remedies. They were indeed the physicians of the hearts, distinct from those who deviated from their path and treated the sicknesses of the hearts with their most severe diseases, similar to those who attempt to cure a disease with a deadly poison.

وَهَكَذَا وَاللَّهِ فَعَلُوا بِكَثِيرٍ مِنَ الْأَدْوِيَةِ الَّتِي رَكَّبُوهَا أَوْ بِأَكْثَرِهَا، فَاتَّفَقَ قِلَّةُ الْأَطِبَّاءِ، وَكَثْرَةُ الْمَرْضَى، وَحُدُوثُ أَمْرَاضٍ مُزْمِنَةٍ لَمْ تَكُنْ فِي السَّلَفِ، وَالْعُدُولُ عَنِ الدَّوَاءِ النَّافِعِ الَّذِي رَكَّبَهُ الشَّارِعُ، وَمَيْلُ الْمَرِيضِ إِلَى مَا يُقَوِّي مَادَّةَ الْمَرَضِ، فَاشْتَدَّ الْمَرَضُ وَتَفَاقَمَ الْأَمْرُ،

And by Allah, they (those who deviated from the way of the Companions) did the same with many or most of the remedies they concocted. The shortage of genuine doctors, the surplus of sick individuals, the rise of chronic conditions that were not prevalent in previous generations, the neglect of beneficial treatments recommended by the Sharī'ah, and the preference of patients towards actions that worsen their illness - all of these elements have led to the intensification and worsening of illnesses.

وَامْتَلَأَتْ الدُّورُ وَالطُّرُقَاتُ وَالْأَسْوَاقُ مِنَ الْمَرْضَى، قَامَ كُلُّ جَاهِلٍ يُطَبِّبُ النَّاسَ".

---

[8] Ighāthah al-Lahfān (1/439).

Consequently, hospitals, streets, and markets filled with patients, and every ignorant person started attempting to treat people."

---

The book before you outlines "*The War Within,*" which is a reference to the never-ending conflict in every human being between their intellect and desires, the faith in their heart and the insistence of the inner self, the angel with them and the *Shayṭān* — a conflict between high aspiration for the loftiest achievements and undignified urges in pursuit of quick satisfaction at the expense of everlasting reward.

I have compiled herein four chapters and a conclusion. The **first chapter** describes *the three types of heart* — healthy, sick, and dead — and the corresponding *three states of the soul or inner-self*: one at peace, one insistent upon commanding evil, and a state of self-reproaching and internal rebuke.

The **second chapter** outlines the necessity of strengthening the heart with *emān* in all facets so that the self and the *Shayṭān* do not destroy the heart.

The **third chapter** highlights how the self sickens the heart and empowers the *Shayṭān* to destroy it.

The **fourth chapter** outlines in greater detail the inner conflict between the heart, the self, and *Shayṭān,* and offers direly needed insights on how to be vigilant and proactive during this life-long conflict.

The **conclusion** is an important extension of the fourth chapter. It discusses how the person's inner-self entrances them, warping their perception of reality and turning their natural potential for good into destructive ideas and traits.

I ask Allah to make this small effort beneficial for its compiler and readers, and to forgive me, you, and all Muslims, for our shortcomings and sins.

Abu Suhailah Umar Quinn | 2 Dhul Ḥijjah, 1444 | Maryland, USA.

# Chapter 1

## 3 Types of Heart & 3 Types of the Self

***The Heart's Function & Disfunction***

***The Heart's Intrinsic Instability***

***The Heart's Firmness or Flimsiness During the Tempests of Trials***

***Two Hearts, Two Thrones***

***3 Types of the Inner-Self***

# 1. Three Types of Heart & Three Types of the Self

## The Heart's Function & Disfunction

Ibn al Qayyim (رَحِمَهُ ٱللَّهُ) explains in detail what makes hearts alive, sick or dead. He writes:[9]

كُلُّ عُضْوٍ مِنْ أَعْضَاءِ الْبَدَنِ خُلِقَ لِفِعْلٍ خَاصٍّ بِهِ، كَمَالُهُ فِي حُصُولِ ذَلِكَ الْفِعْلِ مِنْهُ، وَمَرَضُهُ أَنْ يَتَعَذَّرَ عَلَيْهِ الْفِعْلُ الَّذِي خُلِقَ لَهُ، حَتَّى لَا يَصْدُرَ مِنْهُ، أَوْ يَصْدُرَ مَعَ نَوْعٍ مِنَ الِاضْطِرَابِ.

"Every part of the body was created for a specific function. Its perfection lies in performing that function, and its illness lies in being unable to perform the function it was created for so that it either cannot perform it at all or does so with some disruption.

فَمَرَضُ الْيَدِ: أَنْ يَتَعَذَّرَ عَلَيْهَا الْبَطْشُ، وَمَرَضُ الْعَيْنِ: أَنْ يَتَعَذَّرَ عَلَيْهَا النَّظَرُ وَالرُّؤْيَةُ، وَمَرَضُ اللِّسَانِ: أَنْ يَتَعَذَّرَ عَلَيْهِ النُّطْقُ، وَمَرَضُ الْبَدَنِ: أَنْ يَتَعَذَّرَ عَلَيْهِ حَرَكَتُهُ الطَّبِيعِيَّةُ أَوْ يَضْعُفَ،

Thus, the illness of the hand is to be unable to strike, the illness of the eye is to be unable to see, the illness of the tongue is to be unable to speak and the illness of the body is to be either unable to move naturally or to do so with weakness.

وَمَرَضُ الْقَلْبِ: أَنْ يَتَعَذَّرَ عَلَيْهِ مَا خُلِقَ لَهُ مِنَ الْمَعْرِفَةِ بِاللَّهِ، وَمَحَبَّتِهِ، وَالشَّوْقِ إِلَى لِقَائِهِ، وَالْإِنَابَةِ إِلَيْهِ، وَإِيثَارِ ذَلِكَ عَلَى كُلِّ شَهْوَةٍ.

---

[9] Ighāthah al-Lahfān, chapter 10.

**And the disease of the heart is to be unable to do what it was created for: knowing Allah, loving Him, longing for His meeting, turning to Him, and preferring that over all desires.**

فَلَوْ عَرَفَ الْعَبْدُ كُلَّ شَيْءٍ وَلَمْ يَعْرِفْ رَبَّهُ فَكَأَنَّهُ لَمْ يَعْرِفْ شَيْئًا، وَلَوْ نَالَ كُلَّ حَظٍّ مِنْ حَظُوظِ الدُّنْيَا وَلَذَّاتِهَا وَشَهْوَاتِهَا، وَلَمْ يَظْفَرْ بِمَحَبَّةِ اللَّهِ وَالشَّوْقِ إِلَيْهِ وَالْأُنْسِ بِهِ، فَكَأَنَّهُ لَمْ يَظْفَرْ بِلَذَّةٍ وَلَا نَعِيمٍ وَلَا قُرَّةِ عَيْنٍ،

If a servant knew everything but did not know his Lord, it would be as if he knew nothing. And if he attained every share of the world's pleasures, desires, and indulgences but did not secure the love of Allah, longing for Him and finding comfort in Him, it would be as if he had not achieved any pleasure, bliss, or coolness of the eye.

بَلْ إِذَا كَانَ الْقَلْبُ خَالِيًا مِنْ ذَلِكَ عَادَتْ تِلْكَ الْحَظُوظُ وَاللَّذَّاتُ عَذَابًا لَهُ وَلَا بُدَّ، فَيَصِيرُ مُعَذَّبًا بِنَفْسِ مَا كَانَ مُنَعَّمًا بِهِ مِنْ جِهَتَيْنِ: مِنْ جِهَةِ حَسْرَةِ فَوْتِهِ، وَأَنَّهُ حِيلَ بَيْنَهُ وَبَيْنَهُ، مَعَ شِدَّةِ تَعَلُّقِ رُوحِهِ بِهِ، وَمِنْ جِهَةِ فَوْتِ مَا هُوَ خَيْرٌ لَهُ وَأَنْفَعُ وَأَدْوَمُ حَيْثُ لَمْ يَحْصُلْ لَهُ، فَالْمَحْبُوبُ الْحَاصِلُ فَاتَ، وَالْمَحْبُوبُ الْأَعْظَمُ لَمْ يَظْفَرْ بِهِ.

In fact, if the heart is empty of these, those pleasures inevitably become a torment for him. He becomes tormented by the same things that once gave him pleasure in two ways: firstly, by the regret of missing out and the barrier placed between him and it, despite his soul's severe attachment to it, and secondly, by missing out on what is better, more beneficial and enduring for him, because he did not achieve it. The lesser beloved has gone, and he did not secure the greater beloved.

وَكُلُّ مَنْ عَرَفَ اللَّهَ أَحَبَّهُ وَأَخْلَصَ الْعِبَادَةَ لَهُ وَلَا بُدَّ، وَلَمْ يُؤْثِرْ عَلَيْهِ شَيْئًا مِنَ الْمَحْبُوبَاتِ فَمَنْ آثَرَ عَلَيْهِ شَيْئًا مِنَ الْمَحْبُوبَاتِ؛ فَقَلْبُهُ مَرِيضٌ، كَمَا أَنَّ الْمَعِدَةَ إِذَا اعْتَادَتْ أَكْلَ الْخَبِيثِ، وَآثَرَتْهُ عَلَى الطَّيِّبِ سَقَطَتْ عَنْهَا شَهْوَةُ الطَّيِّبِ، وَتَعَوَّضَتْ بِمَحَبَّةِ غَيْرِهِ.

Everyone who knows Allah loves Him and dedicates their worship sincerely to Him, without any doubt. They don't prefer anything whatsoever that is beloved over Him. Anyone who prefers anything beloved over Him has a sick heart. Just as when the stomach gets used to eating what is impure, preferring it over what is pure, it loses its desire for the pure and is replaced with the love for something else.

وَقَدْ يَمْرُضُ الْقَلْبُ وَيَشْتَدُّ مَرَضُهُ، وَلَا يَعْرِفُ بِهِ صَاحِبُهُ؛ لِاشْتِغَالِهِ وَانْصِرَافِهِ عَنْ مَعْرِفَةِ صِحَّتِهِ وَأَسْبَابِهَا، بَلْ قَدْ يَمُوتُ وَصَاحِبُهُ لَا يَشْعُرُ بِمَوْتِهِ،

The heart may become ill, and its illness may intensify, yet its owner may not recognize it due to being preoccupied and diverting from understanding its health and causes. It might even die, while its owner doesn't realize its death.

وَعَلَامَةُ ذَلِكَ أَنَّهُ لَا تُؤْلِمُهُ جِرَاحَاتُ الْقَبَائِحِ، وَلَا يُوجِعُهُ جَهْلُهُ بِالْحَقِّ وَعَقَائِدُهُ الْبَاطِلَةُ؛ فَإِنَّ الْقَلْبَ إِذَا كَانَ فِيهِ حَيَاةٌ يَأْلَمُ بِوُرُودِ الْقَبِيحِ عَلَيْهِ، وَيَأْلَمُ بِجَهْلِهِ بِالْحَقِّ بِحَسَبِ حَيَاتِهِ، وَ"مَا لِجُرْحٍ بِمَيِّتٍ إِيلَامُ"

The sign of this is that the owner is not pained by the wounds of vileness nor anguished by ignorance of the truth and false beliefs. For if there is life in the heart, it feels pain when ugliness encroaches upon it and pain due to its ignorance of the truth according to its liveliness. As the saying goes, "A wound does not cause pain to the dead."

وَقَدْ يَشْعُرُ بِمَرَضِهِ، وَلَكِنْ يَشْتَدُّ عَلَيْهِ تَحَمُّلُ مَرَارَةِ الدَّوَاءِ وَالصَّبْرُ عَلَيْهَا؛ فَيُؤْثِرُ بَقَاءَ أَلَمِهِ عَلَى مَشَقَّةِ الدَّوَاءِ، فَإِنَّ دَوَاءَهُ فِي مُخَالَفَةِ الْهَوَى، وَذَلِكَ أَصْعَبُ شَيْءٍ عَلَى النَّفْسِ، وَلَيْسَ لَهَا أَنْفَعُ مِنْهُ."

The owner may be aware of the illness of the heart, but the burden of enduring the bitterness of the cure and having patience with it may become too heavy. Therefore, the owner might prefer to keep the pain rather than suffer the hardship of the cure.

Indeed, the cure lies in going against one's desires, which is the most difficult thing for the soul, yet there is nothing more beneficial for it."

## SICK & DEAD HEARTS

Elsewhere, he (رَحِمَهُ ٱللَّهُ) explains that sick and dead hearts possess attributes opposite to those belonging to living and healthy ones; he writes:[10]

"وَالْقَلْبُ الثَّانِي ضِدُّ هَذَا، وَهُوَ الْقَلْبُ الْمَيِّتُ الَّذِي لَا حَيَاةَ بِهِ، فَهُوَ لَا يَعْرِفُ رَبَّهُ، وَلَا يَعْبُدُهُ بِأَمْرِهِ وَمَا يُحِبُّهُ وَيَرْضَاهُ، بَلْ هُوَ وَاقِفٌ مَعَ شَهَوَاتِهِ وَلَذَّاتِهِ، وَلَوْ كَانَ فِيهَا سَخَطُ رَبِّهِ وَغَضَبُهُ، فَهُوَ لَا يُبَالِي — إِذَا فَازَ بِشَهْوَتِهِ وَحَظِّهِ — رَضِيَ رَبُّهُ أَمْ سَخِطَ،

"The second heart is the opposite of this; it is the dead heart that has no life, for it knows not its Lord, and does not worship Him according to His command and what He loves and is pleased with, but instead stands with its desires and pleasures, even if they incur the wrath and anger of its Lord. It does not care whether its Lord is pleased or displeased if it succeeds in its desires and fortune.

فَهُوَ مُتَعَبِّدٌ لِغَيْرِ اللَّهِ: حُبًّا، وَخَوْفًا، وَرَجَاءً، وَرِضًا، وَسَخَطًا، وَتَعْظِيمًا، وَذُلًّا، إِنْ أَحَبَّ أَحَبَّ لِهَوَاهُ، وَإِنْ أَبْغَضَ أَبْغَضَ لِهَوَاهُ، وَإِنْ أَعْطَى أَعْطَى لِهَوَاهُ، وَإِنْ مَنَعَ مَنَعَ لِهَوَاهُ، فَهَوَاهُ آثَرُ عِنْدَهُ وَأَحَبُّ إِلَيْهِ مِنْ رِضَا مَوْلَاهُ؛ فَالْهَوَى إِمَامُهُ، وَالشَّهْوَةُ قَائِدُهُ، وَالْجَهْلُ سَائِسُهُ، وَالْغَفْلَةُ مَرْكَبُهُ،

It is worshipful for other than Allah: in its love, fear, hope, pleasure, anger, veneration, and humility. It loves, hates, gives, and withholds for its desires, for its desires are more important to

---

[10] Ighāthah al-Lahfān, chapter 1.

it and more beloved than the pleasure of its Master; thus, desires are its leader, lust is its guide, ignorance is its driver, and heedlessness is its vessel.

فَهُوَ بِالْفِكْرِ فِي تَحْصِيلِ أَغْرَاضِهِ الدُّنْيَوِيَّةِ مَغْمُورٌ، وَبِسَكْرَةِ الْهَوَى وَحُبِّ الْعَاجِلَةِ مَغْمُورٌ، يُنَادَى إِلَى اللَّهِ وَإِلَى الدَّارِ الْآخِرَةِ مِنْ مَكَانٍ بَعِيدٍ، فَلَا يَسْتَجِيبُ لِلنَّاصِحِ وَيَتَّبِعُ كُلَّ شَيْطَانٍ مَرِيدٍ؛ الدُّنْيَا تُسْخِطُهُ وَتُرْضِيهِ، وَالْهَوَى يُصِمُّهُ عَمَّا سِوَى الْبَاطِلِ وَيُعْمِيهِ؛

It is wholly occupied with thoughts of acquiring worldly goals and immersed in the intoxication of desires and love for the immediate. It is called to Allah and the Hereafter from a far-off place, but does not respond to the sincere adviser and follows instead every rebellious devil. The world angers and pleases it, and desires deafen and blind it.

فَهُوَ فِي الدُّنْيَا كَمَا قِيلَ فِي لَيْلَى:

In this world, it is like what was said about Laylā:

عَدُوٌّ لِمَنْ عَادَتْ وَسِلْمٌ لِأَهْلِهَا ... وَمَنْ قَرَّبَتْ لَيْلَى أَحَبَّ وَقَرَّبَا

An enemy to those who are hostile and at peace with her people... and whomever Layla brings closer, he loves and holds dear.

فَمُخَالَطَةُ صَاحِبِ هَذَا الْقَلْبِ سُقْمٌ، وَمُعَاشَرَتُهُ سُمٌّ، وَمُجَالَسَتُهُ هَلَاكٌ.

Associating with the owner of this heart is a disease; socializing with them is poison, and sitting with them is destruction.

وَالْقَلْبُ الثَّالِثُ قَلْبٌ لَهُ حَيَاةٌ وَبِهِ عِلَّةٌ؛ فَلَهُ مَادَّتَانِ، تَمُدُّهُ هَذِهِ مَرَّةً، وَهَذِهِ أُخْرَى، وَهُوَ لِمَا غَلَبَ عَلَيْهِ مِنْهُمَا، فَفِيهِ مِنْ مَحَبَّةِ اللَّهِ تَعَالَى وَالْإِيمَانِ بِهِ وَالْإِخْلَاصِ لَهُ وَالتَّوَكُّلِ عَلَيْهِ: مَا هُوَ مَادَّةُ حَيَاتِهِ، وَفِيهِ مِنْ مَحَبَّةِ الشَّهَوَاتِ،

وَإِيثَارِهَا، وَالْحِرْصِ عَلَى تَحْصِيلِهَا، وَالْحَسَدِ، وَالْكِبْرِ، وَالْعُجْبِ، وَحُبِّ الْعُلُوِّ فِي الْأَرْضِ بِالرِّيَاسَةِ: مَا هُوَ مَادَّةُ هَلَاكِهِ وَعَطَبِهِ،

The third heart is a heart that has life but also a defect.The sustainability of it relies on two sources, one supporting it at one point in time and the other at a different point. It belongs to whichever of these two prevails over it. In it, there is love for Allah, faith in Him, sincerity towards Him, and reliance upon Him, which is the source of its life. And in it, there is love for desires, preferring them, eagerness to attain them, envy, pride, vanity, and love for high status in the world through leadership, which is the source of its ruin and destruction.

وَهُوَ مُمْتَحَنٌ بَيْنَ دَاعِيَيْنِ: دَاعٍ يَدْعُوهُ إِلَى اللَّهِ وَرَسُولِهِ وَالدَّارِ الْآخِرَةِ، وَدَاعٍ يَدْعُوهُ إِلَى الْعَاجِلَةِ، وَهُوَ إِنَّمَا يُجِيبُ أَقْرَبَهُمَا مِنْهُ بَابًا، وَأَدْنَاهُمَا إِلَيْهِ جِوَارًا.

This heart is tested between two callers: one calling it towards Allah, His Messenger, and the Hereafter, and the other calling it towards immediate enjoyment. It responds to whichever of these callers is closer and more accessible

فَالْقَلْبُ الْأَوَّلُ حَيٌّ مُخْبِتٌ لَيِّنٌ وَاعٍ.

The first heart is living, humble, tender, and aware.

وَالثَّانِي يَابِسٌ مَيِّتٌ

The second heart is dry and dead.

وَالثَّالِثُ مَرِيضٌ؛ فَإِمَّا إِلَى السَّلَامَةِ أَدْنَى، وَإِمَّا إِلَى الْعَطَبِ أَدْنَى".

The third heart is sick, either closer to safety or closer to ruin and destruction..."

Later in the passage, he (رَحِمَهُ ٱللَّهُ) outlines the underlying reasons for this sickness and health:

"وَذَلِكَ أَنَّ الْقَلْبَ وَغَيْرَهُ مِنَ الْأَعْضَاءِ يُرَادُ مِنْهُ أَنْ يَكُونَ صَحِيحًا سَلِيمًا لَا آفَةَ لَهُ، لِيَتَأَتَّى مِنْهُ مَا هُيِّئَ لَهُ وَخُلِقَ لِأَجْلِهِ؛ وَخُرُوجُهُ عَنِ الِاسْتِقَامَةِ إِمَّا بِيُبْسِهِ وَقَسْوَتِهِ، وَعَدَمِ التَّأَتِّي لِمَا يُرَادُ مِنْهُ؛ كَالْيَدِ الشَّلَّاءِ، وَاللِّسَانِ الْأَخْرَسِ، وَالْأَنْفِ الْأَخْشَمِ، وَذَكَرِ الْعِنِّينِ، وَالْعَيْنِ الَّتِي لَا تُبْصِرُ شَيْئًا؛ وَإِمَّا بِمَرَضٍ وَآفَةٍ فِيهِ تَمْنَعُهُ مِنْ كَمَالِ هَذِهِ الْأَفْعَالِ، وَوُقُوعِهَا عَلَى السَّدَادِ. فَلِذَلِكَ انْقَسَمَتِ الْقُلُوبُ إِلَى هَذِهِ الْأَقْسَامِ الثَّلَاثَةِ:

"...The heart and other body parts are meant to be healthy and sound, with no defects, so they can achieve what they were designed and created for. The deviation from the straight path is either due to dryness and hardness, which prevents the fulfillment of the intended purpose, like a paralyzed hand, a mute tongue, a stuffy nose, a defective reproductive organ, and an eye that cannot see anything; or due to sickness and defect that prevents the perfection of these actions and their accuracy. That is why hearts are divided into these three categories:

فَالْقَلْبُ الصَّحِيحُ السَّلِيمُ: لَيْسَ بَيْنَهُ وَبَيْنَ قَبُولِ الْحَقِّ وَمَحَبَّتِهِ وَإِيثَارِهِ سِوَى إِدْرَاكِهِ، فَهُوَ صَحِيحُ الْإِدْرَاكِ لِلْحَقِّ، تَامُّ الِانْقِيَادِ وَالْقَبُولِ لَهُ.

The healthy, sound heart: There is nothing between it and accepting the truth, loving it, and preferring it except for understanding it. It is healthy in recognizing the truth, perfect in compliance and acceptance of it.

وَالْقَلْبُ الْمَيِّتُ الْقَاسِي: لَا يَقْبَلُهُ وَلَا يَنْقَادُ لَهُ.

The dead, hard heart: It does not accept the truth or submit to it.

وَالْقَلْبُ الْمَرِيضُ: إِنْ غَلَبَ عَلَيْهِ مَرَضُهُ الْتَحَقَ بِالْمَيِّتِ الْقَاسِي، وَإِنْ غَلَبَتْ عَلَيْهِ صِحَّتُهُ الْتَحَقَ بِالسَّلِيمِ."

The sick heart: If its sickness prevails, it joins the dead, hard heart; if its health prevails, it joins the sound heart."

## The Heart's Intrinsic Instability

Al Miqdād b. Al Aswad (رَضِيَ ٱللَّهُ عَنْهُ) reported that Allah's Messenger (صَلَّى ٱللَّهُ عَلَيْهِ وَسَلَّمَ) said:[11]

"لَقَلْبُ ابْنِ آدَمَ أَشَدُّ انْقِلَاباً مِنَ الْقِدْرِ إِذَا اسْتَجْمَعَتْ غَلَيَاناً".

**"The heart of the son of Adam fluctuates more intensely than a pot whose contents are boiling."**

Similarly, Abū Mūsā al Ash'arī (رَضِيَ ٱللَّهُ عَنْهُ) reported from Allah's Messenger (صَلَّى ٱللَّهُ عَلَيْهِ وَسَلَّمَ) that he said:[12]

"إِنَّمَا سُمِّيَ الْقَلْبَ مِنْ تَقَلُّبِهِ إِنَّمَا مَثَلُ الْقَلْبِ مَثَلُ رِيشَةٍ بِالْفَلَاةِ تَعَلَّقَتْ فِي أَصْلِ شَجَرَةٍ يُقَلِّبُهَا الرِّيحُ ظَهْراً لِبَطْنٍ".

**"Indeed, the heart is named for its fluctuation. The simile of the heart is like a feather in the wilderness, attached to the base of a tree, being flipped by the wind, back to front."**

---

Ibn al-Qayyim (رَحِمَهُ ٱللَّهُ) summarized some of the greatest reasons that contribute to the hearts instability, saying:[13]

"فَإِذَا اجْتَمَعَ إِلَى ضَعْفِ الْعِلْمِ عَدَمُ اسْتِحْضَارِهِ، أَوْ غَيْبَتُهُ عَنِ الْقَلْبِ فِي كَثِيرٍ مِنْ أَوْقَاتِهِ أَوْ أَكْثَرِهَا لِاشْتِغَالِهِ بِمَا يُضَادُّهُ، وَانْضَمَّ إِلَى ذَلِكَ تَقَاضِي الطَّبْعِ، وَغَلَبَاتُ الْهَوَى، وَاسْتِيلَاءُ الشَّهْوَةِ، وَتَسْوِيلُ النَّفْسِ، وَغُرُورُ الشَّيْطَانِ، وَاسْتِبْطَاءُ الْوَعْدِ، وَطُولُ الْأَمَلِ، وَرَقْدَةُ الْغَفْلَةِ، وَحُبُّ الْعَاجِلَةِ، وَرُخَصُ التَّأْوِيلِ وَإِلْفُ الْعَوَائِدِ، فَهُنَاكَ لَا يُمْسِكُ الْإِيمَانَ إِلَّا الَّذِي يُمْسِكُ السَّمَاوَاتِ وَالْأَرْضَ أَنْ تَزُولَا،

[11] Collected by Ahmad and al Ḥākim. Graded Ṣaḥīḥ by al Albānī in Ṣaḥīḥ al Jāmi' (5147).

[12] Collected by al-Ṭabarānī in al Mu'jam al Kabīr. Graded Ṣaḥīḥ by al Albānī in Ṣaḥīḥ al Jāmi' (2365).

[13] Al-Jawab Al-Kafi

وَبِهَذَا السَّبَبِ يَتَفَاوَتُ النَّاسُ فِي الْإِيمَانِ وَالْأَعْمَالِ، حَتَّى يَنْتَهِيَ إِلَى أَدْنَى مِثْقَالِ ذَرَّةٍ فِي الْقَلْبِ".

"When lack of knowledge is combined with a failure to be mindful of it and its absence from the heart most of the time due to preoccupation with conflicting things, combined with the influence of natural desires, the control of lust, self-justification, deception of Satan, delayed promises, distant hopes, heedlessness, love for instant gratification, the easy resort to misinterpretation, and the familiarity of habits, then only He who keeps the heavens and the earth from vanishing can maintain faith. For this reason, people's faith varies until it reaches the weight of the smallest particle in the heart."

---

## THE HEART'S FIRMNESS OR FLIMSINESS DURING THE TEMPESTS OF TRIALS

Ḥudhayfah b. Al Yamān (رَضِيَ اللَّهُ عَنْهُمَا) reported from Allah's Messenger (صَلَّى اللَّهُ عَلَيْهِ وَسَلَّمَ) that he said:

**"تُعْرَضُ الْفِتَنُ عَلَى الْقُلُوبِ كَالْحَصِيرِ عُودًا عُودًا، فَأَيُّ قَلْبٍ أُشْرِبَهَا نُكِتَ فِيهِ نُكْتَةٌ سَوْدَاءُ، وَأَيُّ قَلْبٍ أَنْكَرَهَا نُكِتَ فِيهِ نُكْتَةٌ بَيْضَاءُ، حَتَّى تَصِيرَ عَلَى قَلْبَيْنِ: عَلَى أَبْيَضَ مِثْلِ الصَّفَا، فَلَا تَضُرُّهُ فِتْنَةٌ مَا دَامَتِ السَّمَاوَاتُ وَالْأَرْضُ، وَالْآخَرُ أَسْوَدُ مُرْبَادًّا كَالْكُوزِ، مُجَخِّيًا لَا يَعْرِفُ مَعْرُوفًا، وَلَا يُنْكِرُ مُنْكَرًا إِلَّا مَا أُشْرِبَ مِنْ هَوَاهُ".**

**"Tribulations *(fitan)* are presented to the heart, one by one, like a straw mat is woven reed by reed. Any heart that absorbs them will have a black spot put into it, and any heart that rejects them will have a white spot. Thus, there will be two types of hearts: one white like a smooth rock, which will not be harmed by any temptation as long as the heavens**

**and earth endure, and the other black and dust-covered like an overturned vessel, not recognizing what is good or rejecting what is evil, but being impregnated with passion."**

---

The great contemporary scholar Muḥammad Adam Atyūbī (d. 1442 AH رَحِمَهُ ٱللَّهُ) explains the meaning of this similitude, saying:[14]

"أَقْرَبُ الأَقْوَالِ عِنْدِي وَأَوْضَحُهَا ضَبْطًا وَمَعْنًى هُوَ الَّذِي رَجَّحَهُ عِيَاضٌ، وَأَشَارَ إِلَيْهِ الْقُرْطُبِيُّ رَحِمَهُمَا اللَّهُ تَعَالَى، وَهُوَ أَنَّهُ بِضَمِّ الْعَيْنِ، وَالْمَرَادُ تَشْبِيهُ عَرْضِ الْفِتَنِ عَلَى الْقُلُوبِ وَاحِدَةً بَعْدَ أُخْرَى بِعَرْضِ عُودِ الْحَصِيرِ عَلَى صَانِعِهَا قَضِيبًا قَضِيبًا، وَاللَّهُ تَعَالَى أَعْلَمُ."

"The closest and clearest statement in my view, both in terms of its pronunciation and meaning, is the one favored by (al Qāḍī) 'Iyāḍ, and alluded to by Al-Qurtubi, may Allah have mercy on them both. It is pronounced with a *Ḍammah* on the 'Ayn (عُوْدًا عُوْدًا – meaning one reed after another). The intended meaning is to liken the presentation of trials to the hearts, one after another, to the process of the assembly of a reed mat by its maker, reed by reed. And Allah knows best."

Additionally, the hadīth scholar Abul 'Abbās al Qurṭubī (d. 656 AH رَحِمَهُ ٱللَّهُ) wrote:[15]

"وَلَيْسَ تَشْبِيهُهُ بِالصَّفَا مِن جِهَةِ بَيَاضِهِ، وَلَكِن مِن جِهَةِ صَلَابَتِهِ عَلَى عَقْدِ الْإِيمَانِ، وَسَلَامَتِهِ مِنَ الْخَلَلِ وَالْفِتَنِ؛ إِذ لَمْ يَلْصَق بِهِ وَلَمْ يُؤَثِّر فِيهِ؛ كَالصَّفَا وَهُوَ الْحَجَرُ الْأَمْلَسُ الَّذِي لَا يَعْلَقُ بِهِ شَيْءٌ، بِخِلَافِ الْقَلْبِ الْآخَرِ الَّذِي شَبَّهَهُ بِالْكُوزِ الْخَاوِي؛ لِأَنَّهُ فَارِغٌ مِنَ الْإِيمَانِ وَالْأَمَانَةِ"

---

[14] *Al Baḥr al Muḥīṭ al-Thajjāj*: A Commentary on the Ṣaḥīḥ of Imam Muslim ibn al-Hajjaj" (4/123).

[15] *Al Mufhim limā Ashkala lk Talkhīṣ Kitāb Muslim* (1/359).

"His likening it to *ṣafa* (a kind of smooth stone) is not because of its whiteness,[16] but because of its solidity in holding onto faith and its integrity from flaws and trials. Nothing sticks to or affects it, just like the *ṣafa*, a smooth stone that nothing sticks to, unlike the other heart, which he compared to an empty water skin because it is devoid of faith and trustworthiness."

Ibn al Qayyim (d. 751 AH رَحِمَهُ ٱللَّهُ) offers some precious additional insights about this amazing similitude, saying:[17]

"فَشَبَّهَ عَرْضَ الْفِتَنَ عَلَى الْقُلُوبِ شَيْئًا فَشَيْئًا؛ كَعَرْضِ عَيْدَانِ الْحَصِيرِ ـ وَهِيَ طَاقَاتُهَا ـ شَيْئًا فَشَيْئًا، وَقَسَّمَ الْقُلُوبَ عِنْدَ عَرْضِهَا عَلَيْهَا إِلَى قِسْمَيْنِ:

"He compared the exposure of trials to hearts bit by bit; like the presentation of the mats' reeds – which are its layers – bit by bit. And he divided the hearts, when they are exposed to these trials, into two categories:

قَلْبٌ إِذَا عُرِضَتْ عَلَيْهِ فِتْنَةٌ أُشْرِبَهَا، كَمَا يَشْرَبُ السِّفِنْجُ الْمَاءَ، فَتُنْكَتُ فِيهِ نَكَتَةٌ سَوْدَاءُ، فَلَا يَزَالُ يَشْرَبُ كُلَّ فِتْنَةٍ تُعَرْضُ عَلَيْهِ، حَتَّى يَسْوَدَّ وَيَنْتَكِسَ، وَهُوَ مَعْنَى قَوْلِهِ: "كَالْكُوزِ مُجَخِّيًا"؛ أَيْ مَكْبُوبًا مَنْكُوسًا، فَإِذَا اسْوَدَّ وَانْتَكَسَ عُرِضَ لَهُ مِنْ هَاتَيْنِ الْآفَتَيْنِ مَرَضَانِ خَطِرَانِ مُتَرَامِيَانِ إِلَى الْهَلَاكِ:

A heart that, when a trial is presented to it, absorbs it, just like a sponge absorbs water. So a black spot is engraved in it, and it continues to absorb every trial presented to it until it turns black and becomes inverted. This is what he meant by the phrase: "like an overturned jug" meaning it is turned upside down. Once it turns black and inverted, it is presented with two dangerous diseases that pose a threat of destruction:

---

[16] Others, like Ibn al Qayyim correctly understood it to be an allusion to the heart's illumination as well as its firmness, as mentioned below.

[17] *Ighātha al-Lahfān.*

أَحَدُهُمَا: اشْتِبَاهُ الْمَعْرُوفِ عَلَيْهِ بِالْمُنْكَرِ، فَلَا يَعْرِفُ مَعْرُوفًا، وَلَا يُنْكِرُ مُنْكَرًا، وَرُبَّمَا اسْتَحْكَمَ فِيهِ هَذَا الْمَرَضُ، حَتَّى يُعْتَقِدَ الْمَعْرُوفُ مُنْكَرًا وَالْمُنْكَرُ مَعْرُوفًا، وَالسُّنَّةُ بِدْعَةً وَالْبِدْعَةُ سُنَّةً، وَالْحَقُّ بَاطِلًا وَالْبَاطِلُ حَقًّا.

The first one is the confusion between good and evil, so it does not recognize good nor reject evil. This disease may get so entrenched in it that it starts to perceive good as evil and evil as good, *Sunnah* (prophetic tradition) as innovation, and innovation as *Sunnah*, truth as falsehood, and falsehood as truth.

الثَّانِيَّ: تَحْكِيمُهُ هَوَاهُ عَلَى مَا جَاءَ بِهِ الرَّسُولُ -صَلَّى اللَّهُ عَلَيْهِ وَسَلَّمَ-، وَانْقِيَادُهُ لِلْهَوَى وَاتِّبَاعُهُ لَهُ.

The second one is the domination of its whims over what the Messenger (ﷺ) brought and its submission to and following these whims.

وَقَلْبٌ أَبْيَضُ، قَدْ أَشْرَقَ فِيهِ نُورُ الْإِيمَانِ، وَأَزْهَرَ فِيهِ مِصْبَاحُهُ، فَإِذَا عُرِضَتْ عَلَيْهِ الْفِتْنَةُ أَنْكَرَهَا وَكَرِهَهَا، فَازْدَادَ نُورُهُ وَإِشْرَاقُهُ وَقُوَّتُهُ.

And the other is a white heart, in which the light of faith has shone, and its lamp has flourished. So when trials are presented to it, it rejects and detests them, and its light, brightness, and strength increase.

وَالْفِتَنُ الَّتِي تُعْرَضُ عَلَى الْقُلُوبِ هِيَ أَسْبَابُ مَرَضِهَا، وَهِيَ فِتَنُ الشَّهَوَاتِ وَفِتَنُ الشُّبُهَاتِ، وَفِتَنُ الْغَيِّ وَالضَّلَالِ، وَفِتَنُ الْمَعَاصِي وَالْبِدَعِ، وَفِتَنُ الظُّلْمِ وَالْجَهْلِ؛ فَالْأُولَى تُوجِبُ فَسَادَ الْقَصْدِ وَالْإِرَادَةِ، وَالثَّانِيَةُ تُوجِبُ فَسَادَ الْعِلْمِ وَالْاعْتِقَادِ".

The trials that are presented to hearts are the causes of their disease, and they are the trials of desires and doubts, the trials of misguidance and deviation, the trials of sins and innovations, and the trials of injustice and ignorance. The first category leads to the corruption of intention and will, and the second leads to the corruption of knowledge and belief."

## TWO HEARTS, TWO THRONES

Elsewhere, Ibn al Qayyim (رَحِمَهُ ٱللَّهُ) explained the difference between living hearts and dead ones in a most captivating way; he said:[18]

"أَنْزَهُ الْمَوْجُودَاتِ وَأَطْهَرُهَا وَأَنْوَرُهَا وَأَشْرَفُهَا وَأَعْلَاهَا ذَاتًا وَقَدْرًا وَأَوْسَعُها عَرْش الرَّحْمَنِ جلّ جلاله، وَلِذَلِكَ صَلُحَ لِاسْتِوَائِهِ عَلَيْهِ.

"The most immaculate, purest, luminous, noblest, and highest of all existing creations, both in essence and status and the vastest of them all is the Throne of the Most Merciful, glorified be His majesty. Therefore, it is fitting for His ascension above it.

وَكُلُّ مَا كَانَ أَقْرَبَ إِلَى الْعَرْشِ؛ كَانَ أَنْوَرَ وَأَنْزَهَ وَأَشْرَفَ مِمَّا بَعُدَ عَنْهُ. وَلِهَذَا كَانَتْ جَنَّةُ الْفِرْدَوْسِ أَعْلَى الْجِنَانِ وَأَشْرَفَهَا وَأَنْوَرَهَا وَأَجَلَّهَا؛ لِقُرْبِهَا مِنَ الْعَرْشِ؛ إِذْ هُوَ سَقْفُهَا.

Everything closer to the Throne is more luminous, purer, and nobler than what is further from it. For this reason, the Garden of *Firdaws* is the highest, noblest, most luminous, and most distinguished of the gardens due to its proximity to the Throne, as it is its ceiling.

وَكُلُّ مَا بَعُدَ عَنْهُ كَانَ أَظْلَمَ وَأَضْيَقَ. وَلِهَذَا كَانَ أَسْفَلَ سَافِلِينَ شَرَّ الْأَمْكِنَةِ وَأَضْيَقَهَا وَأَبْعَدَهَا مِنْ كُلِّ خَيْرٍ.

Everything that is further from it is darker and narrower. Therefore, the lowest of the low is the worst, narrowest, and furthest place from any good.

[18] *al Fawā'id.*

وَخَلَقَ اللَّهُ الْقُلُوبَ وَجَعَلَهَا مَحَلًّا لِمَعْرِفَتِهِ وَمَحَبَّتِهِ وَإِرَادَتِهِ؛ فَهِيَ عَرْشُ الْمِثْلِ الْأَعْلَى الَّذِي هُوَ مَعْرِفَتُهُ وَمَحَبَّتُهُ وَإِرَادَتُهُ. فَهِيَ عَرْشُ الْمَثَلِ الْأَعْلَى الَّذِي هُوَ مَعْرِفَتُهُ وَمَحَبَّتُهُ وَإِرَادَتُهُ.

Allah (جَلَّ وَعَلَا) created hearts and made them a place for knowing Him, loving Him, and wanting Him; thus, they are the throne of the highest description, which is knowing Him, loving Him, and intending for Him.

قال تعالى: {**لِلَّذِينَ لَا يُؤْمِنُونَ بِالْآخِرَةِ مَثَلُ السَّوْءِ وَلِلَّهِ الْمَثَلُ الْأَعْلَى وَهُوَ الْعَزِيزُ الْحَكِيمُ** }، وقال تعالى: {**وَهُوَ الَّذِي يَبْدَأُ الْخَلْقَ ثُمَّ يُعِيدُهُ وَهُوَ أَهْوَنُ عَلَيْهِ وَلَهُ الْمَثَلُ الْأَعْلَى فِي السَّمَاوَاتِ وَالْأَرْضِ وَهُوَ الْعَزِيزُ الْحَكِيمُ**}، وقال تعالى: {**لَيْسَ كَمِثْلِهِ شَيْءٌ**}؛ فَهَذَا مِنَ الْمَثَلِ الْأَعْلَى، وَهُوَ مُسْتَوٍ عَلَى قَلْبِ الْمُؤْمِنِ؛ فَهُوَ عَرْشُهُ.

As Allah (سُبْحَانَهُ وَتَعَالَى) says: "**For those who do not believe in the Hereafter, the similitude is that of evil; and to Allah belongs the highest description. He is the All-Mighty, the All-Wise.**"[19] And He also says: "**He is the one who originates creation, then brings it back again, and that is easier for Him. His is the highest description in the heavens and the earth. He is the All-Mighty, the All-Wise.**"[20] And He says: "**There is nothing like unto Him.**"[21] This is from the highest description and is established on the heart of the believer; thus, it is its throne.

وَإِنْ لَمْ يَكُنْ أَطْهَرَ الْأَشْيَاءِ وَأَنْزَهَهَا وَأَطْيَبَهَا وَأَبْعَدَهَا مِنْ كُلِّ دَنَسٍ وَخَبَثٍ؛ لَمْ يَصْلُحْ لِاسْتِوَاءِ الْمَثَلِ الْأَعْلَى عَلَيْهِ مَعْرِفَةً وَمَحَبَّةً وَإِرَادَةً، فَاسْتَوَى عَلَيْهِ مَثَلُ الدُّنْيَا الْأَسْفَلُ وَمَحَبَّتُهَا وَإِرَادَتُهَا وَالتَّعَلُّقُ بِهَا، فَضَاقَ وَأَظْلَمَ وَبَعُدَ مِنْ كَمَالِهِ وَفَلَاحِهِ.

---

[19] Al-Naḥl: 60.

[20] Al-Rūm: 27.

[21] Al-Shūrā: 11.

If it is not the purest, cleanest, and furthest of all things from any impurity and filth, it will not be suitable for the highest description to ascend upon it with knowledge, love, and will, so the similitude of the lower world —loving it, desiring it and attachment to it — ascend over it, causing it to constrict, darken, and become distant from its perfection and success.

حَتَّى تَعُودَ الْقُلُوبُ عَلَى قَلْبَيْنِ: قَلْبٍ هُوَ عَرْشُ الرَّحْمَنِ؛ فِيهِ النُّورُ وَالْحَيَاةُ وَالْفَرَحُ وَالسُّرُورُ وَالْبَهْجَةُ وَذَخَائِرُ الْخَيْرِ.

Until the hearts return to two hearts: a heart that is the throne of the Merciful; in it is light, life, joy, happiness, delight, and the treasures of goodness.

وَقَلْبٍ هُوَ عَرْشُ الشَّيْطَانِ؛ فَهُنَاكَ الضِّيْقُ وَالظُّلْمَةُ وَالْمَوْتُ وَالْحُزْنُ وَالْغَمُّ وَالْهَمُّ؛ فَهُوَ حَزِينٌ عَلَى مَا مَضَى، مَهْمُومٌ بِمَا يُسْتَقْبَلُ، مَغْمُومٌ فِي الْحَالِ.

And a heart that is the throne of Satan; therein is constriction, darkness, death, sorrow, and anxiety; it is sad for what has passed, worried about what is to come, and distressed in the present moment…

وَالنُّورُ الَّذِي يَدْخُلُ الْقَلْبَ إِنَّمَا هُوَ مِن آثَارِ الْمَثَلِ الْأَعْلَى؛ فَلِذَلِكَ يَنْفَسِحُ وَيَنْشَرِحُ، وَإِذَا لَمْ يَكُنْ فِيهِ مَعْرِفَةُ اللَّهِ وَمَحَبَّتُه؛ فَحَظُّهُ الظُّلْمَةُ والضِّيْقُ."

The light that enters the heart is indeed from the effects of the highest description; therefore, it expands and opens up. And if it does not contain knowledge about Allah and love of Him, darkness and constriction overcome it."

In similar fashion, Ibn al Qayyim (رَحِمَهُ ٱللَّهُ) writes elsewhere:

”فَاعْلَمْ أَنَّ اللَّهَ تَعَالَى خَلَقَ فِي صَدْرِكَ بَيْتًا وَهُوَ الْقَلْبُ، وَوَضَعَ فِي صَدْرِهِ عَرْشًا لِمَعْرِفَتِهِ يَسْتَوِي عَلَيْهِ الْمَثَلُ الْأَعْلَى؛ فَهُوَ مُسْتَوٍّ عَلَى عَرْشِهِ بِذَاتِهِ بَائِنٌ مِنْ خَلْقِهِ، وَالْمَثَلُ الْأَعْلَى مِنْ مَعْرِفَتِهِ وَمَحَبَّتِهِ وَتَوْحِيدِهِ مُسْتَوٍّ عَلَى سَرِيرِ الْقَلْبِ،

"So know that Allah, the Most High, has created within your chest a house, and it is the heart. And He has placed within it a throne for knowing Him, upon which the highest description is established. So He is established upon His throne with His essence, distinct from His creation. And the highest description of knowing Him, loving Him, and singling Him out (with His rights) is established upon the seat of the heart."

وَعَلَى السَّرِيرِ بِسَاطٌ مِنَ الرِّضَا، وَوَضَعَ عَنْ يَمِينِهِ وَشِمَالِهِ مَرَافِقَ شَرَائِعِهِ وَأَوَامِرِهِ، وَفَتَحَ إِلَيْهِ بَابًا مِنْ جَنَّةِ رَحْمَتِهِ وَالْأُنْسِ بِهِ وَالشَّوْقِ إِلَى لِقَائِهِ،

Upon the seat lies a covering of contentment, and to its right and left, He placed the amenities of His laws and commands. He opened a door to it from the garden of His mercy, finding comfort with Him and longing for His meeting.

وَأَمْطَرَهُ مِنْ وَابِلِ كَلَامِهِ مَا أَنْبَتَ فِيهِ أَصْنَافَ الرَّيَاحِينَ وَالْأَشْجَارِ الْمُثْمِرَةِ مِنْ أَنْوَاعِ الطَّاعَاتِ وَالتَّهْلِيلِ وَالتَّسْبِيحِ وَالتَّحْمِيدِ وَالتَّقْدِيسِ،

He showered it with the abundant downpour of His speech, which caused various types of fragrant plants and fruitful trees of obedience, glorification, praise, and sanctification to grow within it.

وَجَعَلَ فِي وَسَطِ الْبُسْتَانِ شَجَرَةَ مَعْرِفَةٍ؛ فَهِيَ {**تُؤْتِي أُكُلَهَا كُلَّ حِينٍ بِإِذْنِ رَبِّهَا**} [إِبْرَاهِيمَ: ٢٥] مِنَ الْمَحَبَّةِ وَالْإِنَابَةِ وَالْخَشْيَةِ وَالْفَرَحِ بِهِ وَالِابْتِهَاجِ بِقُرْبِهِ، وَأَجْرَى إِلَى تِلْكَ الشَّجَرَةِ مَا يَسْقِيهَا مِنْ تَدَبُّرِ كَلَامِهِ وَفَهْمِهِ وَالْعَمَلِ بِوَصَايَاهُ،

He placed in the midst of the garden a tree of knowledge, which "**gives its fruit at every time by the permission of its Lord**",[22] which includes loving Him, turning towards Him, reverencing Him, finding joy in Him, and delighting in His closeness. He directed to that tree what waters it, such as pondering over His words, understanding them, and acting according to His commandments.

وَعَلَّقَ فِي ذَلِكَ الْبَيْتِ قِنْدِيلًا أَسْرَجَهُ بِضِيَاءِ مَعْرِفَتِهِ وَالْإِيمَانِ بِهِ وَتَوْحِيدِهِ؛ فَهُوَ يَسْتَمِدُّ مِنْ {**شَجَرَةٍ مُبَارَكَةٍ زَيْتُونَةٍ لَا شَرْقِيَّةٍ وَلَا غَرْبِيَّةٍ يَكَادُ زَيْتُهَا يُضِيءُ وَلَوْ لَمْ تَمْسَسْهُ نَارٌ**} [النُّور: ٣٥]،

He hung in that house a lantern lit by the light of knowing Him, belief in Him, and singling Him out (with His rights); it draws from "**a blessed olive tree, neither of the east nor of the west, its oil almost gives light even if untouched by fire.**"[23]

ثُمَّ أَحَاطَ عَلَيْهِ حَائِطًا يَمْنَعُهُ مِنْ دُخُولِ الْآفَاتِ وَالْمُفْسِدِينَ وَمَنْ يُؤْذِي الْبُسْتَانَ؛ فَلَا يَلْحَقُهُ أَذَاهُمْ، وَأَقَامَ عَلَيْهِ حَرَسًا مِنَ الْمَلَائِكَةِ يَحْفَظُونَهُ فِي يَقْظَتِهِ وَمَنَامِهِ،

Then He enclosed it with a wall that prevents the entry of pests and corrupters and anyone who would harm the garden, so their harm cannot reach it. He placed over it a guard of angels who protect it during its wakefulness and sleep.

ثُمَّ أَعْلَمَ صَاحِبَ الْبَيْتِ وَالْبُسْتَانِ بِالسَّاكِنِ فِيهِ؛ فَهُوَ دَائِمًا هَمُّهُ إِصْلَاحُ السَّكَنِ وَلَمُّ شَعَثِهِ لِيَرْضَاهُ السَّاكِنُ مَنْزِلًا،

Then He informed the owner of the house and the garden about the resident within. So his constant concern is to repair the residence and groom its disarray to the liking of the resident.

---

[22] Ibrahim: 25.

[23] An-Nur: 35.

وَإِذَا أَحَسَّ بِأَدْنَى شَعَثٍ فِي السَّكَنِ بَادَرَ إِلَى إِصْلَاحِهِ وَلَمِّهُ خَشْيَةَ انْتِقَالِ السَّاكِنِ مِنْهُ؛ فَنِعْمَ السَّاكِنُ وَالْمَسْكَنُ.

If he senses the slightest disarray in the dwelling, he immediately sets to repair and groom it for fear of the resident moving out; what an excellent resident and residence.

فَسُبْحَانَ اللَّهِ رَبِّ الْعَالَمِينَ! كَمْ بَيْنَ هَذَا الْبَيْتِ وَبَيْتٍ قَدْ اسْتَوْلَى عَلَيْهِ الْخَرَابُ وَصَارَ مَأْوَى لِلْحَشَرَاتِ وَالْهَوَامِّ وَمَحَلًّا لِإِلْقَاءِ الْأَنْتَانِ وَالْقَاذُورَاتِ فِيهِ؛ فَمَنْ أَرَادَ التَّخَلِّي وَقَضَاءَ الْحَاجَّةِ وَجَدَ خَرِبَةً لَا سَاكِنَ فِيهَا وَلَا حَافِظًا لَهَا، وَهِيَ مُعَدَّةٌ لِقَضَاءِ الْحَاجَّةِ، مُظْلِمَةُ الْأَرْجَاءِ، مُنْتِنَةُ الرَّائِحَةِ، قَدْ عَمَّهَا الْخَرَابُ وَمَلَأَتْهَا الْقَاذُورَاتُ؛ فَلَا يَأْنَسُ بِهَا وَلَا يَنْزِلُ فِيهَا إِلَّا مَنْ يَنَاسِبُهُ سُكْنَاهَا مِنَ الْحَشَرَاتِ وَالدِّيدَانِ وَالْهَوَامِّ؛

So glory be to Allah, Lord of all the worlds! How different is this house from a house that has been overtaken by ruin, becoming a refuge for insects and pests and a place for casting rubbish and waste into; anyone who desires to relieve themselves and satisfy their needs finds a ruin, with no inhabitant or guardian, prepared for fulfilling such needs. It is dark, filled with an unpleasant smell, engulfed by devastation, and full of rubbish; no one feels comfortable or resides in it except those suited to its habitation, such as insects, worms, and pests.

الشَّيْطَانُ جَالِسٌ عَلَى سَرِيرِهَا، وَعَلَى السَّرِيرِ بِسَاطٌ مِنَ الْجَهْلِ، وَتَخْفِقُ فِيهِ الْأَهْوَاءُ، وَعَنْ يَمِينِهِ وَشِمَالِهِ مَرَافِقُ الشَّهْوَاتِ وَاتِّبَاعُ الْهَوَى، وَقَدْ فُتِحَ إِلَيْهِ بَابٌ مِنْ حَقْلِ الْخِذْلَانِ وَالْوَحْشَةِ وَالرُّكُونِ إِلَى الدُّنْيَا وَالطُّمَأْنِينَةِ بِهَا وَالزُّهْدِ فِي الْآخِرَةِ،

The devil sits on its seat, with a covering of ignorance spread over it, while desires flutter around. To its right and left are amenities of lust and the following of whims. A door has been opened to it from a field of forsakenness and desolation, inclination towards the world, contentment with it, and indifference to the Hereafter.

وَأُمْطِرَ مِنْ وَابِلِ الْجَهْلِ وَالْهَوَى وَالشِّرْكِ وَالْبِدَعِ مَا أَنْبَتَ فِيهِ أَصْنَافَ الشَّوْكِ وَالْحَنْظَلِ وَالْأَشْجَارِ الْمُثْمِرَةِ بِأَنْوَاعِ الْمَعَاصِي وَالْمُخَالَفَاتِ، مِنَ الزَّوَائِدِ وَالتَّنْدِيبَاتِ وَالنَّوَادِرِ وَالْهَزَلِيَّاتِ وَالْمُضْحِكَاتِ وَالْأَشْعَارِ الْغَزَلِيَّاتِ وَالْخَمْرِيَّاتِ الَّتِي تُهَيِّجُ عَلَى ارْتِكَابِ الْمُحَرَّمَاتِ وَتُزَهِّدُ فِي الطَّاعَاتِ،

It has been showered with a downpour of ignorance, desire, polytheism, and innovation, which caused all kinds of thorns, colocynth, and trees bearing various sins and violations to grow within it. From its superfluous matters, useless encouragments, oddities, trivialities, laughable matters, love poems, and wine poems that incite one to commit forbidden acts and make one indifferent to obedience.

وَجُعِلَ فِي وَسَطِ الْحَقْلِ شَجَرَةُ الْجَهْلِ بِهِ وَالْإِعْرَاضِ عَنْهُ؛ فَهِيَ تُؤْتِي أُكُلَهَا كُلَّ حِينٍ مِنَ الْفُسُوقِ وَالْمَعَاصِي وَاللَّهْوِ وَاللَّعِبِ وَالْمَجُونِ وَالذَّهَابِ مَعَ كُلِّ رِيحٍ وَاتِبَاعِ كُلِّ شَهْوَةٍ،

In the middle of the field is the tree of ignorance about (Allah) and turning away from Him; it yields its fruit at every time from wickedness, sins, frivolity, play, indecency, going along with every gust of wind, and following every desire.

وَمِنْ ثَمَرِهَا الْهُمُومُ وَالْغُمُومُ وَالْأَحْزَانُ وَالْآلَامُ، وَلَكِنَّهَا مُتَوَارِيَةٌ بِاشْتِغَالِ النَّفْسِ بِلَهْوِهَا وَلَعِبِهَا؛

From its fruits are worries, sorrows, sadness, and pain, which is hidden by one's preoccupation with their frivolity and play.

فَإِذَا أَفَاقَتْ مِنْ سُكْرِهَا أُحْضِرَتْ كُلَّ هَمٍّ وَغَمٍّ وَحُزْنٍ وَقَلَقٍ وَمَعِيشَةٍ ضَنْكٍ، وَأُجْرِيَ إِلَى تِلْكَ الشَّجَرَةِ مَا يَسْقِيهَا مِنْ اتِبَاعِ الْهَوَى وَطُولِ الْأَمَلِ وَالْغُرُورِ، ثُمَّ تُرِكَ ذَلِكَ الْبَيْتُ وَظُلُمَاتُهُ وَخَرَابُ حُيُوطِهِ؛ بِحَيْثُ لَا يُمْنَعُ مِنْهُ مُفْسِدٌ وَلَا حَيَوَانٌ وَلَا مُؤْذٍ وَلَا قَذَرٌ.

When they sober up from their intoxication, every worry, sorrow, sadness, anxiety, and a miserable life is presented. What waters that tree is the following of whims, long hopes, and delusion. Then, that house and its darkness and the ruin of its walls are left so that no corrupter, animal, harmful creature, or filth is prevented from it.

فَسُبْحَانَ خَالِقِ هَذَا الْبَيْتِ وَذَلِكَ الْبَيْتِ!

So glory be to the Creator of this house and that house!

فَمَنْ عَرَفَ قَدْرَ بَيْتِهِ وَقَدْرَ السَّاكِنِ فِيهِ وَقَدْرَ مَا فِيهِ مِنَ الْكُنُوزِ وَالذَّخَائِرِ وَالْآلَاتِ؛ انْتَفَعَ بِحَيَاتِهِ وَنَفْسِهِ، وَمَنْ جَهِلَ ذَلِكَ جَهِلَ نَفْسَهُ وَأَضَاعَ سَعَادَتَهُ.

Whoever recognizes the value of his house, what inhabits it, and the value of the treasures, resources, and tools in it, benefits from his life and himself. And whoever is ignorant of that is ignorant of himself and squanders his happiness.

وبالله التوفيق."

And with Allah is success."

## 3 TYPES OF THE INNER-SELF

Shaykh al Islām Ibn Taymiyyah (رَحِمَهُ ٱللَّهُ) said:[24]

"كَذَلِكَ النَّفْسُ لَمَّا كَانَتْ حَالُ تَعَلُّقِهَا بِالْبَدَنِ يَكْثُرُ عَلَيْهَا اتِّبَاعُ هَوَاهَا ، صَارَ لَفْظُ "النَّفْسِ" يُعَبَّرُ بِهِ عَنْ النَّفْسِ الْمُتَّبِعَةِ لِهَوَاهَا أَوْ عَنْ اتِّبَاعِهَا الْهَوَى بِخِلَافِ لَفْظِ "الرُّوحِ" فَإِنَّهَا لَا يُعَبَّرُ بِهَا عَنْ ذَلِكَ إذْ كَانَ لَفْظُ "الرُّوحِ" لَيْسَ هُوَ بِاعْتِبَارِ تَدْبِيرِهَا لِلْبَدَنِ.

"Thus, when the self is in a state of attachment to the body, the pursuit of its desires increases. The term 'self' has come to denote the soul that follows its desires or the act of following desires, in contrast to the term 'spirit' (*rūḥ*), which does not express the same idea since the term 'spirit' is not associated with the control of the body.

وَيُقَالُ النُّفُوسُ ثَلَاثَةُ أَنْوَاعٍ: وَهِيَ "**النَّفْسُ الْأَمَّارَةُ بِالسُّوءِ**" الَّتِي يَغْلِبُ عَلَيْهَا اتِّبَاعُ هَوَاهَا بِفِعْلِ الذُّنُوبِ وَالْمَعَاصِي. وَ "**النَّفْسُ اللَّوَّامَةُ**" وَهِيَ الَّتِي تُذْنِبُ وَتَتُوبُ فَعَنْهَا خَيْرٌ وَشَرٌّ لَكِنْ إذَا فَعَلَتْ الشَّرَّ تَابَتْ وَأَنَابَتْ فَتُسَمَّى لَوَّامَةً لِأَنَّهَا تَلُومُ صَاحِبَهَا عَلَى الذُّنُوبِ وَلِأَنَّهَا تَتَلَوَّمُ أَيْ تَتَرَدَّدُ بَيْنَ الْخَيْرِ وَالشَّرِّ.

It is said that there are three types of the self: The first is "*al ammārah*": "the self that insistently commands with evil", which is primarily characterized by following its desires to commit sins and acts of disobedience. The second is "*al-lawwāmah*": "the reproachful soul," which sins and then repents; thus, it possesses both good and evil. However, when it does something evil, it repents and returns to the right path, hence it is called reproachful as it blames its possessor for the sins and because it wavers, i.e., hesitates, between good and evil.

---

[24] *Majmū' al Fatāwā* (9/293).

وَ "**النَّفْسُ الْمُطْمَئِنَّةُ**" وَهِيَ الَّتِي تُحِبُّ الْخَيْرَ وَالْحَسَنَاتِ وَتُرِيدُهُ وَتُبْغِضُ الشَّرَّ وَالسَّيِّئَاتِ وَتَكْرَهُ ذَلِكَ وَقَدْ صَارَ ذَلِكَ لَهَا خُلُقًا وَعَادَةً وَمَلَكَةً.

The third type is al "*muṭma'innah*": "the peaceful soul," which loves good and righteousness, desires them, hates evil deeds, and despises such. This becomes its character, habit, and second nature.

فَهَذِهِ صِفَاتٌ وَأَحْوَالٌ لِذَاتٍ وَاحِدَةٍ وَإِلَّا فَالنَّفْسُ الَّتِي لِكُلِّ إنْسَانٍ هِيَ نَفْسٌ وَاحِدَةٌ وَهَذَا أَمْرٌ يَجِدُهُ الْإِنْسَانُ مِنْ نَفْسِهِ".

These are attributes and states of a single entity. Otherwise, the soul that belongs to each human is one soul. This is a matter that a person finds within themselves."

---

Elsewhere, he (رَحِمَهُ ٱللَّهُ) writes:[25]

"فَالنَّفْسُ فِيهَا دَاعِيُ الظُّلْمِ لِغَيْرِهَا بِالْعُلُوِّ عَلَيْهِ وَالْحَسَدِ لَهُ؛ وَالتَّعَدِّي عَلَيْهِ فِي حَقِّهِ. وَدَاعِيُ الظُّلْمِ لِنَفْسِهَا بِتَنَاوُلِ الشَّهَوَاتِ الْقَبِيحَةِ كَالزِّنَا وَأَكْلِ الْخَبَائِثِ. فَهِيَ قَدْ تَظْلِمُ مَنْ لَا يَظْلِمُهَا؛ وَتُؤْثِرُ هَذِهِ الشَّهَوَاتِ وَإِنْ لَمْ تَفْعَلْهَا؛ فَإِذَا رَأَتْ نُظَرَاءَهَا قَدْ ظَلَمُوا وَتَنَاوَلُوا هَذِهِ الشَّهَوَاتِ صَارَ دَاعِي هَذِهِ الشَّهَوَاتِ أَوْ الظُّلْمِ فِيهَا أَعْظَمَ بِكَثِيرِ

"Within the self is something advocating injustice towards others, by exerting superiority over them and having envy towards them, and transgression upon their rights. It also contains something advocating injustice to oneself by indulging in vile desires, such as adultery and consumption of impurities. It may unjustly harm those who do not harm it and may sometimes favor these desires without enacting them. So, when it sees its peers being unjust and indulging in these desires, that which advocates

---

25 *Majmū' al Fatāwā* (27/142).

for these desires or injustice within it becomes significantly greater.

وَقَدْ تَصْبِرُ؛ وَيَهِيجُ ذَلِكَ لَهَا مِنْ بُغْضِ ذَلِكَ الْغَيْرِ وَحَسَدِهِ وَطَلَبِ عِقَابِهِ وَزَوَالِ الْخَيْرِ عَنْهُ مَا لَمْ يَكُنْ فِيهَا قَبْلَ ذَلِكَ، وَلَهَا حُجَّةٌ عِنْدَ نَفْسِهَا مِنْ جِهَةِ الْعَقْلِ وَالدِّينِ؛ يَكُونُ ذَلِكَ الْغَيْرُ قَدْ ظَلَمَ نَفْسَهُ وَالْمُسْلِمِينَ؛ وَإِنَّ أَمْرَهُ بِالْمَعْرُوفِ وَنَهْيَهُ عَنْ الْمُنْكَرِ وَاجِبٌ؛ وَالْجِهَادَ عَلَى ذَلِكَ مِنْ الدِّينِ .

It might resist the temptation to commit sinful acts, but this can trigger animosity and jealousy towards others, accompanied by a desire for punishment and the removal of good from them. One's inner-self may then resort to an argument from a standpoint of reason and religion; that the other person has wronged himself and the Muslims and that his command for good and forbidding of evil is an obligation, and the struggle for this is from the religion [whilst in fact having ulterior motives].

وَالنَّاسُ هُنَا ثَلَاثَةُ أَقْسَامٍ:

And people here are of three kinds:

(.1) قَوْمٌ لَا يَقُومُونَ إِلَّا فِي أَهْوَاءِ نُفُوسِهِمْ؛ فَلَا يَرْضَوْنَ إِلَّا بِمَا يُعْطُونَهُ وَلَا يَغْضَبُونَ إِلَّا لِمَا يُحَرِّمُونَهُ؛ فَإِذَا أُعْطِيَ أَحَدُهُمْ مَا يَشْتَهِيهِ مِنْ الشَّهَوَاتِ الْحَلَالِ وَالْحَرَامِ زَالَ غَضَبُهُ وَحَصَلَ رِضَاهُ وَصَارَ الْأَمْرُ الَّذِي كَانَ عِنْدَهُ مُنْكَرًا - يُنْهَى عَنْهُ وَيُعَاقَبُ عَلَيْهِ؛ وَيَذُمُّ صَاحِبَهُ وَيَغْضَبُ عَلَيْهِ - مَرْضِيًّا عِنْدَهُ وَصَارَ فَاعِلًا لَهُ وَشَرِيكًا فِيهِ؛ وَمُعَاوِنًا عَلَيْهِ؛ وَمُعَادِيًا لِمَنْ نَهَى عَنْهُ وَيُنْكِرُ عَلَيْهِ. وَهَذَا غَالِبٌ فِي بَنِي آدَمَ يَرَى الْإِنْسَانُ وَيَسْمَعُ مِنْ ذَلِكَ مَا لَا يُحْصِيهِ.

[1.] A group led only by their personal desires; they only become satisfied with what they are given and only become angry about what is denied to them. If one of them is granted what he desires, whether it's halal or haram, his anger subsides, his contentment is achieved, and the act which was once unacceptable to him — an act which he used to forbid and punish for, dispraising its doer and becoming angry with him — becomes acceptable to him. He becomes its doer, a partaker in it, a supporter of it, and an enemy to whoever forbids and condemns it. This is prevalent in the children of Adam; a person sees and hears of such behavior to an extent beyond what he can account for...

(2.) وَقَوْمٌ يَقُومُونَ دِيَانَةً صَحِيحَةً يَكُونُونَ فِي ذَلِكَ مُخْلِصِينَ لِلَّهِ مُصْلِحِينَ فِيمَا عَمِلُوهُ وَيَسْتَقِيمُ لَهُمْ ذَلِكَ حَتَّى يَصْبِرُوا عَلَى مَا أُوذُوا. وَهَؤُلَاءِ هُمْ الَّذِينَ آمَنُوا وَعَمِلُوا الصَّالِحَاتِ وَهُمْ مِنْ خَيْرِ أُمَّةٍ أُخْرِجَتْ لِلنَّاسِ يَأْمُرُونَ بِالْمَعْرُوفِ وَيَنْهَوْنَ عَنْ الْمُنْكَرِ وَيُؤْمِنُونَ بِاَللَّهِ.

[2.] And those who possess authentic religiosity, being sincere to Allah in this and striving to improve in what they do. They remain firm until they persevere despite the harm they endure. These are the ones who believe and do righteous deeds, and they are among the best of nations produced for mankind, enjoining what is good, forbidding what is wrong, and believing in Allah.

(3.) وَقَوْمٌ يَجْتَمِعُ فِيهِمْ هَذَا وَهَذَا؛ وَهُمْ غَالِبُ الْمُؤْمِنِينَ فَمَنْ فِيهِ دِينٌ وَلَهُ شَهْوَةٌ تَجْتَمِعُ فِي قُلُوبِهِمْ إرَادَةُ الطَّاعَةِ وَإِرَادَةُ الْمَعْصِيَةِ وَرُبَّمَا غَلَبَ هَذَا تَارَةً وَهَذَا تَارَةً.

[3.] And there is a group that combines both the aforementioned qualities, and they are the majority of believers. Those among them have religiosity and also have desires. In their hearts the desire to obey and to disobey come together, and perhaps one prevails at times and the other at different times.

وَهَذِهِ الْقِسْمَةُ الثُّلَاثِيَّةُ كَمَا قِيلَ: الْأَنْفُسُ ثَلَاثٌ: أَمَّارَةٌ؛ وَمُطْمَئِنَّةٌ؛ وَلَوَّامَةٌ. فَالْأَوَّلُونَ هُمْ أَهْلُ الْأَنْفُسِ الْأَمَّارَةِ الَّتِي تَأْمُرُهُ بِالسُّوءِ. وَالْأَوْسَطُونَ هُمْ أَهْلُ النُّفُوسِ الْمُطْمَئِنَّةِ الَّتِي قِيلَ فِيهَا: **{يَا أَيَّتُهَا النَّفْسُ الْمُطْمَئِنَّةُ} {ارْجِعِي إِلَى رَبِّكِ رَاضِيَةً مَرْضِيَّةً} {فَادْخُلِي فِي عِبَادِي} {وَادْخُلِي جَنَّتِي}** . وَالْآخَرُونَ هُمْ أَهْلُ

النُّفُوسِ اللَّوَّامَةِ الَّتِي تَفْعَلُ الذَّنْبَ ثُمَّ تَلُومُ عَلَيْهِ؛ وَتَتَلَوَّنُ: تَارَةً كَذَا. وَتَارَةً كَذَا. وَتَخْلِطُ عَمَلًا صَالِحًا وَآخَرَ سَيِّئًا

This three-fold division is as stated: the souls are three: commanding [to evil], at peace, and self-reproaching. The first group is the people of the soul commanding to evil, which orders them to do wrong. The second group is the people of the at-peace soul, about which it is said: "**O reassured soul, return to your Lord, well-pleased and pleasing [to Him], and enter among My [righteous] servants, and enter My Paradise.**" The last group is the people of the self-reproaching soul, who commit a sin and then blame themselves for it. They waver, sometimes in one state, sometimes in another. They mix good deeds with bad ones."

---

Imām Ibn al Qayyim (رَحِمَهُ ٱللَّهُ) explains the different types of souls as follows:[26]

النفوس ثلاثة: نَفْسٌ سَمَاوِيَّةٌ عُلْوِيَّةٌ، فَمَحَبَّتُهَا مُنْصَرِفَةٌ إِلَى الْمَعَارِفِ، وَاكْتِسَابِ الْفَضَائِلِ، وَالْكَمَالَاتِ الْمُمْكِنَةِ لِلْإِنْسَانِ، وَاجْتِنَابِ الرَّذَائِلِ، وَهِيَ مَشْغُوفَةٌ بِمَا يُقَرِّبُهَا مِنْ الرَّفِيقِ الْأَعْلَى، وَذَلِكَ قُوتُهَا، وَغِذَاؤُهَا، وَدَوَاؤُهَا، وَاشْتِغَالُهَا بِغَيْرِهِ هُوَ دَوَاؤُهَا.

There are three types of souls: a heavenly, elevated self whose love is directed towards knowledge, the acquisition of virtues and attainable human perfection while avoiding despicable matters. This soul is impassioned by what brings it closer to *al-rafīq al 'alā* (the heavenly souls), which is its strength, nourishment, and medicine. Its preoccupation with anything else is its sickness.

وَنَفْسٌ سَبْعِيَّةٌ غَضْبِيَّةٌ، فَمَحَبَّتُهَا مُنْصَرِفَةٌ إِلَى الْقَهْرِ، وَالْبَغْيِ، وَالْعُلُوِّ فِي الْأَرْضِ، وَالتَّكَبُّرِ، وَالرِّئَاسَةِ عَلَى النَّاسِ بِالْبَاطِلِ، فَلَذَّتُهَا فِي ذَلِكَ، وَشَغَفُهَا بِهِ.

---

[26] Rawḍah al Muḥibbīn.

The second type is the angry, aggressive soul whose love is directed towards domination, aggression, pride, and leadership through injustice. Its pleasure lies in that, and its desire is strong.

وَنَفْسٌ حَيَوَانِيَّةٌ شَهْوَانِيَّةٌ، فَمَحَبَّتُهَا مُنْصَرِفَةٌ إِلَى الْمَآكِلِ، وَالْمَشْرَبِ، وَالْمَنْكَحِ،

The third type is the animalistic, lustful soul whose love is directed toward food, drink and sex.

وَرُبَّمَا جَمَعَتِ الْأَمْرَيْنِ، فَانْصَرَفَتْ مَحَبَّتُهَا إِلَى الْعُلُوِّ فِي الْأَرْضِ، وَالْفَسَادِ، كَمَا قَالَ تَعَالَى: {**إِنَّ فِرْعَوْنَ عَلَىٰ فِي الْأَرْضِ وَجَعَلَ أَهْلَهَا شِيَعًا يَسْتَضْعِفُ طَائِفَةً مِنْهُمْ يُذَبِّحُ أَبْنَاءَهُمْ وَيَسْتَحْيِي نِسَاءَهُمْ إِنَّهُ كَانَ مِنَ الْمُفْسِدِينَ**} [القصص:4]. وَقَالَ فِي آخِرِ السُّورَةِ: {**تِلْكَ الدَّارُ الْآخِرَةُ نَجْعَلُهَا لِلَّذِينَ لَا يُرِيدُونَ عُلُوًّا فِي الْأَرْضِ وَلَا فَسَادًا وَالْعَاقِبَةُ لِلْمُتَّقِينَ**}

Perhaps it combines both, leading it toward corruption and domination on Earth. Allah (سُبْحَانَهُ وَتَعَالَىٰ) says: "**Verily, Pharaoh exalted himself in the land and made its people sects, weakening (oppressing) a group (i.e., Children of Israel) among them, killing their sons and letting their females live. Verily, he was of the Mufsidoon (those who commit great sins and crimes, oppressors, tyrants, etc.).**"[27] And at the end of the *Surah*: "**That home of the Hereafter (i.e. Paradise), We shall assign to those who rebel not against the truth with pride and oppression in the land nor do mischief by committing crimes. And the good end is for the Muttaqun (pious).**"[28]

وَالْحُبُّ فِي هَذَا الْعَالَمِ دَائِرٌ بَيْنَ هَذِهِ النُّفُوسِ الثَّلَاثَةِ، فَأَيُّ نَفْسٍ مِنْهَا صَادَفَتْ مَا يَلَائِمُ طَبْعَهَا؛ اسْتَحْسَنَتْهُ وَمَالَتْ إِلَيْهِ، وَلَمْ تُصْغِ فِيهِ لِعَاذِلٍ، وَلَمْ يَأْخُذْهَا فِيهِ لَوْمَةُ لَائِمٍ،

---

[27] Al-Qaṣaṣ: 4.

[28] Al-Qaṣaṣ: 83.

Love in this world revolves around these three types of souls. Whichever soul encounters what suits its nature, it approves and inclines towards it, not listening to the dissuaders nor being blamed by the blamers.

وَكُلُّ قِسْمٍ مِنْ هَـذِهِ الْأَقْسَامِ يَرَوْنَ أَنَّ مَا هُـمْ فِيهِ أَوْلَى بِالْإِيثَارِ، وَأَنَّ الاشْتِغَالَ بِغَيْرِهِ، وَالإقْبَالَ عَلَىٰ سِوَاهُ غُبْنٌ، وَفَوَاتُ حَظٍّ،

Each type sees that what they are preoccupied with is worth sacrificing for, and that being preoccupied with anything else and turning away from it is a loss."

# Chapter 2

## The Authority of Faith in the Heart

*The Source of the Heart's Life & Strength*

*A Good Heart is the Key to A Good Life: Knowledge, Ambition & Noble Character*

*Chapter Conclusion: Building the Fortress of Faith upon A Solid Foundation*

# 2. The Authority of Faith in the Heart

Al-Nu'mān b. Bashīr (رَضِيَ ٱللَّهُ عَنْهُمَا) reported from Allah's Messenger (صَلَّى ٱللَّهُ عَلَيْهِ وَسَلَّمَ) who said:

**"أَلَا وَإِنَّ فِي الْجَسَدِ مُضْغَةً: إِذَا صَلَحَتْ صَلَحَ الْجَسَدُ كُلُّهُ، وَإِذَا فَسَدَتْ فَسَدَ الْجَسَدُ كُلُّهُ، أَلَا وَهِيَ الْقَلْبُ".**

**"In the body there is a piece of flesh which, if it is sound, the whole body will be sound, and if it is corrupt, the whole body will be corrupt. It is the heart."[29]**

Abū Hurayrah (رَضِيَ ٱللَّهُ عَنْهُ) said:[30]

**"الْقَلْبُ مَلِكٌ وَلَهُ جُنُودٌ، فَإِذَا صَلُحَ الْمَلِكُ صَلُحَتْ جُنُودُهُ، وإِذَا فَسَدَ الْمَلِكُ فَسَدَتْ جُنُودُهُ".**

**"The heart is a king and it has armies. If the king is righteous, his armies are righteous. And if the king is corrupt, his armies are corrupt."**

Shaykh al Islām Ibn Taymiyyah (d. 728 AH رَحِمَهُ ٱللَّهُ) explains the statement of Abū Hurayrah (رَضِيَ ٱللَّهُ عَنْهُ), saying:[31]

«فَأَصْلُ الْإِيمَانِ فِي الْقَلْبِ وَهُوَ قَوْلُ الْقَلْبِ وَعَمَلُهُ، وَهُوَ: إِقْرَارٌ بِالتَّصْدِيقِ وَالْحُبُّ وَالِانْقِيَادُ،

---

[29] Agreed upon by al Bukhārī and Muslim.

[30] *Muṣannaf* 'Abd al-Razzāq (21445); *Jāmi'* of Ma'mar (20375).

[31] *Majmū' al Fatāwā* (7/644).

"The basis of faith is in the heart, which is the heart's speech and actions. It is an affirmation of belief, along with love and compliance.

وَمَا كَانَ فِي الْقَلْبِ فَلَا بُدَّ أَنْ يَظْهَرَ مُوجِبُهُ وَمُقْتَضَاهُ عَلَى الْجَوَارِحِ وَإِذَا لَمْ يَعْمَلْ بِمُوجِبِهِ وَمُقْتَضَاهُ دَلَّ عَلَى عَدَمِهِ أَوْ ضَعْفِهِ؛

Whatever truly exists in one's heart will naturally manifest in their actions. Failure to act in line with those inner convictions suggests that these beliefs don't truly exist, or that they lack strength.

وَلِهَذَا كَانَتْ الْأَعْمَالُ الظَّاهِرَةُ مِنْ مُوجِبِ إِيمَانِ الْقَلْبِ وَمُقْتَضَاهُ وَهِيَ تَصْدِيقٌ لِمَا فِي الْقَلْبِ وَدَلِيلٌ عَلَيْهِ وَشَاهِدٌ لَهُ وَهِيَ شُعْبَةٌ مِنْ مَجْمُوعِ الْإِيمَانِ الْمُطْلَقِ وَبُعْضٌ لَهُ؛ لَكِنَّ مَا فِي الْقَلْبِ هُوَ الْأَصْلُ لِمَا عَلَى الْجَوَارِحِ كَمَا قَالَ أَبُو هُرَيْرَةَ رضي الله عنه»

This is why outward deeds emanate from what the emān (faith) of the heart requires and necessitates and are an affirmation of what is in the heart, a proof of it, and a witness to it. They are a branch of total absolute faith and a part of it; however, what is in the heart is the basis of what is on the limbs, as Abu Hurayrah (رَضِيَٱللَّهُعَنْهُ) said."

---

Elsewhere, Ibn Taymiyyah (رَحِمَهُٱللَّهُ) explains the centrality of the heart as the origin point of all acts of obedience and disobedience:

"فَصَلَاحُهُ وَفَسَادُهُ يَسْتَلْزِمُ صَلَاحَ الْجَسَدِ وَفَسَادَهُ، فَيَكُونُ هَذَا مِمَّا أَبْدَاهُ لَا مِمَّا أَخْفَاهُ. وَكُلُّ مَا أَوْجَبَهُ اللَّهُ عَلَى الْعِبَادِ لَا بُدَّ أَنْ يَجِبَ عَلَى الْقَلْبِ، فَإِنَّهُ الْأَصْلُ وَإِنْ وَجَبَ عَلَى غَيْرِهِ تَبَعًا،

"So, (the heart's) rectitude and corruption necessitate the rectitude or corruption of the body, and this is what it externalizes, not what it internalizes. Everything Allah has mandated upon His servants, must necessarily be incumbent upon the heart, as it is the foundation. It's being obligatory upon something else is only secondary.

فَالْعَبْدُ الْمَأْمُورُ الْمَنْهِيُّ إِنَّمَا يَعْلَمُ بِالْأَمْرِ وَالنَّهْيِ قَلْبُهُ، وَإِنَّمَا يُقْصَدُ بِالطَّاعَةِ وَالِامْتِثَالِ الْقَلْبُ، وَالْعِلْمُ بِالْمَأْمُورِ وَالِامْتِثَالُ يَكُونُ قَبْلَ وُجُودِ الْفِعْلِ الْمَأْمُورِ بِهِ كَالصَّلَاةِ وَالزَّكَاةِ وَالصِّيَامِ، وَإِذَا كَانَ الْعَبْدُ قَدْ أَعْرَضَ عَنْ مَعْرِفَةِ الْأَمْرِ وَقَصْدِ الِامْتِثَالِ كَانَ أَوَّلَ الْمَعْصِيَةِ مِنْهُ؛ بَلْ كَانَ هُوَ الْعَاصِيَ وَغَيْرُهُ تَبَعٌ لَهُ فِي ذَلِكَ".

The commanded and prohibited servant only *knows* the command and prohibition through his heart. The aim of obedience and *compliance* is the heart. *Knowledge* of the command and *compliance* (in the heart) precedes the performance of the commanded action, like prayer, zakat (charitable giving), and fasting. If a servant turns away from having *knowledge* of the command and *intending to comply*, the first instance of disobedience comes from (the heart); in fact, it is the disobedient one, and other (parts or organs of the body) are just following it in that regard."

---

Elsewhere, Ibn Taymiyyah (رَحِمَهُ ٱللَّهُ) explains the above-mentioned *hadīth* of al-Nu'mān b. Bashīr and the statement of Abū Hurayrah (رَضِيَ ٱللَّهُ عَنْهُمَا), saying:[32]

"وَقَوْلُ أَبِي هُرَيْرَةَ تَقْرِيبٌ، وَقَوْلُ النَّبِيِّ ﷺ أَحْسَنُ بَيَانًا

"Abu Hurayrah's (رَضِيَ ٱللَّهُ عَنْهُ) statement is an approximation, and the Prophet's (صَلَّى ٱللَّهُ عَلَيْهِ وَسَلَّمَ) statement is the best explanation.

فَإِنَّ الْمَلِكَ وَإِنْ كَانَ صَالِحًا فَالْجُنْدُ لَهُمْ اخْتِيَارٌ ، قَدْ يَعْصُونَ بِهِ مَلِكَهُمْ وَبِالْعَكْسِ، فَيَكُونُ فِيهِمْ صَلَاحٌ مَعَ فَسَادِهِ أَوْ فَسَادٌ مَعَ صَلَاحِهِ؛ بِخِلَافِ الْقَلْبِ،

[32] Ibid. (7/187).

فَإِنَّ الْجَسَدَ تَابِعٌ لَهُ لَا يَخْرُجُ عَنْ إرَادَتِهِ قَطُّ كَمَا قَالَ النَّبِيُّ صلى الله عليه وسلم " {**إذَا صَلَحَتْ صَلَحَ لَهَا سَائِرُ الْجَسَدِ وَإِذَا فَسَدَتْ فَسَدَ لَهَا سَائِرُ الْجَسَدِ**} ".

Even if the king is righteous, the army has a choice by which they might disobey their king and vice versa, so there can be righteousness in them despite his corruption or corruption despite his righteousness; unlike the heart, for the body follows it and does not go against its will ever, as the Prophet (ﷺ) said, **"When the heart is righteous, the rest of the body is righteous, and if it is corrupt, the rest of the body is corrupt."**

فَإِذَا كَانَ الْقَلْبُ صَالِحًا بِمَا فِيهِ مِنْ الْإِيمَانِ عِلْمًا وَعَمَلًا قَلْبِيًّا، لَزِمَ ضَرُورَةُ صَلَاحِ الْجَسَدِ بِالْقَوْلِ الظَّاهِرِ وَالْعَمَلِ بِالْإِيمَانِ الْمُطْلَقِ كَمَا قَالَ أَئِمَّةُ أَهْلِ الْحَدِيثِ: قَوْلٌ وَعَمَلٌ قَوْلٌ بَاطِنٌ وَظَاهِرٌ وَعَمَلٌ بَاطِنٌ وَظَاهِرٌ وَالظَّاهِرُ تَابِعٌ لِلْبَاطِنِ لَازِمٌ لَهُ مَتَى صَلَحَ الْبَاطِنُ صَلَحَ الظَّاهِرُ وَإِذَا فَسَدَ فَسَدَ»

So if the heart is righteous due to what it contains of faith, both in knowledge and in heart-centered action, the body must be righteous in outward speech and action with absolute faith, as the *Imāms* of *Ahl al-Hadith* said: 'It (i.e., *emān*) is both statement and action, internal and external, and the external follows the internal and is contingent upon it. When the internal is righteous, the external is righteous, and if it is corrupt, it becomes corrupt.'"

---

Similarly, Imām Ibn al Qayyim (رَحِمَهُ ٱللَّهُ) wrote in the opening pages of his book on the conflict between the heart, the self, and Shayṭān, the following words about the centrality of the heart and it being the king over the remainder of the body:[33]

[33] Ighāthah al-Lahfān, introduction.

وَ لَمَّا كَانَ الْقَلْبُ لِهَذِهِ الْأَعْضَاءِ كَالْمَلِكِ الْمُتَصَرِّفِ فِي الْجُنُودِ، الَّذِي تَصْدُرُ كُلُّهَا عَنْ أَمْرِهِ، وَيَسْتَعْمِلُهَا فِيمَا شَاءَ، فَكُلُّهَا تَحْتَ عَبُودِيَّتِهِ وَقَهْرِهِ، وَتَكْتَسِبُ مِنْهُ الْإِقَامَةَ وَالزَّيْغَ، وَتَتَّبِعُهُ فِيمَا يَعْقِدُهُ مِنَ الْعَزْمِ أَوْ يَحِلُّهُ، قَالَ النَّبِيُّ -صَلَّى اللَّهُ عَلَيْهِ وَسَلَّمَ-: "**أَلَا إِنَّ فِي الْجَسَدِ مُضْغَةً؛ إِذَا صَلَحَتْ صَلَحَ الْجَسَدُ كُلُّهُ، وَإِذَا فَسَدَتْ فَسَدَ الْجَسَدُ كُلُّهُ**".

And since the heart is to these bodily limbs like the king who manages his soldiers, from whose command they all emanate, and he employs them as he pleases, they are all under his servitude and control. They derive from him their uprightness and deviation, and they follow him in what he decides to carry out or abandon as the Prophet (ﷺ) said: "**Indeed, there is a piece of flesh in the body; if it is sound, the whole body is sound, and if it is corrupt, the whole body is corrupt.**"

فَهُوَ مَلِكُهَا، وَهِيَ الْمُنَفِّذَةُ لِمَا يَأْمُرُهَا بِهِ، الْقَابِلَةُ لِمَا يَأْتِيهَا مِنْ هَدِيَّتِهِ، وَلَا يَسْتَقِيمُ لَهَا شَيْءٌ مِنْ أَعْمَالِهَا حَتَّى تَصْدُرَ عَنْ قَصْدِهِ وَنِيَّتِهِ، وَهُوَ الْمَسْؤُولُ عَنْهَا كُلِّهَا؛ لِأَنَّ كُلَّ رَاعٍ مَسْؤُولٌ عَنْ رَعِيَّتِهِ — كَانَ الِاهْتِمَامُ بِتَصْحِيحِهِ وَتَسْدِيدِهِ أَوْلَى مَا اعْتَمَدَ عَلَيْهِ السَّالِكُونَ، وَالنَّظَرُ فِي أَمْرَاضِهِ وَعِلَاجِهَا أَهَمَّ مَا تَنَسَّكَ بِهِ النَّاسِكُونَ.

Thus, it (i,e., the heart) is their king, and they are the executors of what he commands them, receptive to his guidance. Nothing in their actions can be correct unless it comes from his intention and purpose, and he is responsible for them all because every shepherd is responsible for his flock. Therefore, the primary focus for those on the spiritual path must be correcting and directing the heart, while examining its diseases and treating them is the most important task for devoted worshipers.

ولَمَّا عَلِمَ عَدُو اللهِ إِبْلِيسُ أَنَّ الْمَدَارَ عَلَى الْقَلْبِ وَالِاعْتِمَادَ عَلَيْهِ؛ أَجْلَبَ عَلَيْهِ بِالْوَسَاوِسِ، وَأَقْبَلَ بِوُجُوهِ الشَّهَوَاتِ إِلَيْهِ، وَزَيَّنَ لَهُ مِنَ الْأَحْوَالِ وَالْأَعْمَالِ مَا يَصُدُّهُ بِهِ عَنِ الطَّرِيقِ، وَأَمَدَّهُ مِنْ أَسْبَابِ الْغَيِّ بِمَا يَقْطَعُهُ عَنْ أَسْبَابِ التَّوْفِيقِ، وَنَصَبَ

لَهُ مِنَ الْمَصَايِدَ وَالْحَبَائِلَ مَا إِنْ سَلِمَ مِنَ الْوُقُوعِ فِيهَا لَمْ يَسلَمْ مِنْ أَنْ يَحْصُلَ لَهُ بِهَا التَّعْوِيقُ،

When the enemy of Allah, *Shayṭān*, knew that the heart is central and primarily depended on, he overwhelmed it with whispers and turned the focus of desires towards it. He adorned for it conditions and acts that would distract it from the path, extended to it the causes of misguidance that would cut it off from the causes of success, and set traps and snares for it. If one were to escape falling into them, they would not escape what they present of obstacles.

فَلا نَجَاةَ مِنْ مَصَايِدِهِ وَمَكَايِدِهِ إِلَّا بِدَوَامِ الاسْتِعَانَةِ بِاللَّهِ تَعَالَى، وَالتَّعَرُّضِ لِأَسْبَابِ مَرْضَاتِهِ، وَالْتِجَاءِ الْقَلْبِ إِلَيْهِ وَإِقْبَالِهِ عَلَيْهِ فِي حَرَكَاتِهِ وَسَكَنَاتِهِ، وَالتَّحَقُّقِ بِذُلِّ الْعُبُودِيَّةِ الَّذِي هُوَ أَوْلَى مَا تَلَبَّسَ بِهِ الْإِنْسَانُ لِيَحْصُلَ لَهُ الدُّخُولُ فِي ضِمَانِ {**إِنَّ عِبَادِي لَيْسَ لَكَ عَلَيْهِمْ سُلْطَانٌ**}؛

There is no escape from his traps and schemes except by constantly seeking the help of Allah exposing oneself to the causes of His pleasure, turning one's heart towards Him and focusing on Him in all actions and stillness, and realizing the humility of servitude, which is the first condition for a person to enter the guarantee of, "**Indeed, My servants - no authority will you have over them.**"[34]

فَهَذِهِ الْإِضَافَةُ هِيَ الْقَاطِعَةُ بَيْنَ الْعَبْدِ وَبَيْنَ الشَّيَاطِينِ، وَحُصُولُهَا بِسَبَبِ تَحْقِيقِ مَقَامِ الْعُبُودِيَّةِ لِرَبِّ الْعَالَمِينَ، وَإِشْعَارِ الْقَلْبِ بِإِخْلَاصِ الْعِلْمِ وَدَوَامِ الْيَقِينِ، فَإِذَا أُشْرِبَ الْقَلْبُ الْعُبُودِيَّةَ وَالْإِخْلَاصَ صَارَ عِنْدَ اللَّهِ مِنَ الْمُقَرَّبِينَ، وَشَمِلَهُ اسْتِثْنَاءُ {**إِلَّا عِبَادَكَ مِنْهُمُ الْمُخْلَصِينَ**}.

This possessive ascription (i.e. My servants) is the decisive factor between the servant and the devils, and its attainment is

[34] Al-Hijr: 42.

due to the realization of the station of servitude to the Lord of the Worlds and making the heart aware of the sincerity of knowledge and the constancy of certainty. When the heart is imbued with servitude and sincerity, it becomes one of those who are close to Allah, and it is included in the exception of "**Except Your sincere servants among them.**"[35]

وَلَمَّا مَنَّ اللَّهُ الْكَرِيمُ بِلُطْفِهِ بِالإِطِّلاعِ عَلَى مَا أَطْلَعَ عَلَيْهِ مِنْ أَمْرَاضِ الْقُلُوبِ وَأَدْوَائِهَا، وَمَا يَعْرِضُ لَهَا مِنْ وَسَاوِسِ الشَّيَاطِينِ أَعْدَائِهَا، وَمَا تُثْمِرُهَا تِلْكَ الْوَسَاوِسُ مِنَ الْأَعْمَالِ، وَمَا يَكْتَسِبُ الْقَلْبُ بَعْدَهَا مِنَ الْأَحْوَالِ، فَإِنَّ الْعَمَلَ السَّيِّءَ مَصْدَرُهُ عَنْ فَسَادِ قَصْدِ الْقَلْبِ، ثُمَّ يُعْرَضُ لِلْقَلْبِ مِنْ فَسَادِ الْعَمَلِ قَسْوَةٌ، فَيَزْدَادُ مَرَضًا عَلَى مَرَضِهِ حَتَّى يَمُوتَ، وَيَبْقَى لَا حَيَاةَ فِيهِ وَلَا نُورَ لَهُ، وَكُلُّ ذَلِكَ مِنْ انْفِعَالِهِ لَوَسْوَسَةِ الشَّيْطَانِ، وَرُكُونِهِ إِلَى عَدُوِّهِ الَّذِي لَا يُفْلِحُ إِلَّا مَنْ جَاهَرَهُ بِالْعُصِيَانِ — أَرَدْتُ أَنْ أُقَيِّدَ ذَلِكَ فِي هَذَا الْكِتَابِ.

Allah, The Most Generous, in His grace, allowed insight into the diseases of the hearts and their remedies, as well as the whispers of the devils that afflict them and the actions that these whispers produce, and the conditions that the heart acquires thereafter — it becomes clear that the source of evil deeds is the corruption of the heart's intention. Then, the heart is exposed to the hardness caused by the corruption of the deed, which adds to its illness until it dies, leaving it with no life or light. All of this is due to the influence of Satan's whispers and its submission to its enemy, who only succeeds against those who openly disobey. I wanted to compile all of this in this book."[36]

---

[35] Al-Hijr: 40.

[36] i.e., *Ighāthah al-Lahfān*. The first thirteen chapters lay a detailed framework for the interplay of the conflict between the heart, the self and the Shayṭān. These chapters have been translated and published by our esteemed brothers at *Hikmah Publications* under the title, "*Purification of the Heart: Its Diseases & Their Cures*" (2023).

# THE SOURCE OF THE HEART'S LIFE & STRENGTH

Ibn al Qayyim (رَحِمَهُ ٱللَّهُ) said:[37]

"وَالْقَلْبُ خُلِقَ لِمَعْرِفَةِ فَاطِرِهِ وَمَحَبَّتِهِ وَتَوْحِيدِهِ وَالسُّرُورِ بِهِ، وَالِابْتِهَاجِ بِحُبِّهِ، وَالرِّضَى عَنْهُ، وَالتَّوَكُّلِ عَلَيْهِ، وَالْحُبِّ فِيهِ، وَالْبُغْضِ فِيهِ، وَالْمُوَالَاةِ فِيهِ، وَالْمُعَادَاةِ فِيهِ، وَدَوَامِ ذِكْرِهِ، وَأَنْ يَكُونَ أَحَبَّ إِلَيْهِ مِنْ كُلِّ مَا سِوَاهُ، وَأَرْجَى عِنْدَهُ مِنْ كُلِّ مَا سِوَاهُ، وَأَجَلَّ فِي قَلْبِهِ مِنْ كُلِّ مَا سِوَاهُ،

"And the heart was created for knowing its Creator, loving Him, singling Him out (with His rights), rejoicing in Him, delighting in His love, being pleased with Him, reliance on Him, love and aversion for His sake, allegiance and enmity for His sake, perpetual remembrance of Him, and His being dearer to it than anything else, more hopeful with it than anything else, and more venerable in its heart than anything else.

وَلَا نَعِيمَ لَهُ وَلَا سُرُورَ وَلَا لَذَّةَ بَلْ وَلَا حَيَاةَ إِلَّا بِذَلِكَ، وَهَذَا لَهُ بِمَنْزِلَةِ الْغِذَاءِ، وَالصِّحَّةِ، وَالْحَيَاةِ، فَإِذَا فَقَدَ غِذَاءَهُ، وَصِحَّتَهُ، وَحَيَاتَهُ؛ فَالْهُمُومُ وَالْغُمُومُ وَالْأَحْزَانُ مُسَارِعَةٌ مِنْ كُلِّ صَوْبٍ إِلَيْهِ، وَرَهْنٌ مُقِيمٌ عَلَيْهِ".

There is no bliss, joy, pleasure, or even life for it except through this. This is to it like food, health, and life. If it loses food, health, life, worries, sadness, and sorrows, rush towards it from all sides, and a perpetual pledge hangs over it."

---

Elsewhere, Ibn al Qayyim (رَحِمَهُ ٱللَّهُ) explained that the heart's main function is *knowledge* — the most important of which is to know Allah — and *intention*, the most important

---

[37] *al-Ṭibb al-Nabawī* from *Zād al Ma'ād* (4/289).

of which is to sincerely draw near to him and seek His good pleasure. He writes:[38]

وَالْمَقْصُودُ أَنَّ اللَّهَ سُبْحَانَهُ وَتَعَالَى لَمَّا اقْتَضَتْ حِكْمَتُهُ وَرَحْمَتُهُ إِخْرَاجَ آدَمَ وَذُرِّيَّتَهُ مِنَ الْجَنَّةِ أَعَاضَهُمْ أَفْضَلَ مِنْهَا، وَهُوَ مَا أَعْطَاهُمْ مِنْ عَهْدِهِ الَّذِي جَعَلَهُ سَبَبًا مُوْصِلًا لَهُمْ إِلَيْهِ، وَطَرِيقًا وَاضِحًا بَيِّنَ الدَّلَالَةِ عَلَيْهِ، مَنْ تَمَسَّكَ بِهِ فَازَ وَاهْتَدَى، وَمَنْ أَعْرَضَ عَنْهُ شَقِيَ وَغَوَى.

"The intent is that when Allah's wisdom and mercy, glory be unto Him, necessitated the expulsion of Adam and his offspring from Paradise, He compensated them with something better than it, which is what He gave them of His covenant through which He made a means for them to reach Him and a clear path that distinctly leads to Him. Whoever clings to it succeeds and is guided, and whoever turns away from it suffers and goes astray.

وَلَمَّا كَانَ هَذَا الْعَهْدُ الْكَرِيمُ، وَالصِّرَاطُ الْمُسْتَقِيمُ، وَالنَّبَأُ الْعَظِيمُ، لَا يُوَصَّلُ إِلَيْهِ أَبَدًا إِلَّا مِنْ بَابِ الْعِلْمِ وَالْإِرَادَةِ؛ فَالْإِرَادَةُ بَابُ الْوُصُولِ إِلَيْهِ، وَالْعِلْمُ مِفْتَاحُ ذَلِكَ الْبَابِ الْمُتَوَقِّفُ فَتْحُهُ عَلَيْهِ، **وَكَمَالُ كُلِّ إِنْسَانٍ إِنَّمَا يَتِمُّ بِهَذَيْنِ النَّوْعَيْنِ: هِمَّةٌ تُرْقِيهِ، وَعِلْمٌ يُبَصِّرُهُ وَيَهْدِيهِ.** فَإِنَّ مَرَاتِبَ السَّعَادَةِ وَالْفَلَاحِ إِنَّمَا تَفُوتُ الْعَبْدَ مِنْ هَاتَيْنِ الْجِهَتَيْنِ، أَوْ مِنْ إِحْدَاهُمَا:

Given that this honorable covenant, this straight path, and this great news can never be reached except through the gate of knowledge and intention; thus, the intention is the gate to reach Him, and knowledge is the key to that gate whose opening depends on it. *The perfection of every person can only be achieved with these two kinds: ambition that uplifts him and knowledge that enlightens and guides him.* The degrees of happiness and success only escape the servant from these two aspects or one of them:

---

[38] Miftāḥ Dār al-Sa'ādah, introduction. Ibn al Qayyim wrote the book Miftāḥ Dār al-Sa'ādah as an explanation of the first principle, which is love. He wrote another book, Rawḍah al Muḥibbīn, about love, which is the second principle function of the heart.

* إِمَّا أَنَّ لَا يَكُونَ لَهُ عِلْمٌ بِهَا، فَلَا يَتَحَرَّكُ فِي طَلَبِهَا.

* Either he has no knowledge of it (i.e., happiness and success), so he does not move to seek them.

* أَوْ يَكُونُ عَالِمًا بِهَا وَلَا تَنْهَضُ هَمَّتُهُ إِلَيْهَا.

* Or he is knowledgeable about it but his determination does not rise towards it.

فَلَا يَزَالُ فِي حَضِيضِ طَبْعِهِ مَحْبُوسًا، وَقَلْبُهُ عَنْ كَمَالِهِ الَّذِي خُلِقَ لَهُ مَصْدُودًا مُنْكَوِسًا، قَدْ أَسَامَ نَفْسَهُ مَعَ الْأَنْعَامِ رَاعِيًا مَعَ الْهَمَلِ، وَاسْتَطَابَ لُقَيْمَاتِ الرَّاحَةِ وَالْبَطَالَةِ، وَاسْتَلَانَ فِرَاشَ الْعَجْزِ وَالْكَسَلِ، لَا كَمَنْ رُفِعَ لَهُ عَلَمٌ فَشَمَّرَ إِلَيْهِ، وَبُورِكَ لَهُ فِي تَفَرُّدِهِ فِي طَرِيقِ طَلَبِهِ فَلَزِمَهُ وَاسْتَقَامَ عَلَيْهِ، قَدْ أَبَتْ غَلَبَاتُ شَوْقِهِ إِلَّا الْهِجْرَةَ إِلَى اللَّهِ وَرَسُولِهِ، وَمَقَتَتْ نَفْسُهُ الرُّفَقَاءَ إِلَّا ابْنَ سَبِيلٍ يُرَافِقُهُ فِي سَبِيلِهِ.

So he remains confined in the lowlands of his nature, and his heart is repelled and turned away from the perfection for which he was created. He degrades himself among the cattle, shepherding among the sheep, enjoying the taste of comfort and idleness, reclining on the bed of incapacity and laziness. Unlike the one for whom a guidepost is raised, he rolls up his sleeves towards it, is blessed in his isolation on the path of seeking it, adheres to it and remains steadfast upon it. The overpowering waves of his longing refuse anything but migration to Allah, His messenger, and his self detests any companions except a wayfarer accompanying him on his path.

وَلَمَّا كَانَ كَمَالُ الْإِرَادَةِ بِحَسَبِ كَمَالِ مُرَادِهَا، وَشَرَفُ الْعِلْمِ تَابِعٌ لِشَرَفِ مَعْلُومِهِ، كَانَتْ نِهَايَةُ سَعَادَةِ الْعَبْدِ الَّتِي لَا سَعَادَةَ لَهُ بِدُونِهَا وَلَا حَيَاةَ لَهُ إِلَّا بِهَا أَنْ تَكُونَ إِرَادَتُهُ مُتَعَلِّقَةً بِالْمُرَادِ الَّذِي لَا يَبْلَى وَلَا يَفُوتُ، وَعَزَمَاتُ هِمَّتِهِ مُسَافِرَةً إِلَى حَضْرَةِ الْحَيِّ الَّذِي لَا يَمُوتُ.

And since the perfection of will is according to the perfection of its object, and the nobility of knowledge follows the nobility of what is known, the ultimate happiness of the servant, which he has no happiness without, nor life except with it, is that his intention is attached to the desired object that does not fade or miss, and the resolutions of his determination journey to the presence of the Ever-Living who does not die.

وَلَا سَبِيلَ لَهُ إِلَى هَذَا الْمَطْلَبِ الْأَسْنَى وَالْحَظِّ الْأَوْفَى إِلَّا بِالْعِلْمِ الْمَوْرُوثِ عَنْ عَبْدِهِ وَرَسُولِهِ وَخَلِيلِهِ وَحَبِيبِهِ، الَّذِي بَعَثَهُ لِذَلِكَ دَاعِيًا، وَأَقَامَهُ عَلَى هَذَا الطَّرِيقِ هَادِيًا، وَجَعَلَهُ وَاسِطَةً بَيْنَهُ وَبَيْنَ الْأَنَامِ، وَدَاعِيًا لَهُمْ بِإِذْنِهِ إِلَى دَارِ السَّلَامِ،

And there is no way for him to this highest request and fullest portion of fortune except through the inherited knowledge from His servant, messenger, friend, and beloved (ﷺ), who was sent for this purpose, established on this path as a guide. And He made him a mediator between Him and the people, calling them by His permission to the home of peace.

وَأَبَى سُبْحَانَهُ أَنْ يَفْتَحَ لِأَحَدٍ مِنْهُمْ إِلَّا عَلَى يَدَيْهِ، أَوْ يَقْبَلَ مِنْ أَحَدٍ مِنْهُمْ سَعْيًا إِلَّا أَنْ يَكُونَ مُبْتَدَئًا مِنْهُ وَمُنْتَهِيًا إِلَيْهِ، فَالطُّرُقُ كُلُّهَا إِلَّا طَرِيقَهُ صَلَّى اللَّهُ عَلَيْهِ وَسَلَّمَ مَسْدُودَةٌ، وَالْقُلُوبُ بِأَسْرِهَا إِلا قُلُوبَ أَتْبَاعِهِ الْمُنْقَادَةِ إِلَيْهِ عَنِ اللَّهِ مَحْبُوسَةٌ مَصْدُودَةٌ.

He (سُبْحَانَهُ وَتَعَالَى) refused to open for any of them except through his hands or accept any striving from them unless it begins with him and ends with him. So all paths except his path (ﷺ) are blocked, and all hearts, except those of his followers who surrender to Him (جَلَّ وَعَلَا), are confined and obstructed from Allah.

فَحَقٌّ عَلَى مَنْ كَانَ فِي سَعَادَةِ نَفْسِهِ سَاعِيًا، وَكَانَ قَلْبُهُ حَيًّا عَنِ اللَّهِ وَاعِيًا، أَنْ يَجْعَلَ عَلَى هَذَيْنِ الْأَصْلَيْنِ مَدَارَ أَقْوَالِهِ وَأَعْمَالِهِ، وَأَنْ يُصَيِّرَهُمَا آخِيَّتَهُ الَّتِي إِلَيْهَا مَفْزَعُهُ فِي حَيَاتِهِ وَمَآلِهِ.

It is incumbent upon whoever is pursuing his own happiness, and whose heart is alive and aware of Allah, to make his statements and deeds revolve around these two principles and make them their ultimate resort in their life and their final destination."

## A GOOD HEART IS THE KEY TO A GOOD LIFE

Ibn al Qayyim (رَحِمَهُ ٱللَّهُ) explains that the keys to the good life are knowledge, determination, and character. He says:[39]

"وَقَدْ جَعَلَ اللَّهُ الْحَيَاةَ الطَّيِّبَةَ لِأَهْلِ مَعْرِفَتِهِ وَمَحَبَّتِهِ وَعِبَادَتِهِ، فَقَالَ تَعَالَى: {مَنْ عَمِلَ صَالِحًا مِنْ ذَكَرٍ أَوْ أُنْثَى وَهُوَ مُؤْمِنٌ فَلَنُحْيِيَنَّهُ حَيَاةً طَيِّبَةً وَلَنَجْزِيَنَّهُمْ أَجْرَهُمْ بِأَحْسَنِ مَا كَانُوا يَعْمَلُونَ}

"And Allah has made the good life for those who know Him, love Him, and worship Him. So He says: "**Whoever does righteousness, whether male or female, while he is a believer - We will surely cause him to live a good life, and We will surely give them their reward [in the Hereafter] according to the best of what they used to do.**"[40]

وَقَدْ فُسِّرَتِ الْحَيَاةُ الطَّيِّبَةُ بِالْقَنَاعَةِ وَالرِّضَا، وَالرِّزْقِ الْحَسَنِ وَغَيْرِ ذَلِكَ، وَالصَّوَابُ: **أَنَّهَا حَيَاةُ الْقَلْبِ وَنَعِيمُهُ، وَبَهْجَتُهُ وَسُرُورُهُ بِالْإِيمَانِ وَمَعْرِفَةُ اللَّهِ، وَمَحَبَّتُهُ، وَالْإِنَابَةُ إِلَيْهِ، وَالتَّوَكُّلُ عَلَيْهِ**، فَإِنَّهُ لَا حَيَاةَ أَطْيَبُ مِنْ حَيَاةِ صَاحِبِهَا، وَلَا نَعِيمَ فَوْقَ نَعِيمِهِ إِلَّا نَعِيمَ الْجَنَّةِ،

The '*good life*' has been interpreted to mean contentment, satisfaction, sound sustenance, and other things. *The most accurate interpretation is that it is the life of the heart and its delight, its joy and happiness in faith and knowledge of Allah, and love for Him, turning to Him, and reliance upon Him.* There is no life better than that of its

---

[39] Madārij al-Sālikīn.

[40] Al-Nahl: 97.

possessor, no bliss above its bliss, except for the pleasure of Paradise.

كَمَا كَانَ بَعْضُ الْعَارِفِينَ يَقُولُ: إِنَّهُ لَتَمُرُّ بِي أَوْقَاتٌ أَقُولُ فِيهَا إِنْ كَانَ أَهْلُ الْجَنَّةِ فِي مِثْلِ هَذَا إِنَّهُمْ لَفِي عَيْشٍ طَيِّبٍ، وَقَالَ غَيْرُهُ: إِنَّهُ لَيَمُرُّ بِالْقَلْبِ أَوْقَاتٌ يَرْقُصُ فِيهَا طَرَبًا.

As some of the enlightened people of knowledge used to say: 'There are times when I think that if the people of Paradise are in a state like this, they are surely living a good life.' Another said: 'There are times when the heart dances with joy.'

وَإِذَا كَانَتْ حَيَاةُ الْقَلْبِ حَيَاةً طَيِّبَةً تَبِعَتْهُ حَيَاةُ الْجَوَارِحِ، فَإِنَّهُ مَلِكُهَا، وَلِهَذَا جَعَلَ اللَّهُ الْمَعِيشَةَ الضَّنْكَ لِمَنْ أَعْرَضَ عَنْ ذِكْرِهِ، وَهِيَ عَكْسُ الْحَيَاةِ الطَّيِّبَةِ.

If the life of the heart is good, then the life of the limbs will follow it, for it is their king. For this reason, Allah has constricted life for those who turn away from His remembrance, which is the opposite of the good life.

وَهَذِهِ الْحَيَاةُ الطَّيِّبَةُ تَكُونُ فِي الدُّورِ الثَّلَاثِ، أَعْنِي: دَارَ الدُّنْيَا، وَدَارَ الْبَرْزَخِ، وَدَارَ الْقَرَارِ، وَالْمَعِيشَةُ الضَّنْكُ أَيْضًا تَكُونُ فِي الدُّورِ الثَّلَاثِ، فَالْأَبْرَارُ فِي النَّعِيمِ هُنَا وَهُنَالِكَ، وَالْفُجَّارُ فِي الْجَحِيمِ هُنَا وَهُنَالِكَ، قَالَ اللَّهُ تَعَالَى: {**لِلَّذِينَ أَحْسَنُوا فِي هَذِهِ الدُّنْيَا حَسَنَةٌ وَلَدَارُ الْآخِرَةِ خَيْرٌ**}، وَقَالَ تَعَالَى: {**وَأَنِ اسْتَغْفِرُوا رَبَّكُمْ ثُمَّ تُوبُوا إِلَيْهِ يُمَتِّعْكُمْ مَتَاعًا حَسَنًا إِلَى أَجَلٍ مُسَمًّى وَيُؤْتِ كُلَّ ذِي فَضْلٍ فَضْلَهُ**}

This good life takes place in the three abodes, namely: the worldly life (*dunya*), the intermediate stage (*barzakh*), and the eternal abode (*dar al-qarar*). The constricted life also occurs in these three abodes. The righteous live in bliss here and in the hereafter, while the wicked live in hell in this life and the next. Allah (سُبْحَانَهُ وَتَعَالَىٰ) says: "**For those who have done good is the best [reward] and extra.**"[41] And He (سُبْحَانَهُ وَتَعَالَىٰ) says: "**And ask**

[41] An-Nahl: 30.

**forgiveness of your Lord and then repent to Him. He will let you enjoy a good provision for a specified term and give every doer of favor his favor."**[42]

فَذِكْرُ اللَّهِ سبحانه وتعالى، وَمَحَبَّتُهُ وَطَاعَتُهُ، وَالْإِقْبَالُ عَلَيْهِ ضَامِنٌ لِأَطْيَبِ الْحَيَاةِ فِي الدُّنْيَا وَالْآخِرَةِ، وَالْإِعْرَاضُ عَنْهُ وَالْغَفْلَةُ وَمَعْصِيَتُهُ كَفِيلٌ بِالْحَيَاةِ الْمُنَغَّصَةِ، وَالْمَعِيشَةِ الضَّنْكِ فِي الدُّنْيَا وَالْآخِرَةِ

Therefore, remembering Allah (سُبْحَانَهُ وَتَعَالَىٰ), loving Him, obeying Him, and turning to Him guarantees the best life in this world and the hereafter. Turning away from Him, neglecting Him, and disobeying Him ensures a constricted life of hardship in this world and the hereafter."

## KNOWLEDGE ENLIVENS THE HEART

Ibn al Qayyim (رَحِمَهُ ٱللَّهُ) then proceeds to provide a detailed framework for the life of the heart that manifest in the righteous deeds of the body. He writes:

"(1.) **حَيَاةُ الْعِلْمِ مِنْ مَوْتِ الْجَهْلِ**، فَإِنَّ الْجَهْلَ مَوْتٌ لِأَصْحَابِهِ، كَمَا قِيلَ:

"(1.) The life of knowledge from the death of ignorance, for ignorance is death to its possessors, as it is said:

**وَفِي الْجَهْلِ قَبْلَ الْمَوْتِ مَوْتٌ لِأَهْلِهِ ... وَأَجْسَامُهُمْ قَبْلَ الْقُبُورِ قُبُورُ**

'In ignorance, before death, there is death for its people... and their bodies before the graves are graves.

وَأَرْوَاحُهُمْ فِي وَحْشَةٍ مِنْ جُسُومِهِمْ ... فَلَيْسَ لَهُمْ حَتَّى النُّشُورِ نُشُورُ

[42] Hud: 3.

And their souls are in estrangement from their bodies... so there is no resurrection for them until the Day of Resurrection.'

فَإِنَّ الْجَاهِلَ مَيِّتُ الْقَلْبِ وَالرُّوحِ، وَإِنْ كَانَ حَيَّ الْبَدَنِ فَجَسَدُهُ قَبْرٌ يَمْشِي بِهِ عَلَى وَجْهِ الْأَرْضِ،

Indeed, the ignorant is dead in heart and spirit, even if his body is alive; his body is a grave walking on the face of the earth.

قَالَ اللَّهُ تَعَالَى: {**أَوَمَنْ كَانَ مَيْتًا فَأَحْيَيْنَاهُ وَجَعَلْنَا لَهُ نُورًا يَمْشِي بِهِ فِي النَّاسِ كَمَنْ مَثَلُهُ فِي الظُّلُمَاتِ لَيْسَ بِخَارِجٍ مِنْهَا**}، وَقَالَ تَعَالَى: {**إِنْ هُوَ إِلَّا ذِكْرٌ وَقُرْآنٌ مُبِينٌ - لِيُنْذِرَ مَنْ كَانَ حَيًّا وَيَحِقَّ الْقَوْلُ عَلَى الْكَافِرِينَ**} ، وَقَالَ تَعَالَى: {**إِنَّكَ لَا تُسْمِعُ الْمَوْتَى وَلَا تُسْمِعُ الصُّمَّ الدُّعَاءَ**}، وَقَالَ تَعَالَى: {**إِنَّ اللَّهَ يُسْمِعُ مَنْ يَشَاءُ وَمَا أَنْتَ بِمُسْمِعٍ مَنْ فِي الْقُبُورِ**}

Allah (سُبْحَانَهُ وَتَعَالَىٰ) says: "**Or [he who] was dead and We gave him life and made for him light by which to walk among the people be like he who is in darkness, never to emerge from it?**"[43] And Allah (سُبْحَانَهُ وَتَعَالَىٰ) says: "**Indeed, it is nothing but a reminder and a clear Qur'an - to warn whoever is alive and justify the word against the disbelievers.**"[44] Allah (سُبْحَانَهُ وَتَعَالَىٰ) also says: "**Indeed, you will not make the dead hear, nor will you make the deaf hear the call.**"[45] And Allah (سُبْحَانَهُ وَتَعَالَىٰ) says: "**Indeed, Allah makes whom He wills to hear, and you cannot make those in the grave hear.**"[46]

وَشَبَّهَهُمْ فِي مَوْتِ قُلُوبِهِمْ بِأَهْلِ الْقُبُورِ، فَإِنَّهُمْ قَدْ مَاتَتْ أَرْوَاحُهُمْ، وَصَارَتْ أَجْسَامُهُمْ قُبُورًا لَهَا، فَكَمَا أَنَّهُ لَا يَسْمَعُ أَصْحَابُ الْقُبُورِ، كَذَلِكَ لَا يَسْمَعُ هَؤُلَاءِ،

---

[43] Surah Al-Anam: 122.

[44] Yasin: 69 - 70.

[45] An-Naml: 80.

[46] Fatir: 22.

He likened them — in the death of their hearts — to the people of the graves, for their spirits have died, and their bodies have become graves for them. Just as the people of the graves do not hear, nor do these people hear.

وَإِذَا كَانَتِ الْحَيَاةُ هِيَ الْحِسُّ وَالْحَرَكَةُ وَمَلْزُومُهُمَا، فَهَذِهِ الْقُلُوبُ لَمَّا لَمْ تُحِسَّ بِالْعِلْمِ وَالْإِيمَانِ، وَلَمْ تَتَحَرَّكْ لَهُ: كَانَتْ مَيْتَةً حَقِيقَةً، وَلَيْسَ هَذَا تَشْبِيهًا لِمَوْتِهَا بِمَوْتِ الْبَدَنِ، بَلْ ذَلِكَ مَوْتُ الْقَلْبِ وَالرُّوحِ.

And since life is about feeling and movement, and what is premised on both of them, these hearts, when they do not perceive knowledge and faith and do not move towards it, are *indeed dead.* This is not an analogy of their death with the death of the body, but it is the [actual] death of the heart and the spirit."

## SINCERITY & SOUND DETERMINATION

Ibn al Qayyim (رَحِمَهُ ٱللَّهُ) then explains the second element of the good life of the heart, which is sound intention and ambition. He writes:

"(2.) **حَيَاةُ الْإِرَادَةِ وَالْهِمَّةِ.** وَضَعْفُ الْإِرَادَةِ وَالطَّلَبِ: مِنْ ضَعْفِ حَيَاةِ الْقَلْبِ، وَكُلَّمَا كَانَ الْقَلْبُ أَتَمَّ حَيَاةٍ، كَانَتْ هِمَّتُهُ أَعْلَى وَإِرَادَتُهُ وَمَحَبَّتُهُ أَقْوَى،

(2.) The life of [sound] intention and ambition. The weakness of intention and seeking is from the weakness of the life of the heart, and the more the heart is full of life, the higher its ambition and the stronger its intention and love

فَإِنَّ الْإِرَادَةَ وَالْمَحَبَّةَ تَتْبَعُ الشُّعُورَ بِالْمُرَادِ الْمَحْبُوبِ، وَسَلَامَةُ الْقَلْبِ مِنَ الْآفَةِ الَّتِي تَحُولُ بَيْنَهُ وَبَيْنَ طَلَبِهِ وَإِرَادَتِهِ، فَضَعْفُ الطَّلَبِ، وَفُتُورُ الْهِمَّةِ إِمَّا مِنْ نُقْصَانِ الشُّعُورِ وَالْإِحْسَاسِ، وَإِمَّا مِنْ وُجُودِ الْآفَةِ الْمُضْعِفَةِ لِلْحَيَاةِ،

Intention and love are guided by one's perception of the beloved and the soundness of their heart, unburdened by any ailment that might hinder their pursuit and devotion. So the weakness of pursuing and the decline of ambition are either from the deficiency of feeling and perception or from an ailment debilitating the (heart's) life.

فَقُوَّةُ الشُّعُورِ، وَقُوَّةُ الْإِرَادَةِ دَلِيلٌ عَلَى قُوَّةِ الْحَيَاةِ، وَضَعْفُهَا دَلِيلٌ عَلَى ضَعْفِهَا،

The strength of feeling and the strength of the will is an indication of the strength of life, and its weakness is an indication of its weakness.

وَكَمَا أَنَّ عُلُوَّ الْهِمَّةِ، وَصِدْقَ الْإِرَادَةِ وَالطَّلَبِ مِنْ كَمَالِ الْحَيَاةِ: فَهُوَ سَبَبٌ إِلَى حُصُولِ أَكْمَلِ الْحَيَاةِ وَأَطْيَبِهَا، فَإِنَّ الْحَيَاةَ الطَّيِّبَةَ إِنَّمَا تُنَالُ بِالْهِمَّةِ الْعَالِيَةِ، وَالْمَحَبَّةِ الصَّادِقَةِ، وَالْإِرَادَةِ الْخَالِصَةِ،

And just as high ambition and sincerity of intention and seeking are from the perfection of life: it is a cause for achieving the most complete and best life, for the good life is only attained by high ambition, sincere love, and pure will.

فَعَلَى قَدْرِ ذَلِكَ تَكُونُ الْحَيَاةُ الطَّيِّبَةُ، وَأَخَسُّ النَّاسِ حَيَاةً أَخَسُّهُمْ هِمَّةً، وَأَضْعَفُهُمْ مَحَبَّةً وَطَلَبًا، وَحَيَاةُ الْبَهَائِمِ خَيْرٌ مِنْ حَيَاتِهِ. كَمَا قِيلَ:

According to that, the good life is achieved, and the most miserable people in life are those with the least ambition, and the weakest in loving and seeking, and the life of beasts is better than theirs. As it was said:

نَهَارُكَ يَا مَغْرُورُ سَهْوٌ وَغَفْلَةٌ ... وَلَيْلُكَ نَوْمٌ وَالرَّدَى لَكَ لَازِمُ

Your day, O deluded one, is negligence and oblivion... and your night is sleep, and ruin is a constant for you,

وَتَكْدَحُ فِيمَا سَوْفَ تُنْكِرُ غِبَّهُ ... كَذَلِكَ فِي الدُّنْيَا تَعِيشُ الْبَهَائِمُ

And you work hard for what you will eventually despise...
thus in the world, the beasts live,

تُسَرُّ بِمَا يَفْنَى وَتَفْرَحُ بِالْمُنَى ... كَمَا غُرَّ بِاللَّذَّاتِ فِي النَّوْمِ حَالِمُ

You delight in what will perish and rejoice in illusions... as
one does when deceived by pleasures in a dream.

وَالْمَقْصُودُ: أَنَّ حَيَاةَ الْقَلْبِ بِالْعِلْمِ وَالْإِرَادَةِ وَالْهِمَّةِ، وَالنَّاسُ إِذَا شَاهَدُوا ذَلِكَ مِنَ الرَّجُلِ قَالُوا: هُوَ حَيُّ الْقَلْبِ،

And the intended meaning is: the life of the heart is achieved by knowledge, intention, and ambition, and when people witness that from a man, they say: he has a heart that is alive.

وَحَيَاةُ الْقَلْبِ بِدَوَامِ الذِّكْرِ، وَتَرْكِ الذُّنُوبِ، كَمَا قَالَ عَبْدُ اللَّهِ بْنُ الْمُبَارَكِ. رحمه الله:

And the life of the heart is with the constant remembrance, and avoidance of sins. As Abdullah bin Al-Mubarak (رَحِمَهُ ٱللَّهُ) said:

رَأَيْتُ الذُّنُوبَ تُمِيتُ الْقُلُوبَ ... وَقَدْ يُورِثُ الذُّلَّ إِدْمَانُهَا

I have seen sins cause the death of hearts ... and addiction to
them could lead to disgrace

وَتَرْكُ الذُّنُوبِ حَيَاةُ الْقُلُوبِ ... وَخَيْرٌ لِنَفْسِكَ عِصْيَانُهَا

And the abandonment of sins is the life of hearts ... it is better
for yourself to disobey it (i.e., your inner-self).

وَهَلْ أَفْسَدَ الدِّينَ إِلَّا الْمُلُوكُ وَأَحْبَارُ سُوءٍ وَرُهْبَانُهَا

Have any but corrupt kings and evil clerics and their monks
spoiled the religion?

وَبَاعُوا النُّفُوسَ وَلَمْ يَرْبَحُوا ...وَلَمْ يَغْلُ فِي الْبَيْعِ أَثْمَانُهَا

And they sold themselves but gained no profit ... and the prices were not made high for their sale

فَقَدْ رَتَعَ الْقَوْمُ فِي جِيفَةٍ ...يَبِينُ لِذِي اللُّبِّ خُسْرَانُهَا

Indeed, people have indulged in a carcass (i.e. this world) ... the loss of which is clear to the wise.

وَكَمَا أَنَّ اللَّهَ سُبْحَانَهُ جَعَلَ حَيَاةَ الْبَدَنِ بِالطَّعَامِ وَالشَّرَابِ، فَحَيَاةُ الْقَلْبِ بِدَوَامِ الذِّكْرِ، وَالْإِنَابَةِ إِلَى اللَّهِ، وَتَرْكِ الذُّنُوبِ، وَالْغَفْلَةِ الْجَاثِمَةِ عَلَى الْقَلْبِ، وَالتَّعَلُّقِ بِالرَّذَائِلِ وَالشَّهَوَاتِ الْمُنْقَطِعَةِ عَنْ قَرِيبٍ يُضْعِفُ هَذِهِ الْحَيَاةَ،

And just as Allah (سُبْحَانَهُۥوَتَعَالَىٰ) made the life of the body to occur by way of food and drink, the life of the heart is nourished through constant remembrance and turning to Allah while abstaining from sins. Negligence clouds the heart, leading to attachment to vices and temporary desires, which weakens this this life.

وَلَا يَزَالُ الضَّعْفُ يَتَوَالَى عَلَيْهِ حَتَّى يَمُوتَ، وَعَلَامَةُ مَوْتِهِ: أَنَّهُ لَا يَعْرِفُ مَعْرُوفًا، وَلَا يُنْكِرُ مُنْكَرًا، كَمَا قَالَ عَبْدُ اللَّهِ بْنُ مَسْعُودٍ: أَتَدْرُونَ مَنْ مَيِّتُ الْقَلْبِ الَّذِي قِيلَ فِيهِ:

Weakness continues to befall it until it dies. The sign of its death is that it does not discern between good and evil, as Abdullah bin Mas'ūd (رَضِيَ اللَّهُ عَنْهُ) said: Do you know who is the dead heart that it was said about?

لَيْسَ مَنْ مَاتَ فَاسْتَرَاحَ بِمَيِّتٍ ... إِنَّمَا الْمَيِّتُ مَيِّتُ الْأَحْيَاءِ

He is not dead who died and rested ... rather the dead are the dead of the living

قَالُوا: وَمَنْ هُوَ؟ قَالَ: الَّذِي لَا يَعْرِفُ مَعْرُوفًا وَلَا يُنْكِرُ مُنْكَرًا.

They said: Whose is it? He said: the one who does not discern between good and evil.

## FEARING THE DEATH OF THE HEART MORE THAN THE DEATH OF THE BODY

وَالرَّجُلُ: هُوَ الَّذِي يَخَافُ مَوْتَ قَلْبِهِ، لَا مَوْتَ بَدَنِهِ، إِذْ أَكْثَرُ هَؤُلَاءِ الْخَلْقِ يَخَافُونَ مَوْتَ أَبْدَانِهِمْ، وَلَا يُبَالُونَ بِمَوْتِ قُلُوبِهِمْ، وَلَا يَعْرِفُونَ مِنَ الْحَيَاةِ إِلَّا الْحَيَاةَ الطَّبِيعِيَّةَ، وَذَلِكَ مِنْ مَوْتِ الْقَلْبِ وَالرُّوحِ،

A true man is one who fears the death of his heart, not the death of his body. Most of these creatures fear the death of their bodies but pay no heed to the death of their hearts. They know of life only as a natural life, and that itself is from the death of the heart and spirit.

فَإِنَّ هَذِهِ الْحَيَاةَ الطَّبِيعِيَّةَ شَبِيهَةٌ بِالظِّلِّ الزَّائِلِ، وَالنَّبَاتِ السَّرِيعِ الْجَفَافِ، وَالْمَنَامِ الَّذِي يُخَيَّلُ كَأَنَّهُ حَقِيقَةٌ، فَإِذَا اسْتَيْقَظَ عَرَفَ أَنَّهُ كَانَ خَيَالًا، كَمَا قَالَ عُمَرُ بْنُ الْخَطَّابِ رضي الله عنه: لَوْ أَنَّ الْحَيَاةَ الدُّنْيَا مِنْ أَوَّلِهَا إِلَى آخِرِهَا أُوتِيَهَا رَجُلٌ وَاحِدٌ، ثُمَّ جَاءَهُ الْمَوْتُ: لَكَانَ بِمَنْزِلَةِ مَنْ رَأَى فِي مَنَامِهِ مَا يَسُرُّهُ ثُمَّ اسْتَيْقَظَ، فَإِذَا لَيْسَ فِي يَدِهِ شَيْءٌ.

Indeed, this earthly existence resembles a passing shadow, fleeting plants that wither away swiftly, and dreams that seem to be reality. When they wake up, they realize it is only a fantasy. As 'Umar b. al-Khaṭṭāb (رَضِيَ اللَّهُ عَنْهُ) said: "If the worldly life from its beginning to its end were given to a single man, then death comes, it would be as if one saw what pleases him in his dream, then woke up to find he has nothing."

وَقَدْ قِيلَ: إِنَّ الْمَوْتَ مَوْتَانِ: مَوْتٌ إِرَادِيٌّ، وَمَوْتٌ طَبِيعِيٌّ، فَمَنْ أَمَاتَ نَفْسَهُ مَوْتًا إِرَادِيًّا كَانَ مَوْتُهُ الطَّبِيعِيُّ حَيَاةً لَهُ،

It has been said that there are two kinds of death: death of desire and natural death. Whoever kills the desires of the self, his natural death becomes a true life for him.

وَمَعْنَى هَذَا أَنَّ الْمَوْتَ الْإِرَادِيَّ: هُوَ قَمْعُ الشَّهَوَاتِ الْمُرْدِيَةِ، وَإِخْمَادُ نِيرَانِهَا الْمُحْرِقَةِ، وَتَسْكِينُ هَوَائِجِهَا الْمُتْلِفَةِ، فَحِينَئِذٍ يَتَفَرَّغُ الْقَلْبُ وَالرُّوحُ لِلتَّفَكُّرِ فِيمَا فِيهِ كَمَالُ الْعَبْدِ، وَمَعْرِفَتِهِ، وَالِاشْتِغَالِ بِهِ.

This means voluntary death suppresses harmful desires, extinguishes their blazing fires, and calms their destructive urges. Then, the heart and spirit can be free to contemplate matters that lead to the perfection and understanding of the servant and engage in them.

وَيَرَى حِينَئِذٍ أَنَّ إِيثَارَ الظِّلِّ الزَّائِلِ عَنْ قَرِيبٍ عَلَى الْعَيْشِ اللَّذِيذِ الدَّائِمِ أَخْسَرُ الْخُسْرَانِ، فَأَمَّا إِذَا كَانَتِ الشَّهَوَاتُ وَافِدَةً، وَاللَّذَّاتُ مُؤْثَرَةً، وَالْعَوَائِدُ غَالِبَةً، وَالطَّبِيعَةُ حَاكِمَةً، فَالْقَلْبُ حِينَئِذٍ إِمَّا أَنْ يَكُونَ أَسِيرًا ذَلِيلًا، أَوْ مَهْزُومًا مُخْرَجًا عَنْ وَطَنِهِ وَمُسْتَقَرِّهِ الَّذِي لَا قَرَارَ لَهُ إِلَّا فِيهِ أَوْ قَتِيلًا مَيِّتًا، وَمَا لِجُرْحٍ بِهِ إِيلَامٌ، وَأَحْسَنُ أَحْوَالِهِ: أَنْ يَكُونَ فِي حَرْبٍ، يُدَالُ لَهُ فِيهَا مَرَّةً، وَيُدَالُ عَلَيْهِ مَرَّةً،

They then realize that preferring a fleeting shadow over a pleasurable and permanent life is the tremendous loss. However, when desires run rampant, pleasures prevail, habits dominate, and nature rules, the heart then is either a humiliated prisoner or a defeated exile from its homeland and its permanent abode, outside of which it can find no rest, or a dead victim that no longer feels pain if wounded. The best-case scenario is that one is at war, winning sometimes and losing sometimes.

فَإِذَا مَاتَ الْعَبْدُ مَوْتَهُ الطَّبِيعِيَّ، كَانَتْ بَعْدَهُ حَيَاةُ رُوحِهِ بِتِلْكَ الْعُلُومِ النَّافِعَةِ، وَالْأَعْمَالِ الصَّالِحَةِ، وَالْأَحْوَالِ الْفَاضِلَةِ الَّتِي حَصَلَتْ لَهُ بِإِمَاتَةِ نَفْسِهِ، فَتَكُونُ حَيَاتُهُ هَاهُنَا عَلَى حَسَبِ مَوْتِهِ الْإِرَادِيِّ فِي هَذِهِ الدَّارِ.

Then when the servant dies a natural death, his life after that is the life of his spirit achieved through beneficial knowledge, righteous deeds, and the virtuous states he attained by killing his inner self. At that point, his life is according to the death of his desire in this life.

وَهَذَا مَوْضِعٌ لَا يَفْهَمُهُ إِلَّا أَلِبَّاءُ النَّاسِ وَعُقَلَاؤُهُمْ، وَلَا يَعْمَلُ بِمُقْتَضَاهُ إِلَّا أَهْلُ الْهِمَمِ الْعَلِيَّةِ، وَالنُّفُوسِ الزَّكِيَّةِ الْأَبِيَّةِ.

This is a matter only comprehended by the intelligent and wise among people, and what it requires is only acted upon by those possessing high aspirations and pure, brave souls."

## Lofty Moral Character is the Sign of a Healthy Heart

Ibn al Qayyim (رَحِمَهُ ٱللَّهُ) adds a third component to the life of the heart after expounding upon the dire importance of knowledge and lofty ambition. He writes:

"(3.) **حَيَاةُ الْأَخْلَاقِ، وَالصِّفَاتِ الْمَحْمُودَةِ**، الَّتِي هِيَ حَيَاةٌ رَاسِخَةٌ لِلْمَوْصُوفِ بِهَا، فَهُوَ لَا يَتَكَلَّفُ التَّرَقِّيَ فِي دَرَجَاتِ الْكَمَالِ، وَلَا يَشُقُّ عَلَيْهِ، لِاقْتِضَاءِ أَخْلَاقِهِ وَصِفَاتِهِ لِذَلِكَ، بِحَيْثُ لَوْ فَارَقَهُ ذَلِكَ لَفَارَقَ مَا هُوَ مِنْ طَبِيعَتِهِ وَسَجِيَّتِهِ،

"(3.) The life of moral character and praiseworthy qualities constitute a steadfast life for the one characterized by them, such that they do not have to exert effort to ascend the ranks of perfection, nor does it cause them hardship. This is due to the requirements of their morals and characteristics, such that if they were devoid of these qualities, they would be devoid of what is natural and innate.

فَحَيَاةُ مَنْ قَدْ طُبِعَ عَلَى الْحَيَاءِ وَالْعِفَّةِ وَالْجُودِ وَالسَّخَاءِ، وَالْمُرُوءَةِ وَالصِّدْقِ وَالْوَفَاءِ وَنَحْوِهَا أَتَمُّ مِنْ حَيَاةِ مَنْ يَقْهَرُ نَفْسَهُ، وَيُغَالِبُ طَبْعَهُ، حَتَّى يَكُونَ كَذَلِكَ، فَإِنَّ هَذَا بِمَنْزِلَةِ مَنْ تُعَارِضُهُ أَسْبَابُ الدَّاءِ وَهُوَ يُعَالِجُهَا وَيَقْهَرُهَا بِأَضْدَادِهَا، وَذَلِكَ بِمَنْزِلَةِ مَنْ قَدْ عُوفِيَ مِنْ ذَلِكَ. وَكُلَّمَا كَانَتْ هَذِهِ الْأَخْلَاقُ فِي صَاحِبِهَا أَكْمَلَ كَانَتْ حَيَاتُهُ أَقْوَى وَأَتَمَّ،

Thus, the life of one naturally instilled with modesty, chastity, generosity, benevolence, dignity, honesty, loyalty and the like is more perfect than the life of someone who suppresses themselves and overcomes their nature to be like that. The latter is comparable to someone who is faced with the causes of disease and is treating and overcoming them with their opposites, and the former is equivalent to someone who has been spared from that. The more complete these characteristics are in their possessor, the stronger and more perfect their life will be.

وَلِهَذَا كَانَ خُلُقُ الْحَيَاءِ مُشْتَقًّا مِنَ الْحَيَاةِ اسْمًا وَحَقِيقَةً، فَأَكْمَلُ النَّاسِ حَيَاةً: أَكْمَلُهُمْ حَيَاءً، وَنُقْصَانُ حَيَاءِ الْمَرْءِ مِنْ نُقْصَانِ حَيَاتِهِ، فَإِنَّ الرُّوحَ إِذَا مَاتَتْ لَمْ تُحِسَّ بِمَا يُؤْلِمُهَا مِنَ الْقَبَائِحِ، فَلَا تَسْتَحِي مِنْهَا، فَإِذَا كَانَتْ صَحِيحَةَ الْحَيَاةِ أَحَسَّتْ بِذَلِكَ، فَاسْتَحْيَتْ مِنْهُ، وَكَذَلِكَ سَائِرُ الْأَخْلَاقِ الْفَاضِلَةِ، وَالصِّفَاتِ الْمَمْدُوحَةِ تَابِعَةٌ لِقُوَّةِ الْحَيَاةِ، وَضِدُّهَا مِنْ نُقْصَانِ الْحَيَاةِ،

This is why the moral characteristic of modesty (*ḥayā'*) is derived from life (*ḥayāt*) in both its linguistic name and its actuality. The most complete people in life are the most modest, and a person's lack of modesty is from the deficiency of his life. When the soul dies, it does not feel what (usually) pains it of reprehensible matters, so it does not feel ashamed of them. But if it is sound in its life, it senses that, and therefore feels ashamed of it. And so too, all other noble characteristics, and praiseworthy qualities are contingent upon the strength of life, and their opposites are from the deficiency of life.

وَلِهَذَا كَانَتْ حَيَاةُ الشُّجَاعِ أَكْمَلَ مِنْ حَيَاةِ الْجَبَانِ، وَحَيَاةُ السَّخِيِّ أَكْمَلَ مِنْ حَيَاةِ الْبَخِيلِ، وَحَيَاةُ الْفَطِنِ الذَّكِيِّ أَكْمَلَ مِنْ حَيَاةِ الْفَدْمِ الْبَلِيدِ،

Therefore, the life of the brave is more complete than the life of the coward, the life of the generous is more complete than the life of the miser, and the life of the sharp and intelligent is more complete than the life of the dull and ignorant.

وَلِهَذَا لَمَّا كَانَ الْأَنْبِيَاءُ صَلَوَاتُ اللَّهِ وَسَلَامُهُ عَلَيْهِمْ أَكْمَلَ النَّاسِ حَيَاةً حَتَّى إِنَّ قُوَّةَ حَيَاتِهِمْ تَمْنَعُ الْأَرْضَ أَنْ تُبْلِيَ أَجْسَامَهُمْ كَانُوا أَكْمَلَ النَّاسِ فِي هَذِهِ الْأَخْلَاقِ، ثُمَّ الْأَمْثَلُ فَالْأَمْثَلُ مِنْ أَتْبَاعِهِمْ.

Therefore, when the Prophets, may Allah's blessings and peace be upon them, were the most complete in life to the point that the strength of their life prevented the earth from decomposing their bodies, they were the most complete people in these qualities, then the next best, and then the next best of their followers.

فَانْظُرِ الْآنَ إِلَى حَيَاةِ {**حَلَّافٍ مَهِينٍ هَمَّازٍ مَشَّاءٍ بِنَمِيمٍ ، مَنَّاعٍ لِلْخَيْرِ مُعْتَدٍ أَثِيمٍ، عُتُلٍّ بَعْدَ ذَلِكَ زَنِيمٍ**} ، وَحَيَاةِ جَوَّادٍ شُجَاعٍ، بَرٍّ عَادِلٍ عَفِيفٍ مُحْسِنٍ تَجِدُ الْأَوَّلَ مَيِّتًا بِالنِّسْبَةِ إِلَى الثَّانِي، وَلِلَّهِ دَرُّ الْقَائِلِ:

Now look at the life of **"A slanderer, going about with calumnies, hinderer of the good, transgressor, sinful, coarse, besides all that, base-born."**,[47] and the life of a generous, brave, righteous, fair, chaste, benevolent person. You will find the former is dead in comparison to the latter. A poet said:

وَمَا لِلْمَرْءِ خَيْرٌ فِي حَيَاةٍ ... إِذَا مَا عُدَّ مَنْ سَقَطِ الْمَتَاعِ

"What good is there for a man in living... if it is counted among worthless belongings?"

## A DETAILED DESCRIPTION OF THE TRULY HAPPY LIFE

(4.) **حَيَاةُ الْفَرَحِ وَالسُّرُورِ**، وَقُرَّةُ الْعَيْنِ بِاللَّهِ، وَهَذِهِ الْحَيَاةُ إِنَّمَا تَكُونُ بَعْدَ الظَّفَرِ بِالْمَطْلُوبِ، الَّذِي تَقَرُّ بِهِ عَيْنُ طَالِبِهِ، فَلَا حَيَاةَ نَافِعَةً لَهُ بِدُونِهِ، وَحَوْلَ

47 Al-Qalam: 10-13.

هَذِهِ الْحَيَاةِ يُدَنْدِنُ النَّاسُ كُلُّهُمْ، وَكُلُّهُمْ قَدْ أَخْطَأَ طَرِيقَهَا، وَسَلَكَ طُرُقًا لَا تُفْضِي إِلَيْهَا، بَلْ تَقْطَعُهُ عَنْهَا، إِلَّا أَقَلَّ الْقَلِيلِ.

(4.) The life of joy, happiness, and the eye's delight in Allah. This life only comes after achieving the goal, which pleases the eye of its pursuer, for there is no beneficial life for him without it. This is the life that people commonly speak of. And all of them have lost their way to it, taking paths instead that do not lead to it but rather cut them off from it, except for the very few.

فَدَارَ طَلَبُ الْكُلِّ حَوْلَ هَذِهِ الْحَيَاةِ، وَحُرِمَهَا أَكْثَرُهُمْ. وَسَبَبُ حِرْمَانِهِمْ إِيَّاهَا: ضَعْفُ الْعَقْلِ وَالتَّمْيِيزِ وَالْبَصِيرَةِ، وَضَعْفُ الْهِمَّةِ وَالْإِرَادَةِ، فَإِنَّ مَادَّتَهَا بَصِيرَةٌ وَقَّادَةٌ، وَهِمَّةٌ نَفَّاذَةٌ، وَالْبَصِيرَةُ كَالْبَصَرِ تَكُونُ عَمًى وَعَوَرًا وَعَمَشًا وَرَمَدًا، وَتَامَّةَ النُّورِ وَالضِّيَاءِ، وَهَذِهِ الْآفَاتُ قَدْ تَكُونُ لَهَا بِالْخِلْقَةِ فِي الْأَصْلِ، وَقَدْ تَحْدُثُ فِيهَا بِالْعَوَارِضِ الْكَسْبِيَّةِ.

Everyone's pursuit revolves around this life, yet most of them are deprived of it. Their deprivation is a weakness of intellect, discernment, and insight and a weakness of ambition and intention. For its substance is a fueled guidance and a penetrating ambition. Insight is like sight; it can be blind, defective, cloudy, or filled with light and brightness. These afflictions can either be inherent from its creation or occur due to circumstantial factors that are earned.

وَالْمَقْصُودُ: أَنَّ هَذِهِ الْمَرْتَبَةَ مِنْ مَرَاتِبِ الْحَيَاةِ هِيَ أَعْلَى مَرَاتِبِهَا، وَلَكِنْ كَيْفَ يَصِلُ إِلَيْهَا مَنْ عَقْلُهُ مَسْبِيٌّ فِي بِلَادِ الشَّهَوَاتِ، وَأَمَلُهُ مَوْقُوفٌ عَلَى اجْتِنَاءِ اللَّذَّاتِ، وَسِيرَتُهُ جَارِيَةٌ عَلَى أَسْوَأِ الْعَادَاتِ، وَدِينُهُ مُسْتَهْلَكٌ بِالْمَعَاصِي وَالْمُخَالَفَاتِ، وَهِمَّتُهُ وَاقِفَةٌ مَعَ السُّفْلِيَّاتِ، وَعَقِيدَتُهُ غَيْرُ مُتَلَقَّاةٍ مِنْ مِشْكَاةِ النُّبُوَّاتِ؟!

The point is that this level of life is the highest of its levels. But how can one reach it if their mind is enslaved in the land of desires, their hope is dependent on the accumulation of pleasures, their lifestyle follows the worst of habits, sins and transgressions consume their religiosity, their ambition stands with the lowest of things, and the lantern of prophecy does not illuminate their belief?

فَهُوَ فِي الشَّهَوَاتِ مُنْغَمِسٌ، وَفِي الشُّبُهَاتِ مُنْتَكِسٌ، وَعَنِ النَّاصِحِ مُعْرِضٌ، وَعَلَى الْمُرْشِدِ مُعْتَرِضٌ، وَعَنِ السَّرَّاءِ نَائِمٌ، وَقَلْبُهُ فِي كُلِّ وَادٍ هَائِمٌ،

He is immersed in desires, ensnared in doubts, averse to any good advisor, disagreeable with guidance, sleeps through prosperity, and his heart is wandering in every valley.

فَلَوْ أَنَّهُ تَجَرَّدَ مِنْ نَفْسِهِ، وَرَغِبَ عَنْ مُشَارَكَةِ أَبْنَاءِ جِنْسِهِ، وَخَرَجَ مِنْ ضِيقِ الْجَهْلِ إِلَى فَضَاءِ الْعِلْمِ، وَمِنْ سِجْنِ الْهَوَى إِلَى سَاحَةِ الْهُدَى، وَمِنْ نَجَاسَةِ النَّفْسِ، إِلَى طَهَارَةِ الْقُدْسِ لَرَأَى الْإِلْفَ الَّذِي نَشَأَ بِنَشْأَتِهِ، وَزَادَ بِزِيَادَتِهِ، وَقَوِيَ بِقُوَّتِهِ، وَشَرُفَ عِنْدَ نَفْسِهِ وَأَبْنَاءِ جِنْسِهِ بِحُصُولِهِ، قَذًى فِي عَيْنِ بَصِيرَتِهِ، وَشَجًا فِي حَلْقِ إِيمَانِهِ، وَمَرَضًا مُتَرَامِيًا إِلَى هَلَاكِهِ،

If he could detach from his self, give up competing with his peers, exit from the confines of ignorance to the expanse of knowledge, from the prison of desire to the arena of guidance, from the impurity of the soul to the purity of sanctity, he would see the (reality of) the habits and customs that developed as he grew up, increased as he increased, strengthened as he strengthened, the attainment of which gained him both self esteem and the esteem of his peers, is actually a piercing thorn in the eye of his insight, a knot in the throat of his faith, and a pervasive disease leading to his destruction.

فَإِنْ قُلْتَ: قَدْ أَشَرْتَ إِلَى حَيَاةٍ غَيْرِ مَعْهُودَةٍ بَيْنَ أَمْوَاتِ الْأَحْيَاءِ، فَهَلْ يُمْكِنُكَ وَصْفُ طَرِيقِهَا، لِأَصِلَ إِلَى شَيْءٍ مِنْ أَذْوَاقِهَا، فَقَدْ بَانَ لِي أَنَّ مَا نَحْنُ فِيهِ مِنَ الْحَيَاةِ حَيَاةٌ بَهِيمِيَّةٌ، رُبَّمَا زَادَتْ عَلَيْنَا فِيهِ الْبَهَائِمُ بِخُلُوِّهَا عَنِ الْمُنْكَرَاتِ وَالْمُنَغِّصَاتِ وَسَلَامَةِ الْعَاقِبَةِ؟

If you say: You have pointed to an unfamiliar life among the living-dead. Can you describe its path, so I may reach some of its experiences? It has become clear to me that our current life is animalistic, perhaps animals exceed us in it by their avoidance of evils and troubling things, and reaching a safe end?

قُلْتُ: لَعَمْرُ اللَّهِ إِنَّ اشْتِيَاقَكَ إِلَى هَذِهِ الْحَيَاةِ، وَطَلَبَ عِلْمِهَا وَمَعْرِفَتِهَا: لَدَلِيلٌ عَلَى حَيَاتِكَ، وَأَنَّكَ لَسْتَ مِنْ جُمْلَةِ الْأَمْوَاتِ.

I would say: By Allah's Life, your longing for this life and seeking its knowledge and understanding is evidence of your life and that you are not from amongst the dead.

فَأَوَّلُ طَرِيقِهَا: أَنْ تَعْرِفَ اللَّهَ، وَتَهْتَدِيَ إِلَيْهِ طَرِيقًا يُوَصِّلُكَ إِلَيْهِ، وَيُحْرِقُ ظُلُمَاتِ الطَّبْعِ بِأَشِعَّةِ الْبَصِيرَةِ،

The first step on this path is to recognize Allah and to find a way to Him that will take you there, burning the darkness of instinct with the rays of insight.

فَيَقُومُ بِقَلْبِهِ شَاهِدٌ مِنْ شَوَاهِدِ الْآخِرَةِ، فَيَنْجَذِبُ إِلَيْهَا بِكُلِّيَّتِهِ، وَيَزْهَدُ فِي التَّعَلُّقَاتِ الْفَانِيَةِ، وَيَدْأَبُ فِي تَصْحِيحِ التَّوْبَةِ، وَالْقِيَامِ بِالْمَأْمُورَاتِ الظَّاهِرَةِ وَالْبَاطِنَةِ، وَتَرْكِ الْمَنْهِيَّاتِ الظَّاهِرَةِ وَالْبَاطِنَةِ،

So a witness from the witnesses of the hereafter would rise in his heart, drawing him entirely towards it, causing him to disdain transient attachments. He should diligently correct repentance, comply with the outward and inward commands, and abandon the prohibited outward and inward acts.

ثُمَّ يَقُومُ حَارِسًا عَلَى قَلْبِهِ، فَلَا يُسَامِحُهُ بِخَطْرَةٍ يَكْرَهُهَا اللَّهُ، وَلَا بِخَطْرَةِ فُضُولٍ لَا تَنْفَعُهُ،

Then he should stand guard over his heart, not permitting any thought that Allah dislikes, nor any unnecessary thought that brings no benefit.

فَـيَصْفُو بِـذَلِـكَ قَـلْبُهُ عَـنْ حَـدِيـثِ الـنَّفْسِ وَوَسْـوَاسِـهَا، فَـيُفْدَى مِـنْ أَسْـرِهَـا، وَيَـصِيرُ طَـلِيقًا، فَـحِينَئِذٍ يَخْـلُو قَـلْبُهُ بِـذِكْـرِ رَبِّـهِ، وَمَـحَبَّتِهِ وَالْإِنَـابَـةِ إِلَـيْهِ، وَيَخْـرُجُ مِـنْ بَـيْنِ بُـيُوتِ طَـبْعِهِ وَنَـفْسِهِ، إِلَـى فَـضَاءِ الْخَـلْوَةِ بِـرَبِّـهِ وَذِكْـرِهِ، كَمَا قِيلَ:

This would purify his heart from the chatter of the self and its whispers, freeing him from its imprisonment, making him liberated. Then his heart would be secluded in remembrance of his Lord, and in His love and turning to Him, and he would leave the confines of his nature and self to the vastness of solitude with his Lord and His remembrance. As it is said:

وَأَخْرُجُ مِنْ بَيْنِ الْبُيُوتِ لَعَلَّنِي ... أُحَدِّثُ عَنْكَ النَّفْسَ فِي السِّرِّ خَالِيًا

"And I leave to beyond houses so that perhaps... I will converse about You with my soul alone in solitude."

فَحِينَئِذٍ يَجْتَمِعُ قَلْبُهُ وَخَوَاطِرُهُ وَحَدِيثُ نَفْسِهِ عَلَى إِرَادَةِ رَبِّهِ، وَطَلَبِهِ وَالشَّوْقِ إِلَيْهِ.

Then his heart, his thoughts, and his inner dialogue would all converge on intending his Lord, seeking Him and yearning for Him.

فَإِذَا صَدَقَ فِي ذَلِكَ رُزِقَ مَحَبَّةَ الرَّسُولِ صلى الله عليه وسلم، وَاسْتَوْلَتْ رُوحَانِيَّتُهُ عَلَى قَلْبِهِ، فَجَعَلَهُ إِمَامَهُ وَمُعَلِّمَهُ، وَأُسْتَاذَهُ وَشَيْخَهُ وَقُدْوَتَهُ، كَمَا جَعَلَهُ اللَّهُ نَبِيَّهُ وَرَسُولَهُ وَهَادِيًا إِلَيْهِ،

When he is truthful in that, he would be blessed with the love of the Messenger (ﷺ) and his spiritual example would take over his heart, making him his leader, his teacher, his mentor, his spiritual guide, and his role model, just as Allah made him His Prophet, His Messenger, and His guide to Him.

فَيُطَالِعُ سِيرَتَهُ وَمَبَادِئَ أَمْرِهِ، وَكَيْفِيَّةَ نُزُولِ الْوَحْيِ عَلَيْهِ، وَيَعْرِفُ صِفَاتِهُ وَأَخْلَاقَهُ، وَآدَابَهُ فِي حَرَكَاتِهِ وَسُكُونِهِ وَيَقْظَتِهِ وَمَنَامِهِ، وَعِبَادَتِهِ وَمُعَاشَرَتِهِ لِأَهْلِهِ وَأَصْحَابِهِ، حَتَّى يَصِيرَ كَأَنَّهُ مَعَهُ مِنْ بَعْضِ أَصْحَابِهِ.

He would study his biography, the beginning stages of his life, how revelation descended upon him, and would know of his characteristics, his morals, and his etiquettes in his activities and stillness, his wakefulness and sleep, his worship and his treatment of his family and companions, until it is as if he were with him among his companions.

فَإِذَا رَسَخَ قَلْبُهُ فِي ذَلِكَ: فَتَحَ عَلَيْهِ بِفَهْمِ الْوَحْيِ الْمُنَزَّلِ عَلَيْهِ مِنْ رَبِّهِ، بِحَيْثُ لَوْ قَرَأَ السُّورَةَ شَاهَدَ قَلْبُهُ مَا أُنْزِلَتْ فِيهِ، وَمَا أُرِيدَ بِهَا، وَحَظَّهُ الْمُخْتَصَّ بِهِ مِنْهَا مِنَ الصِّفَاتِ وَالْأَخْلَاقِ وَالْأَفْعَالِ الْمَذْمُومَةِ، فَيَجْتَهِدُ فِي التَّخَلُّصِ مِنْهَا كَمَا يَجْتَهِدُ فِي الشِّفَاءِ مِنَ الْمَرَضِ الْمَخُوفِ، وَشَاهَدَ حَظَّهُ مِنَ الصِّفَاتِ وَالْأَفْعَالِ الْمَمْدُوحَةِ، فَيَجْتَهِدُ فِي تَكْمِيلِهَا وَإِتْمَامِهَا.

When his heart is firmly grounded in this, it opens him to the understanding of the revelation sent down to him (ﷺ) from his Lord, so much so that if he reads a *Surah*, his heart witnesses what it was revealed about and what was intended by it. It also discerns the portion specifically addressed to him in terms of blameworthy traits and actions. He makes an effort to rid himself of the blameworthy as one strives to heal from a fearful disease, and he recognizes his share of the praiseworthy traits and actions, working hard to perfect and complete them.

فَإِذَا تَمَكَّنَ مِنْ ذَلِكَ انْفَتَحَ فِي قَلْبِهِ عَيْنٌ أُخْرَى، يُشَاهِدُ بِهَا صِفَاتِ الرَّبِّ جل جلاله، حَتَّى تَصِيرَ لِقَلْبِهِ بِمَنْزِلَةِ الْمَرْئِيِّ لِعَيْنِهِ، فَيَشْهَدُ عُلُوَّ الرَّبِّ سُبْحَانَهُ فَوْقَ خَلْقِهِ، وَاسْتِوَاءَهُ عَلَى عَرْشِهِ، وَنُزُولَ الْأَمْرِ مِنْ عِنْدِهِ بِتَدْبِيرِ مَمْلَكَتِهِ، وَتَكْلِيمَهُ بِالْوَحْيِ، وَتَكْلِيمَهُ لِعَبْدِهِ جِبْرِيلَ بِهِ، وَإِرْسَالَهُ إِلَى مَنْ يَشَاءُ بِمَا يَشَاءُ، وَصُعُودَ الْأُمُورِ إِلَيْهِ، وَعَرْضَهَا عَلَيْهِ.

When he has mastered this, another eye opens in his heart, with which he perceives the attributes of his Lord (جَلَّ وَعَلَا) until these become to his heart as what is seen is to his physical eye. He witnesses the Highness of his Lord (سُبْحَانَهُ وَتَعَالَىٰ) above His creation, His ascension over His throne, the descent of His command in the management of His dominion, His speaking through revelation, His addressing His servant Jibrīl (عَلَيْهِ ٱلصَّلَاةُ وَٱلسَّلَامُ) with it, sending him to whom He wills with what He wills, the ascension of all matters to Him, and their presentation before Him.

فَيُشَاهِدُ قَلْبُهُ رَبًّا قَاهِرًا فَوْقَ عِبَادِهِ، آمِرًا نَاهِيًا، بَاعِثًا لِرُسُلِهِ، مُنْزِلًا لِكُتُبِهِ، مَعْبُودًا مُطَاعًا، لَا شَرِيكَ لَهُ، وَلَا مَثِيلَ، وَلَا عَدْلَ لَهُ، لَيْسَ لِأَحَدٍ مَعَهُ مِنَ الْأَمْرِ شَيْءٌ، بَلِ الْأَمْرُ كُلُّهُ لَهُ، فَيَشْهَدُ رَبَّهُ سُبْحَانَهُ قَائِمًا بِالْمُلْكِ وَالتَّدْبِيرِ،

His heart witnesses a Lord who is dominant over His servants, commanding and prohibiting, sending His messengers, revealing His books, worshiped and obeyed, with no partner, no equal, and no rival. No one shares in His command, but all command belongs to Him. He sees his Lord (سُبْحَانَهُ وَتَعَالَىٰ) in control of all affairs and management.

فَلَا حَرَكَةَ وَلَا سُكُونَ، وَلَا نَفْعَ وَلَا ضَرَّ، وَلَا عَطَاءَ وَلَا مَنْعَ، وَلَا قَبْضَ وَلَا بَسْطَ إِلَّا بِقُدْرَتِهِ وَتَدْبِيرِهِ، فَيَشْهَدُ قِيَامَ الْكَوْنِ كُلِّهِ بِهِ، وَقِيَامَهُ سُبْحَانَهُ بِنَفْسِهِ، فَهُوَ الْقَائِمُ بِنَفْسِهِ، الْمُقِيمُ لِكُلِّ مَا سِوَاهُ.

So there is no motion or stillness, no benefit or harm, no giving or withholding, no taking or extending except by His power and His management. He witnesses the whole universe being sustained by Him, while He (سُبْحَانَهُ وَتَعَالَىٰ) is Self-sustaining. So He is the Self-Sustaining while being the Sustainer of all else.

فَإِذَا رَسَخَ قَلْبُهُ فِي ذَلِكَ شَهِدَ الصِّفَةَ الْمُصَحِّحَةَ لِجَمِيعِ صِفَاتِ الْكَمَالِ، وَهِيَ الْحَيَاةُ الَّتِي كَمَالُهَا يَسْتَلْزِمُ كَمَالَ السَّمْعِ وَالْبَصَرِ وَالْقُدْرَةِ وَالْإِرَادَةِ وَالْكَلَامِ وَسَائِرِ

صِفَاتِ الْكَمَالِ، وَصِفَةَ الْقَيُّومِيَّةِ الصَّحِيحَةِ الْمُصَحِّحَةِ لِجَمِيعِ الْأَفْعَالِ، فَالْحَيُّ الْقَيُّومُ: مَنْ لَهُ كُلُّ صِفَةِ كَمَالٍ، وَهُوَ الْفَعَّالُ لِمَا يُرِيدُ.

When his heart is firmly grounded in this, he witnesses the divine attribute that validates all the attributes of perfection, and that is life. The perfection of life necessitates the perfection of hearing, sight, power, will, speech, and all other attributes of perfection, and the attribute of Self-Sustaining, which validates all actions. So the Ever-Living, the Self-Sustaining, Sustainer (*al Ḥayy al Qayyūm*) is He to whom every attribute of perfection belongs, and He is the One who does whatever He wills."

فَإِذَا رَسَخَ قَلْبُهُ فِي ذَلِكَ: فَتَحَ لَهُ مَشْهَدَ الْقُرْبِ وَالْمَعِيَّةِ فَيَشْهَدُهُ سُبْحَانَهُ مَعَهُ، غَيْرَ غَائِبٍ عَنْهُ، قَرِيبًا غَيْرَ بَعِيدٍ، مَعَ كَوْنِهِ فَوْقَ سَمَاوَاتِهِ عَلَى عَرْشِهِ، بَائِنًا مِنْ خَلْقِهِ، قَائِمًا بِالصُّنْعِ وَالتَّدْبِيرِ، وَالْخَلْقِ وَالْأَمْرِ،

When his heart becomes firmly established in that (belief), the scene of proximity and companionship opens up to him, and he witnesses His (Allah's) being with him, not absent from him, close and not far away, despite His being above His heavens on His Throne, distinct from His creation, managing creation and administration, creating and commanding.

فَيَحْصُلُ لَهُ مَعَ التَّعْظِيمِ وَالْإِجْلَالِ الْأُنْسُ بِهَذِهِ الصِّفَةِ، فَيَأْنَسُ بِهِ بَعْدَ أَنْ كَانَ مُسْتَوْحِشًا، وَيَقْوَى بِهِ بَعْدَ أَنْ كَانَ ضَعِيفًا، وَيَفْرَحُ بِهِ بَعْدَ أَنْ كَانَ حَزِينًا، وَيَجِدُ بَعْدَ أَنْ كَانَ فَاقِدًا،

So he attains, with veneration and respect, a sense of comfort with this attribute. He feels comfort with it after he had been feeling isolated, he becomes strong after he had been weak, he becomes happy after he had been sad, and he is found after he had been missing.

فَحِينَئِذٍ يَجِدُ طَعْمَ قَوْلِهِ: " **«وَلَا يَزَالُ عَبْدِي يَتَقَرَّبُ إِلَيَّ بِالنَّوَافِلِ حَتَّى أُحِبَّهُ، فَإِذَا أَحْبَبْتُهُ كُنْتُ سَمْعَهُ الَّذِي يَسْمَعُ بِهِ، وَبَصَرَهُ الَّذِي يُبْصِرُ بِهِ، وَيَدَهُ الَّتِي يَبْطِشُ بِهَا، وَرِجْلَهُ الَّتِي يَمْشِي بِهَا، وَلَئِنْ سَأَلَنِي لَأُعْطِيَنَّهُ، وَلَئِن اسْتَعَاذَنِي لَأُعِيذَنَّهُ»** .

At that point, he tastes the meaning of His saying: "**And My servant continues to draw near to Me with voluntary acts of worship so that I shall love him. When I love him, I am his hearing with which he hears, his sight with which he sees, his hand with which he strikes, and his foot with which he walks. If he asks (something) of Me, I shall surely give it to him, and if he takes refuge in Me, I shall certainly grant him it**".

فَأَطْيَبُ الْحَيَاةِ عَلَى الْإِطْلَاقِ حَيَاةُ هَذَا الْعَبْدِ، فَإِنَّهُ مُحِبٌّ مَحْبُوبٌ، مُتَقَرِّبٌ إِلَى رَبِّهِ، وَرَبُّهُ قَرِيبٌ مِنْهُ، قَدْ صَارَ لَهُ حَبِيبُهُ لِفَرْطِ اسْتِيلَائِهِ عَلَى قَلْبِهِ وَلَهَجِهِ بِذِكْرِهِ وَعُكُوفِ هِمَّتِهِ عَلَى مَرْضَاتِهِ بِمَنْزِلَةِ سَمْعِهِ وَبَصَرِهِ وَيَدِهِ وَرِجْلِهِ، وَهَذِهِ آلَاتُ إِدْرَاكِهِ وَعَمَلِهِ وَسَعْيِهِ، فَإِنْ سَمِعَ سَمِعَ بِحَبِيبِهِ، وَإِنْ أَبْصَرَ أَبْصَرَ بِهِ، وَإِنْ بَطَشَ بَطَشَ بِهِ، وَإِنْ مَشَى مَشَى بِهِ.

So, the best life of all is the life of this servant, absolutely, for he both loves and is loved, he draws near to his Lord, and his Lord is close to him. His Beloved has become — due to His overwhelming authority on his heart and his constant remembrance of Him and commitment to pleasing Him — as if He is his hearing, sight, hand, and foot. And these are the tools of his perception, action, and striving. So if he hears, he hears by way of his Beloved; if he sees, he sees by Him; if he strikes, he strikes by Him; if he walks, he walks by way of Him.

فَإِنْ صَعُبَ عَلَيْكَ فَهْمُ هَذَا الْمَعْنَى، وَكَوْنُ الْمُحِبِّ الْكَامِلِ الْمَحَبَّةِ يَسْمَعُ وَيُبْصِرُ وَيَبْطِشُ وَيَمْشِي بِمَحْبُوبِهِ، وَذَاتُهُ غَائِبَةٌ عَنْهُ، فَاضْرِبْ عَنْهُ صَفْحًا، وَخَلِّ هَذَا الشَّأْنَ لِأَهْلِهِ.

If you find it difficult to understand this concept, and how the one who has perfect love hears, sees, strikes, and walks by way of his beloved, while his self is absent from him, then turn the page, and leave this matter to its people.

خَلِّ الْهَوَى لِأُنَاسٍ يُعْرَفُونَ بِهِ ... قَدْ كَابَدُوا الْحُبَّ حَتَّى لَانَ أَصْعَبُهُ

Leave love to people who are known for it... They have endured love until even the most difficult parts of it became easy for them.

فَإِنَّ السَّالِكَ إِلَى رَبِّهِ لَا تَزَالُ هِمَّتُهُ عَاكِفَةً عَلَى أَمْرَيْنِ: اسْتِفْرَاغُ الْقَلْبِ فِي صِدْقِ الْحُبِّ، وَبَذْلُ الْجُهْدِ فِي امْتِثَالِ الْأَمْرِ، فَلَا يَزَالُ كَذَلِكَ حَتَّى يَبْدُوَ عَلَى سِرِّهِ شَوَاهِدُ مَعْرِفَتِهِ، وَآثَارُ صِفَاتِهِ وَأَسْمَائِهِ.

Indeed, the seeker of his Lord's path constantly focuses on two matters: using the full capacity of the heart for genuine love, and exerting effort in complying with the divine command. And he remains like this until the signs of knowing (Allah) and the effects of His attributes and names become apparent upon his heart and private conduct."

## CHAPTER CONCLUSION: BUILDING THE FORTRESS OF FAITH UPON A SOLID FOUNDATION

Imām Ibn al Qayyim (رَحِمَهُ ٱللَّهُ) says:[48]

"مَنْ أَرَادَ عُلُوَّ بُنْيَانِهِ فَعَلَيْهِ بِتَوْثِيقِ أَسَاسِهِ وَإِحْكَامِهِ وَشِدَّةِ الاعْتِنَاءِ بِهِ؛ فَإِنَّ عُلُوَّ الْبُنْيَانِ عَلَى قَدْرِ تَوْثِيقِ الْأَسَاسِ وَإِحْكَامِهِ.

"Whoever wants to build his structure high must reinforce and stabilize its foundation, paying great attention to it; for the height of a structure is determined by the firmness and stability of its foundation.

فَالْأَعْمَالُ وَالدَّرَجَاتُ بُنْيَانٌ، وَأَسَاسُهَا الْإِيمَانُ، وَمَتَى كَانَ الْأَسَاسُ وَثِيقًا حَمَلَ الْبُنْيَانَ وَاعْتَلَى عَلَيْهِ، وَإِذَا تَهَدَّمَ شَيْءٌ مِنَ الْبُنْيَانِ سَهُلَ تَدَارُكُهُ، وَإِذَا كَانَ الْأَسَاسُ غَيْرَ وَثِيقٍ لَمْ يَرْتَفِعِ الْبُنْيَانُ وَلَمْ يَثْبُتْ، وَإِذَا تَهَدَّمَ شَيْءٌ مِنَ الْأَسَاسِ سَقَطَ الْبُنْيَانُ أَوْ كَادَ.

Deeds and degrees (of virtue) are like a structure, the foundation of which is faith. When the foundation is solid, it can bear the structure, which can then be built high. If something from the structure collapses, it's easy to fix. However, if the foundation is not solid, the structure will not rise and remain stable. If something from the foundation collapses, the structure will fall or almost fall.

فَالْعَارِفُ هِمَّتُهُ تَصْحِيحُ الْأَسَاسِ وَإِحْكَامُهُ، وَالْجَاهِلُ يَرْفَعُ فِي الْبِنَاءِ عَنْ غَيْرِ أَسَاسٍ؛ فَلَا يَلْبَثُ بُنْيَانُهُ أَنْ يَسْقُطَ. قَالَ تَعَالَى: {أَفَمَنْ أَسَّسَ بُنْيَانَهُ عَلَى تَقْوَى مِنَ اللَّهِ وَرِضْوَانٍ خَيْرٌ أَمْ مَنْ أَسَّسَ بُنْيَانَهُ عَلَى شَفَا جُرُفٍ هَارٍ فَانْهَارَ بِهِ فِي نَارِ جَهَنَّمَ} [التوبة: 109].

[48] *Al Fawā'id.*

The wise person focuses on solidifying and stabilizing the foundation, while the ignorant person builds without foundation; their structure will soon collapse. He (سُبْحَانَهُ وَتَعَالَىٰ) says: "**Then is one who laid the foundation of his building on righteousness [with fear] from Allah and [seeking] His approval better or one who laid the foundation of his building on the edge of a bank about to collapse, so it collapsed with him into the fire of Hell? And Allah does not guide the wrongdoing people.**?" [Al-Tawbah: 109].

فَالْأَسَاسُ لِبِنَاءِ الْأَعْمَالِ كَالْقُوَّةِ لِبَدَنِ الْإِنْسَانِ؛ فَإِذَا كَانَتِ الْقُوَّةُ قَوِيَّةً حَمَلَتِ الْبَدَنَ وَدَفَعَتْ عَنْهُ كَثِيرًا مِنَ الْآفَاتِ، وَإِذَا كَانَتِ الْقُوَّةُ ضَعِيفَةً ضَعُفَ حَمْلُهَا لِلْبَدَنِ وَكَانَتِ الْآفَاتُ إِلَيْهِ أَسْرَعَ شَيْءٍ.

The foundation for the structure of deeds is like strength to the human body; when one's strength is strong, it carries the body and deflects many afflictions. When one's strength is weak, its ability to carry the body is weak, and afflictions come quickly.

فَاحْمِلْ بُنْيَانَكَ عَلَى قُوَّةِ أَسَاسِ الْإِيمَانِ؛ فَإِذَا تَشَعَّثَ شَيْءٌ مِنْ أَعَالِي الْبُنْيَانِ وَسَطْحِهِ كَانَ تَدَارُكُهُ أَسْهَلَ عَلَيْكَ مِنْ خَرَابِ الْأَسَاسِ.

So, place the weight of your structure upon the strength of the foundation of faith; if something falls into disarray from the top or roof of the structure, it is easier for you to fix than the collapse of the foundation.

وَهَذَا الْأَسَاسُ أَمْرَانِ: صِحَّةُ الْمَعْرِفَةِ بِاللَّهِ وَأَمْرِهِ وَأَسْمَائِهِ وَصِفَاتِهِ. **وَالثَّانِي:** تَجْرِيدُ الِانْقِيَادِ لَهُ وَلِرَسُولِهِ دُونَ مَا سِوَاهُ. فَهَذَا أَوْثَقُ أَسَاسٍ أَسَّسَ الْعَبْدُ عَلَيْهِ بُنْيَانَهُ، وَبِحَسَبِهِ يَعْتَلِي الْبُنْيَانُ مَا شَاءَ.

This foundation has two components: (1.) accurate knowledge of Allah, His commandments, His names, and His attributes. And the second: unreserved obedience to Him and His Messenger, to the exclusion of anything else. This is the firmest foundation a servant can base his structure on, and according to it, the structure will ascend as he wishes.

فَأَحْكِمِ الْأَسَاسَ، وَاحْفَظِ الْقُوَّةَ، وَدُمْ عَلَى الْحِمْيَةِ، وَاسْتَفْرِغْ إِذَا زَادَ بِكَ الْخَلَطُ، وَالْقَصْدَ الْقَصْدَ وَقَدْ بَلَغْتَ الْمُرَادَ، وَإِلَّا فَمَا دَامَتِ الْقُوَّةُ ضَعِيفَةً وَالْمَادَّةُ الْفَاسِدَةُ مَوْجُودَةً وَالِاسْتِفْرَاغُ مُعْدَمًا:

So, reinforce the foundation, preserve the strength, persist in your regimen *(al ḥimyah)*, rid yourself from impure excess, practice moderation and you will reach your goal. Otherwise, as long as one's strength is weak, their sustenance is corrupt and one does not rid himself (of harmful matters), [then his situation is as a poet said]:

فَاقْرأ السَّلَامَ عَلَى الْحَيَاةِ فَإِنَّهَا ... قَدْ آذَنَتْكَ بِسُرْعَةِ التَّوْدِيعِ

'Bid life farewell, for it has already... declared that you must
offer it a quick farewell.'

فَإِذَا كَمُلَ الْبُنْيَانُ؛ فَبَيِّضْهُ بِحُسْنِ الْخُلُقِ وَالْإِحْسَانِ إِلَى النَّاسِ، ثُمَّ حُطَّهُ بِسُورٍ مِنَ الْحَذَرِ لَا يَقْتَحِمُهُ عَدُوٌّ وَلَا تَبْدُو مِنْهُ الْعَوْرَةُ،

Then, once the structure is complete, brighten the exterior with a sealing coat of good character and benevolence towards people, then surround it with a wall of vigilance so that no enemy invades it and no flaws are exposed.

ثُمَّ أَرْخِ السُّتُورَ عَلَى أَبْوَابِهِ، ثُمَّ أَقْفِلِ الْبَابَ الْأَعْظَمَ بِالسُّكُوتِ عَمَّا تَخْشَى عَاقِبَتَهُ، ثُمَّ رَكِّبْ لَهُ مِفْتَاحًا مِنْ ذِكْرِ اللَّهِ بِهِ تَفْتَحُهُ وَتُغْلِقُهُ؛ فَإِنْ فَتَحْتَ فَتَحْتَ بِالْمِفْتَاحِ، وَإِنْ أَغْلَقْتَ الْبَابَ أَغْلَقْتَهُ بِهِ، فَتَكُونُ حِينَئِذٍ قَدْ بَنَيْتَ حِصْنًا تَحَصَّنْتَ فِيهِ مِنْ أَعْدَائِكَ؛ إِذَا طَافَ بِهِ الْعَدُوُّ لَمْ يَجِدْ مِنْهُ مَدْخَلًا، فَيَيْأَسَ مِنْكَ.

Then hang the coverings on its doors, and close the main door by keeping silent about matters whose consequence you fear. Then install for it a key of Allah's remembrance, with which you open and close it. If you open it, you open it with the key, and if you close the door, you close it with it. Then, you would have built a fortress in which you protect yourself from your enemies; when the enemy encircles it, they find no entrance; thus, they despair of you.

ثُمَّ تَعَاهَدْ بِنَاءَ الْحِصْنِ كُلَّ وَقْتٍ؛ فَإِنَّ الْعَدُوَّ إِذَا لَمْ يَطْمَعْ فِي الدُّخُولِ مِنَ الْبَابِ نَقَبَ عَلَيْكَ النُّقُوبَ مِنْ بَعِيدٍ بِمَعَاوِلِ الذُّنُوبِ.

Then constantly take care of the fortress's structure at every moment; if the enemy doesn't aspire to enter through the door, he will start undermining you from afar with the pickaxes of sins.

فَإِنْ أَهْمَلْتَ أَمْرَهُ وَصَلَ إِلَيْكَ النَّقْبُ؛ فَإِذَا الْعَدُوُّ مَعَكَ فِي دَاخِلِ الْحِصْنِ، فَيَصْعَبُ عَلَيْكَ إِخْرَاجُهُ،

If you neglect his matter, the digging will reach your position. Suddenly the enemy will be inside the fortification with you, at which point you will find it difficult to expel him.

وَتَكُونُ مَعَهُ عَلَى ثَلَاثِ خِلَالٍ: إِمَّا أَنْ يَغْلِبَكَ عَلَى الْحِصْنِ وَيَسْتَوْلِيَ عَلَيْهِ، وَإِمَّا أَنْ يُسَاكِنَكَ فِيهِ، وَإِمَّا أَنْ يَشْغَلَكَ بِمُقَابَلَتِهِ عَنْ تَمَامِ مَصْلَحَتِكَ وَتَعُودَ إِلَى سَدِّ النَّقْبِ وَلَمِّ شَعَثِ الْحِصْنِ.

You will be in one of three situations with him: either he defeats you and takes over the fort, cohabitates it with you, or keeps you busy fighting him. Rather than fully attending to your interests, you resort to sealing the holes and repairing the fortress's disarray.

وَإِذَا دَخَلَ نَقْبُهُ إِلَيْكَ نَالَكَ مِنْهُ ثَلَاثُ آفَاتٍ: إِفْسَادُ الْحِصْنِ، وَالْإِغَارَةُ عَلَى حَوَاصِلِهِ وَذَخَائِرِهِ، وَدَلَالَةُ السُّرَّاقِ مِنْ بَنِي جِنْسِهِ عَلَى عَوْرَتِهِ.

Once his digging reaches you, you will suffer from three afflictions: the corruption of the fort, the raiding of its storehouses and treasures, and signaling to the thieves of his kind about its vulnerabilities.

فَلَا يَزَالُ يُبْلَى مِنْهُ بِغَارَةٍ بَعْدَ غَارَةٍ حَتَّى يُضَعِّفُوا قُوَاهُ وَيُوهِنُوا عَزْمَهُ فَيَتَخَلَّى عَنِ الْحِصْنِ وَيُخَلِّي بَيْنَهُمْ وَبَيْنَهُ.

Thus, you will be continuously afflicted by one raid after another until they weaken your power and dilute your determination, leading you to abandon the fort and evacuate the ground between you and them.

وَهَذِهِ حَالُ أَكْثَرِ النُّفُوسِ مَعَ هَذَا الْعَدُوِّ، وَلِهَذَا تَرَاهُمْ يُسْخِطُونَ رَبَّهُمْ بِرِضَا أَنْفُسِهِمْ بَلْ بِرِضَا مَخْلُوقٍ مِثْلِهِمْ لَا يَمْلِكُ لَهُمْ ضَرًّا وَلَا نَفْعًا،

This is the situation of most souls with this enemy, so you see them angering their Lord by pleasing themselves or even by pleasing someone created like them, who has neither the power to harm nor benefit them.

وَيُضِيعُونَ كَسْبَ الدِّينِ بِكَسْبِ الْأَمْوَالِ، وَيُهْلِكُونَ أَنْفُسَهُمْ بِمَا لَا يَبْقَى لَهُمْ، وَيَحْرِصُونَ عَلَى الدُّنْيَا وَقَدْ أَدْبَرَتْ عَنْهُمْ، وَيَزْهَدُونَ فِي الْآخِرَةِ وَقَدْ هَجَمَتْ عَلَيْهِمْ،

They waste what they earn from the religion with their wealth, destroying themselves for things that will not remain with them. They ardently yearn for the world that has turned its back on them while showing indifference to the afterlife, which is rushing toward them.

وَيُخَالِفُونَ رَبَّهُمْ بِاتِّبَاعِ أَهْوَائِهِمْ، وَيَتَّكِلُونَ عَلَى الْحَيَاةِ وَلَا يَذْكُرُونَ الْمَوْتَ، وَيَذْكُرُونَ شَهَوَاتِهِمْ وَحَظُوظَهُمْ وَيَنْسَونَ مَا عَهِدَ اللَّهُ إِلَيْهِمْ،

They show opposition to their Lord by following their desires and rely on life without remembering death. They remember their desires and self-interests, forgetting the covenant that Allah has entrusted to them.

وَيَهْتَمُّونَ بِمَا ضَمِنَهُ اللَّهُ لَهُمْ وَلَا يَهْتَمُّونَ بِمَا أَمَرَهُمْ بِهِ، وَيَفْرَحُونَ بِالدُّنْيَا وَيَحْزَنُونَ عَلَى فَوَاتِ حَظِّهِمْ مِنْهَا وَلَا يَحْزَنُونَ عَلَى فَوَاتِ الْجَنَّةِ وما فيها،

They concern themselves with what Allah has guaranteed for them but pay no heed to His commands. They rejoice in this world and grieve over losing a share of it but don't grieve over losing paradise and what is in it.

ولا يَفْرَحُونَ بِالْإِيمَانِ فَرَحَهُمْ بِالدِّرْهَمِ وَالدِّينَارِ، وَيُفسِدُونَ حَقَّهُمْ بِبَاطِلِهِمْ وَهُدَاهُمْ بِضَلَالِهِمْ وَمَعْرُوفَهُمْ بِمُنْكَرِهِمْ، وَيَلبِسُون إِيْمَانَهُمْ بِظُنُونِهِمْ، ويَخلِطُونَ حَلَالَهُمْ بِحَرَامِهِمْ، وَيَتَرَدَّدُونَ فِي حيرَة آرائِهم وأَفْكَارِهِمْ، وَيَتْرُكُونَ هُدَى اللَّهِ الَّذي أهداه إليهم.

Their joy for faith doesn't match their joy for a dirham or a dinar. They corrupt the truth they have with their falsehood, their guidance with their misguidance, their goodness with their evil. They taint their faith with their suspicions, mix their lawful with their unlawful, hesitate in the confusion of their opinions and ideas, and abandon Allah's guidance which He has granted to them.

وَمِنَ الْعَجَبِ أَنَّ هَذَا الْعَدُوَّ يَسْتَعْمِلُ صَاحِبَ الْحِصْنِ فِي هَدمِ حِصْنِهِ بِيَدَيْهِ".

It is amazing that this enemy makes the master of the fort destroy his own fort with his hands."

# Chapter 3

## The Untamed Self Kills The Heart & Empowers Shaytān

# 3. The Untamed Self Sickens & Kills The Heart while Empowering Shaytān

Allah (سُبْحَانَهُ وَتَعَالَىٰ) said:[49]

﴿وَأَمَّا مَنْ خَافَ مَقَامَ رَبِّهِ وَنَهَى النَّفْسَ عَنِ الْهَوَىٰ ۝٤٠ فَإِنَّ الْجَنَّةَ هِيَ الْمَأْوَىٰ ۝٤١﴾

**"But as for him who feared standing before his Lord, and restrained himself from impure evil desires, and lusts. Verily, Paradise will be his abode."**

---

Shaykh al Islām Ibn Taymiyyah (d. 728 AH رَحِمَهُ اللَّهُ) makes a valuable comment on this verse, saying:[50]

"وَيَحْتَاجُ الْمُسْلِمُ فِي ذَلِكَ إِلَى أَنْ يَخَافَ اللَّهَ وَيَنْهَى النَّفْسَ عَنْ الْهَوَى ، وَنَفْسُ الْهَوَى وَالشَّهْوَةِ لَا يُعَاقَبُ عَلَيْهِ بَلْ عَلَى اتِّبَاعِهِ وَالْعَمَلِ بِهِ فَإِذَا كَانَتْ النَّفْسُ تَهْوَى وَهُوَ يَنْهَاهَا كَانَ نَهْيُهُ عِبَادَةً لِلَّهِ وَعَمَلًا صَالِحًا".

"The Muslim needs to fear Allah and restrain the self from desires. One is not punished because of having desire and lust but rather for following and acting upon them. If the self has desires and restrains it, his act of restraint is an act of worship to Allah and a righteous deed."

---

[49] Al-Nāzi'āt: 40-41.

[50] Faṣl fī Tazkiyyah al-Nafs (p. 33); Majmū' al Fatāwā (10/635).

Likewise, Allah (سُبْحَانَهُۥوَتَعَالَىٰ) said:[51]

﴿قَدْ أَفْلَحَ مَن تَزَكَّىٰ ۝١٤ وَذَكَرَ اسْمَ رَبِّهِۦ فَصَلَّىٰ ۝١٥﴾

**"He will indeed be successful who purifies himself, And remembers the name of his Lord, and prays."**

Similarly, Allah (جَلَّ وَعَلَا) says:

﴿ قَدْ أَفْلَحَ مَن زَكَّاهَا ۝٩ وَقَدْ خَابَ مَن دَسَّاهَا ﴾

**"He has succeeded who purifies it (the self), And indeed he fails who corrupts it."**[52]

There are similar exhortations in the authentic Sunnah about striving against the self. Faḍālah b. 'Ubayd (رَضِيَ ٱللَّهُ عَنْهُ) reported that Allah's Messenger (صَلَّى ٱللَّهُ عَلَيْهِ وَسَلَّمَ) said:[53]

«الْمُجَاهِدُ مَنْ جَاهَدَ نَفْسَهُ فِي اللَّهِ (عَزَّوَجَلَّ)»

**"The mujahid is the one who struggles against his own self for the sake of Allah (عَزَّوَجَلَّ) ."**

Similarly, Abū Hurayrah (رَضِيَ ٱللَّهُ عَنْهُ) reported that Allah's Messenger (صَلَّى ٱللَّهُ عَلَيْهِ وَسَلَّمَ) said:[54]

«لَيْسَ الشَّدِيدُ مَنْ غَلَبَ، إِنَّمَا الشَّدِيدُ مَنْ غَلَبَ نَفْسَهُ»

**"Indeed, the strong one is not the one who overcomes others, but the strong one is the one who overcomes his self."**

---

51 Al-A'la: 14 - 15

52 Al-Shams: 9 - 10.

53 Reported by Ahmad, Abu Dawūd, and al-Tirmidhī who graded it *ḥasan ṣaḥīḥ*. See *al Jāmi' al-Ṣaḥīḥ* by Sh. Muqbil b. Hādī al Wādi'ī (1057, 3424).

54 Reported by Ibn Ḥibbān in al-Taqāsīm wal Anwā' (Ṣaḥīḥ Ibn Ḥibbān).

Commenting on this *ḥadīth* of Abū Hurayrah, Al Ajurri (d. 360 AH رَحِمَهُ ٱللَّهُ) said:[55]

"فَإِنْ قَالَ قَائِلٌ: فَعَلَى مَا أُجَاهِدُ نَفْسِي حَتَّى أَغْلِبَهَا ؟ قِيلَ لَهُ: تُجَاهِدُهَا حَتَّى تَلْزَمَ أَدَاءَ فَرَائِضِ اللَّهِ عَزَّ وَجَلَّ ، وَتَنْتَهِيَ عَنْ مَعَاصِيهِ.

"If someone says: How can I struggle with my self until I overcome it? It was said to him: You struggle with it until you commit to performing the obligations of Allah, the Mighty and Sublime, and you abstain from his disobedience.

فَإِنْ قَالَ: صِفْ لِي مِنْ أَخْلَاقِهَا الَّتِي تَمِيلُ إِلَيْهِ مِمَّا لَا يَحْسُنُ ، حَتَّى أَحْذَرَهَا ، وَأَمْقُتَهَا ، وَأُجَاهِدَهَا ، إِذَا عَلِمْتُ أَنَّ فِيهَا شَيْئًا مِنْ تِلْكَ الْخِصَالِ.

If he says: Describe to me its characteristics that I tend to, which are not good so that I can be cautious of them, hate them, and struggle against them when I know they have any of those qualities.

قِيلَ لَهُ: إِنَّ النَّفْسَ أَهْلٌ أَنْ تُمْقَتَ فِي اللَّهِ عَزَّ وَجَلَّ ، وَمَنْ مَقَتَ نَفْسَهُ فِي ذَاتِ اللَّهِ عَزَّ وَجَلَّ رَجَوْتُ أَنْ يُؤَمِّنَهُ اللَّهُ عَزَّ وَجَلَّ مِنْ مَقْتِهِ ، كَذَا رُوِيَ عَنِ الْفُضَيْلِ بْنِ عِيَاضٍ".

It is said to him in response: Indeed, the self deserves to be hated for the sake of Allah, the Mighty and Sublime, and whoever hates his self for the sake of Allah, the Mighty and Sublime, I hope that Allah will keep him safe from His hatred. It was narrated from al-Fuḍayl ibn 'Iyāḍ."

---

[55] See the treatise *Adab al-Nufūs* by al Ājurri.

Likewise the Qāḍī Abul Hasan al Mawārdī (d. 450 AH رَحِمَهُ ٱللَّهُ) commented, saying:[56]

"وَقَالَ عَوْنُ بْنُ عَبْدِ اللَّهِ: إِذَا عَصَتْكَ نَفْسُكَ فِيمَا كَرِهَتْ فَلَا تُطِعْهَا فِيمَا أَحَبَّتْ، وَلَا يَغُرَّنَّكَ ثَنَاءُ مَنْ جَهِلَ أَمْرَكَ.

"And Awn ibn Abdullah said: 'If your soul disobeys you in what it dislikes, then do not obey it in what it likes. And do not be deceived by the praise of those ignorant of your affairs.'

وَقَالَ بَعْضُ الْبُلَغَاءِ: مَنْ قَوِيَ عَلَى نَفْسِهِ تَنَاهَى فِي الْقُوَّةِ، وَمَنْ صَبَرَ عَنْ شَهْوَتِهِ بَالَغَ فِي الْمُرُوَّةِ.

And some eloquent speakers have said: 'The one who has mastery over themselves restrains their desires, and the one who exercises patience in controlling their lust excels in manhood.'

فَحِينَئِذٍ يَأْخُذُ نَفْسَهُ عِنْدَ مَعْرِفَةِ مَا أَكَنَّتْ، وَخِبْرَةِ مَا أَجَنَّتْ بِتَقْوِيمِ عِوَجِهَا وَإِصْلَاحِ فَسَادِهَا...

At that point, one takes control of their soul, knowing its inclinations and understanding the consequences it may bring by rectifying its distortions and mending its corruptions...

ثُمَّ يُرَاعِي مِنْهَا مَا صَلُحَ وَاسْتَقَامَ مِنْ زَيْغٍ يَحْدُثُ عَنْ إِغْفَالٍ، أَوْ مَيْلٍ يَكُونُ عَنْ إِهْمَالٍ؛ لِيَتِمَّ لَهُ الصَّلَاحُ وَتَسْتَدِيمَ لَهُ السَّعَادَةُ، فَإِنَّ الْمُغَفَّلَ بَعْدَ الْمُعَانَاةِ ضَائِعٌ، وَالْمُهْمِلَ بَعْدَ الْمُرَاعَاةِ زَائِغٌ".

Then, one carefully watches and guards what one possesses that is good and upright, guarding against deviance caused by heedlessness or inclinations caused by negligence. This enables one to attain righteousness and establish lasting happiness fully. Indeed, the one who remains foolishly heedless after suffering is

[56] Adab al-Dunyā wal-Dīn by al Mawārdī (p. 236).

lost and who becomes negligent after careful-mindedness is deviant."

---

Another important ḥadīth that highlights the need to strive against the self is the report in which 'Imrān bin Ḥuṣayn (رَضِيَ اللَّهُ عَنْهُمَا) narrated from his father (Ḥuṣayn b. 'Ubayd al Khuzā'ī), saying:[57]

"أَتَى رَسُولَ اللهِ صلى الله عليه وسلم فَقَالَ: يَا مُحَمَّدُ بَنُ عَبْدِ الْمُطَّلِبِ خَيْرٌ لِقَوْمِكَ مِنْكَ، كَانَ يُطْعِمُهُمْ بِالْكَبِدِ وَالسَّنَامِ، وَأَنْتَ تَنْحَرُهُمْ،

"He (Huṣayn) went to Allah's Messenger (صَلَّى اللَّهُ عَلَيْهِ وَسَلَّمَ) and said: 'O Muhammad, son of Abd al-Muṭṭalib, he (i.e., 'Abd al Muṭṭalib) was more better to his people than you. He used to feed them liver and camel, but now you slaughter them.' The Prophet (صَلَّى اللَّهُ عَلَيْهِ وَسَلَّمَ) said:

"مَا شَاءَ اللَّهُ".

**'As Allah wills.'** (i.e., what you said is simply a test from Allah).

فَلَمَّا أَرَادَ أَنْ يَنْصَرِفَ قَالَ: مَا أَقُولُ؟

When he (i.e., Ḥuṣayn) was about to leave, he asked: 'What should I say?'

قَالَ: " قُلِ: **اللهُمَّ قِنِي شَرَّ نَفْسِي، وَاعْزِمْ لِي عَلَى رُشْدِ أَمْرِي،**

He (صَلَّى اللَّهُ عَلَيْهِ وَسَلَّمَ) replied: 'Say: **O Allah, protect me from the evils of my self, and guide me to the best of my affairs.'**

---

[57] Reported by al-Nasā'ī. Graded Authentic by al-Nawawī in the introduction of his explanation of Ṣaḥīḥ Muslim, Ibn Ḥajr in al Iṣābah and by al Albānī in al-Ṣaḥieḥah, and Imām Muqbil in al Jāmi' al-Ṣaḥīḥ (1538, 3397). Ibn al Qayyim says in al Wābil al-Ṣayyib that its isnād meets the conditions of Bukhārī and Muslim.

فَانْطَلَقَ وَلَمْ يَكُنْ أَسْلَمَ، ثُمَّ إِنَّهُ أَسْلَمَ فَقَالَ: يَا رَسُولَ اللهِ، إِنِّي كُنْتُ أَتَيْتُكَ فَقُلْتُ: عَلِّمْنِي، قُلْتَ: " قُلِ: اللهُمَّ قِنِي شَرَّ نَفْسِي، وَاعْزِمْ لِي عَلَى رُشْدِ أَمْرِي " فَمَا أَقُولُ الْآنَ حِينَ أَسْلَمْتُ؟

He left, and at that time, he had not yet embraced Islam. Later, he converted to Islam and said: 'O Messenger of God, I came to you previously and asked you to teach me, and you said: 'Say: O Allah, protect me from the evils of my soul, and guide me to the best of my affairs.' What should I say now that I have embraced Islam?'

قَالَ: " قُلِ: اللهُمَّ قِنِي شَرَّ نَفْسِي، وَاعْزِمْ لِي عَلَى رُشْدِ أَمْرِي، اللهُمَّ اغْفِرْ لِي مَا أَسْرَرْتُ وَمَا أَعْلَنْتُ، وَمَا أَخْطَأْتُ وَمَا عَمَدْتُ، وَمَا عَلِمْتُ وَمَا جَهِلْتُ "

He (صَلَّى ٱللَّهُ عَلَيْهِ وَسَلَّمَ) replied: **'Say: O Allah, protect me from the evils of my soul, and guide me to the best of my affairs. O Allah, forgive what I have concealed and what I have declared, what I have done in error and what I have done deliberately, what I know and what I am ignorant of.'"**

---

Imam Ibn al Qayyim (رَحِمَهُ ٱللَّهُ) explains that all sicknesses of the heart come from the self commanding evil. He writes:[58]

"فَإِنَّ سَائِرَ أَمْرَاضِ الْقَلْبِ إِنَّمَا تَنْشَأُ مِنْ جَانِبِ النَّفْسِ، فَالْمَوَادُّ الْفَاسِدَةُ كُلُّهَا إِلَيْهَا تَنْصَبُّ، ثُمَّ تَنْبَعِثُ مِنْهَا إِلَى الْأَعْضَاءِ، وَأَوَّلُ مَا تَنَالُ الْقَلْبَ".

"Indeed, all of the heart's diseases originate from the self. All corrupt substances are poured (the self), and then they emerge from it to the body parts, and the first part that they reach is the heart."

---

[58] Ighāthah al-Lahfān, chapter 11.

...وَقَدِ اتَّفَقَ السَّالِكُونَ إِلَى اللَّهِ -عَلَى اخْتِلَافِ طُرُقِهِمْ وَتَبَايُنِ سُلُوكِهِمْ- عَلَى أَنَّ النَّفْسَ قَاطِعَةٌ بَيْنَ الْقَلْبِ وَبَيْنَ الْوُصُولِ إِلَى الرَّبِّ، وَأَنَّهُ لَا يُدْخَلُ عَلَيْهِ سُبْحَانَهُ وَلَا يُوصَلُ إِلَيْهِ إِلَّا بَعْدَ تَرْكِهَا، وَإِمَاتَتِهَا بِمُخَالَفَتِهَا، وَالظَّفَرِ بِهَا.

Despite their varied paths and diverse approaches, those journeying to Allah have agreed that the soul is a barrier between the heart and reaching the Lord. No one is allowed to approach Him, and no one reaches Him, except after abandoning it (i.e., the self) and 'killing' it through opposing and defeating it.

فَإِنَّ النَّاسَ عَلَى قِسْمَيْنِ: قِسْمٌ ظَفِرَتْ بِهِ نَفْسُهُ؛ فَمَلَكَتْهُ وَأَهْلَكَتْهُ، وَصَارَ طَوْعًا لَهَا تَحْتَ أَوَامِرِهَا. وَقِسْمٌ ظَفِرُوا بِنُفُوسِهِمْ؛ فَقَهَرُوهَا، فَصَارَتْ طَوْعًا لَهُمْ، مُنْقَادَةً لِأَوَامِرِهِمْ.

Indeed, people are of two categories: A category whose selves have overcome them; thus, their selves have dominated and destroyed them, and they willingly follow the commands of their inner-self. Another category is those who have overcome their souls; thus, they have dominated them, and their souls have willingly obeyed to their commands.

كَمَا قَالَ بَعْضُ الْعَارِفِينَ: انتَهَى سَفَرُ الطَّالِبِينَ إِلَى الظَّفَرِ بِأَنْفُسِهِمْ، فَمَنْ ظَفِرَ بِنَفْسِهِ أَفْلَحَ وَأَنْجَحَ، وَمَنْ ظَفِرَتْ بِهِ نَفْسُهُ خَسِرَ وَهَلَكَ. قال تعالى: {**فَأَمَّا مَنْ طَغَى (37) وَآثَرَ الْحَيَاةَ الدُّنْيَا (38) فَإِنَّ الْجَحِيمَ هِيَ الْمَأْوَى (39) وَأَمَّا مَنْ خَافَ مَقَامَ رَبِّهِ وَنَهَى النَّفْسَ عَنِ الْهَوَى (40) فَإِنَّ الْجَنَّةَ هِيَ الْمَأْوَى**}.

As one of the knowledgeable said: "The journey of the seekers ends when they overcome their souls. Whoever overcomes his soul is successful and prosperous, and whoever is overcome by his soul is a loser and perishes." As Allah said: "But as for him who transgressed and preferred the life of this world, Hell will be his abode. But as for him who feared standing before his Lord and restrained his soul from impure evil desires and lusts, Paradise will be his abode."[59]

فَالنَّفْسُ تَدْعُو إِلَى الطُّغْيَانِ وَإِيثَارِ الْحَيَاةِ الدُّنْيَا، وَالرَّبُّ تَعَالَى يَدْعُو الْعَبْدَ إِلَى خَوْفِهِ وَنَهْيِ النَّفْسِ عَنِ الْهَوَى، وَالْقَلْبُ بَيْنَ الدَّاعِيَيْنِ، يَمِيلُ إِلَى هَذَا الدَّاعِي مَرَّةً وَإِلَى هَذَا مَرَّةً، وَهَذَا مَوْضِعُ الْمِحْنَةِ وَالْابْتِلَاءِ.

The soul invites one to transgress and to prefer the life of this world, and the Lord (سُبْحَانَهُ وَتَعَالَىٰ) invites the servant to fear Him and to restrain the soul from its desires. The heart is between these two callers, inclining to this caller at one time and to that caller at another, and this is the place of trial and tribulation."

...والمقصود ذكر علاج مرض القلب باستيلاء النفس الأمارة عليه، وله علاجان: محاسبتها، ومخالفتها.

The purpose here is to mention the treatment of heart disease when the insistent self takes control over it, and there are two treatments: holding it accountable and opposing it."

---

Abul Faraj Ibn al Jawzī (d. 597 AH رَحِمَهُ ٱللَّهُ) said:[60]

"اعْلَمْ وَفَّقَكَ اللَّهُ أَنَّ النَّفْسَ مَجْبُولَةٌ عَلَى حُبِّ الْهَوَى وَقَدْ سَبَقَ بَيَانُ أَذَاهُ فَافْتَقَرَتْ لِذَلِكَ إِلَى الْمُجَاهَدَةِ وَالْمُخَالَفَةِ، وَمَتَى لَمْ تُزْجَرْ عَنِ الْهَوَى هَجَمَ عَلَيْهَا الْفِكْرُ فِي طَلَبِ مَا شُغِفَتْ بِهِ

Know, may Allah guide you, that the soul is inclined towards love for whimsical desires. Its harms have already been explained, so it is in need of struggling against these desires and contradicting them. When it is not checked from indulging in

---

[59] An-Nazi'at: 37-41.

[60] *Dhamm al Hawā.*

desires, the thought of seeking what it is passionate about attacks it.

فَاسْتَأْنَسَتْ بِالآرَاءِ الْفَاسِدَةِ وَالأَطْمَاعِ الْكَاذِبَةِ وَالأَمَانِي الْعَجِيبَةِ خُصُوصًا إِنْ سَاعَدَ الشَّبَابُ الَّذِي هُوَ شُعْبَةٌ مِنَ الْجُنُونِ وَامْتَدَّ سَاعِدُ الْقُدْرَةِ إِلَى نَيْلِ الْمَطْلُوبِ...

Then, it finds comfort in corrupt opinions, false ambitions, and strange hopes, especially if it is assisted by youth, which is a branch of insanity, and when the ability extends to achieve the desired...

اعْلَمْ أَنَّهُ إِنَّمَا كَانَ جِهَادُ النَّفْسِ أَكْبَرَ مِنْ جِهَادِ الأَعْدَاءِ لأَنَّ النَّفْسَ مَحْبُوبَةٌ وَمَا تَدْعُو إِلَيْهِ مَحْبُوبٌ، لأَنَّهَا لَا تَدْعُو إلا إِلَى مَا تَشْتَهِي، وَمُوَافَقَةُ الْمَحْبُوبِ فِي الْمَكْرُوهِ مَحْبُوبَةٌ، فَكَيْفَ إِذا دَعَا إِلَى مَحْبُوب

Know that the struggle against the self is greater than the struggle against enemies because the soul is beloved, and what it calls for is beloved. For it calls only for what it desires, and pleasing one's beloved in what is personally disliked is beloved, so how much more so if it calls for what is beloved?

فَإِذْ عَكَسْتَ الْحَالَ وَخُولِفَ الْمَحْبُوبُ فِيمَا يَدْعُو إِلَيْهِ مِنَ الْمَحْبُوبِ اشْتَدَّ الْجِهَادُ وَصَعُبَ الأَمْرُ بِخِلافِ جِهَادِ الْكُفَّارِ فَإِنَّ الطِّبَاعَ تَحْمِلُ عَلَى خُصُومَةِ الأَعْدَاءِ

But when the situation is reversed, and the beloved is opposed to what it calls for from the beloved, the struggle intensifies, and the matter becomes difficult. This contrasts the struggle against disbelievers, for natural dispositions drive people to oppose their enemies.

وَقَالَ ابْنُ الْمُبَارَكِ فِي قَوْله تعال: {وَجَاهِدُوا فِي اللَّهِ حَقَّ جِهَادِهِ}، قَالَ هُوَ جِهَادُ النَّفْسِ وَالْهَوَى..."

In his interpretation of the verse, Ibn Al-Mubarak said, "And strive hard for Allah's cause as you ought to strive." He said: "It is the struggle against the self and desires..."

The great scholar, Muḥammad b. Ḥussayn al Aajurī (d. 360 AH رَحِمَهُ ٱللَّهُ) opened his essay on disciplining the self with a chapter titled, "Being Careful of One's Self", saying:[61]

"اعْلَمُوا أَنَّ اللَّهَ جَلَّ ذِكْرُهُ ذَكَرَ النَّفْسَ فِي غَيْرِ مَوْضِعٍ مِنْ كِتَابِهِ ، مُنَبِّهٌ بِمَعَانِي كَثِيرَةٍ ، كُلُّهَا تَدُلُّ عَلَى الْحَذَرِ مِنَ النَّفْسِ. أَخْبَرَنَا مَوْلَانَا الْكَرِيمُ أَنَّهَا تَمِيلُ إِلَى مَا تَهْوَاهُ مِمَّا لَهَا فِيهِ مِنَ اللَّذَّةِ ، وَقَدْ عَلِمَتْ أَنَّهَا قَدْ نُهِيَتْ عَنْهُ. ثُمَّ أَعْلَمَنَا مَوْلَانَا الْكَرِيمُ مَنْ نَهَى نَفْسَهُ عَمَّا تَهْوَى فَإِنَّ الْجَنَّةَ مَأْوَاهُ ،

"Know that Allah (جَلَّ وَعَلَا) has mentioned the self in more than one place in His Book, hinting at many meanings, all indicating caution against the self. Our Generous Master informed us that it inclines to what it desires from what pleases it, even though it knows it has been prohibited. Then our Generous Master informed us that whoever prohibits his soul from what it desires, indeed, Paradise is his dwelling.

قَالَ اللَّهُ تَبَارَكَ وَتَعَالَى: {**فَإِذَا جَاءَتِ الطَّامَّةُ الْكُبْرَى يَوْمَ يَتَذَكَّرُ الْإِنسَانُ مَا سَعَى وَبُرِّزَتِ الْجَحِيمُ لِمَن يَرَى فَأَمَّا مَن طَغَى وَآثَرَ الْحَيَاةَ الدُّنْيَا فَإِنَّ الْجَحِيمَ هِيَ الْمَأْوَى وَأَمَّا مَنْ خَافَ مَقَامَ رَبِّهِ وَنَهَى النَّفْسَ عَنِ الْهَوَى فَإِنَّ الْجَنَّةَ هِيَ الْمَأْوَى**}،

Allah, Blessed and Exalted, said: "**But as for him who feared the position of his Lord and prevented the soul from [following] desire, then indeed, Paradise will be [his] refuge.**"[62]

فَإِنْ كَانَ اللَّهُ تَعَالَى قَدْ نَهَى عَنْهُ انْزَجَرَ عَنْهُ ، فَإِنْ تَابَعَتْهُ نَفْسُهُ إِلَى مَا زَجَرَهَا عَنْهُ ، فَلْيَعْلَمْ أَنَّهُ مِنَ اللَّهِ عَزَّ وَجَلَّ بِبَالٍ ، وَأَنَّ هَذِهِ نَفْسٌ مَرْحُومَةٌ ، فَلْيَشْكُرِ اللَّهَ الْكَرِيمَ عَلَى ذَلِكَ.

[61] *Adab al-Nufūs.*

[62] Al-Nazi'at: 35.

So, since Allah has prohibited (desires), one should be dissuaded. And if his self followed in what He warned it from, let him know that Allah cares for him and that this is a soul that has been shown mercy, so let him thank Allah the Generous for that.

أَلَمْ تَسْمَعُوا - رَحِمَكُمُ اللَّهُ - إِلَى مَا أَخْبَرَكُمْ مَوْلَاكُمُ الْكَرِيمُ عَنْ نَبِيٍّ مِنْ أَنْبِيَائِهِ ، وَهُوَ يُوسُفُ عَلَيْهِ السَّلَامُ ، قَوْلَهُ: {**وَمَا أُبَرِّئُ نَفْسِي إِنَّ النَّفْسَ لَأَمَّارَةٌ بِالسُّوءِ إِلَّا مَا رَحِمَ رَبِّي إِنَّ رَبِّي غَفُورٌ رَحِيمٌ**} ،

Have you not heard, may Allah have mercy on you, what your Generous Master informed you about a prophet from His prophets, Yūsuf (عَلَيْهِ ٱلصَّلَاةُ وَٱلسَّلَامُ), and his saying: "**And I do not acquit myself. Indeed, the soul is a persistent enjoiner of evil, except those upon which my Lord has mercy. Indeed, my Lord is Forgiving and Merciful.**"[63]

فَيُقَالُ: إِنَّ النَّفْسَ الْأَمَّارَةَ الْمَرْحُومَةَ هِيَ الْمَعْصُومَةُ الَّتِي عَصَمَهَا اللَّهُ عَزَّ وَجَلَّ.

So it is said: Indeed, the insistent self that has been shown mercy is the protected one, which Allah (عَزَّوَجَلَّ) has preserved.

ثُمَّ اعْلَمُوا - رَحِمَكُمُ اللَّهُ - أَنَّ النَّفْسَ إِذَا رَكِبَتْ مَا تَهْوَى مِمَّا قَدْ نُهِيَتْ عَنْهُ ، فَإِنَّهَا سَتَلُومُ صَاحِبَهَا يَوْمَ الْقِيَامَةِ ، تَقُولُ: لِمَ فَعَلْتَ؟ لِمَ قَصَّرْتَ؟ لِمَ بَلَّغْتَنِي مَا أُحِبُّ وَقَدْ عَلِمْتَ أَنَّ فِيهِ عَطَبِي؟ أَلَمْ تَسْمَعُوا رَحِمَكُمُ اللَّهُ إِلَى قَوْلِ اللَّهِ عَزَّ وَجَلَّ: {**لَا أُقْسِمُ بِيَوْمِ الْقِيَامَةِ وَلَا أُقْسِمُ بِالنَّفْسِ اللَّوَّامَةِ**}،

"Then, know —may Allah have mercy on you— that the self, when it indulges in what it desires from what it has been forbidden, will blame its owner on the Day of Resurrection, saying: 'Why did you do that? Why did you fall short? Why did you let me reach what I love while you knew it harmed me?' Have you not heard (may Allah have mercy on you) the words of

[63] Yusuf: 53.

Allah, the Mighty and Majestic: 'Nay, I swear by the Day of Resurrection; And nay, I swear by the reproaching soul.'[64]

فَالْوَاجِبُ عَلَى مَنْ سَمِعَ هَذَا مِنَ اللَّهِ عَزَّ وَجَلَّ أَنْ يَحْذَرَ مِنْ نَفْسِهِ أَشَدَّ حَذَرًا مِنْ عَدُوٍّ يُرِيدُ قَتْلَهُ ، أَوْ أَخْذَ مَالِهِ ، أَوِ انْتِهَاكَ عِرْضِهِ.

It is obligatory for whoever hears this from Allah, the Mighty and Majestic, to be more cautious of his soul than an enemy who wants to kill him, take his wealth, or violate his honor.

فَإِنْ قَالَ قَائِلٌ: لِمَ أَلْزَمْتَنِي هَذَا الْحَذَرَ مِنَ النَّفْسِ حَتَّى جَعَلْتَهُ أَشَدَّ حَالًا مِنْ عَدُوٍّ وَقَدْ تَبَيَّنْتُ عَدَاوَتَهُ؟ قِيلَ لَهُ: إِنَّ عَدُوَّكَ الَّذِي يُرِيدُ قَتْلَكَ ، أَوْ أَخْذَ مَالِكَ ، أَوِ انْتِهَاكَ عِرْضِكَ ، إِنْ ظَفِرَ مِنْكَ بِمَا يُؤَمِّلُهُ مِنْكَ فَإِنَّ اللَّهَ عَزَّ وَجَلَّ يُكَفِّرُ عَنْكَ بِهِ السَّيِّئَاتِ ، وَيَرْفَعُ لَكَ بِهِ الدَّرَجَاتِ ،

If someone asks, 'Why do you impose this caution towards the self to the extent that you make it more severe than an enemy when I already recognize the enemy's hostility?' It will be said to him: 'Your enemy, who wants to kill you, take your wealth, or violate your honor, if he achieves from you what he hopes, Allah (عَزَّوَجَلَّ) will expiate your sins and elevate your rank.

وَلَيْسَ النَّفْسُ كَذَلِكَ؛ لِأَنَّ النَّفْسَ إِنْ ظَفِرَتْ مِنْكَ بِمَا تَهْوَى مِمَّا قَدْ نُهِيتَ عَنْهُ ، كَانَ فِيهِ هَلَكَتُكَ فِي الدُّنْيَا وَالْآخِرَةِ ،

However, the soul is not like that; if the soul achieves from you what it desires from what it has been forbidden, it leads to your destruction in this world and the Hereafter.

أَمَّا فِي الدُّنْيَا فَالْفَضِيحَةُ مَعَ شِدَّةِ الْعُقُوبَةِ ، وَسُوءُ الْمَنْزِلَةِ عِنْدَ اللَّهِ عَزَّ وَجَلَّ مَعَ سُوءِ الْمُنْقَلَبِ فِي الْآخِرَةِ.

[64] Al-Qiyama: 1-2.

In this world, there is being exposed to severe punishment. a poor status before Allah, the Mighty and Majestic, and a bad ending in the Hereafter.

فَالْعَاقِلُ، يَرْحَمُكُمُ اللَّهُ، يُلْزِمُ نَفْسَهُ الْحَذَرَ وَالْجِهَادَ لَهُ أَشَدَّ مِنْ مُجَاهَدَةِ الْأَقْرَانِ مِمَّنْ يُرِيدُ مَالَهُ وَنَفْسَهُ ، فَجَاهِدْهَا عِنْدَ الرِّضَا وَالْغَضَبِ ، كَذَا أَدَّبَنَا نَبِيُّنَا صَلَّى اللَّهُ عَلَيْهِ وَسَلَّمَ فِي غَيْرِ حَدِيثٍ بِقَوْلِهِ صَلَّى اللَّهُ عَلَيْهِ وَسَلَّمَ: «الْمُجَاهِدُ مَنْ جَاهَدَ نَفْسَهُ فِي طَاعَةِ اللَّهِ عَزَّ وَجَلَّ»

Therefore, the wise person, may Allah have mercy on you, imposes caution upon himself and strives against it more fiercely than striving against a peer who wants his wealth and his life. Struggle against it when pleased and angry. This is how our Prophet (ﷺ) taught us in an authentic hadith when he said: **'The Mujahid is the one who strives against himself in obedience to Allah (عَزَّوَجَلَّ).'**

## THE SELF IS A VESSEL TO EITHER PARADISE OR HELL

Ibn al Qayyim (d. 751 AH رَحِمَهُ ٱللَّهُ) says:[65]

"وَالنَّفْسُ مَطِيَّةُ الْعَبْدِ الَّذِي يَسِيرُ عَلَيْهَا إِلَى الْجَنَّةِ أَوِ النَّارِ، وَالصَّبْرُ لَهَا بِمَنْزِلَةِ الْخِطَامِ وَالزِّمَامِ لِلْمَطِيَّةِ، فَإِنْ لَمْ يَكُنْ لِلْمَطِيَّةِ خِطَامٌ وَلَا زِمَامٌ شَرَدَتْ فِي كُلِّ مَذْهَبٍ.

And the self is the servant's mount on which he travels to Paradise or Hell, and patience for it is like the harness and the rein for the mount. If the mount does not have a harness or rein, it will stray in every direction.

وَحُفِظَ مِنْ خُطَبِ الْحَجَّاجِ: "اقْدَعُوا هَذِهِ النُّفُوسَ؛ فَإِنَّهَا طُلَعَةٌ إِلَى كُلِّ سَوْءٍ، فَرَحِمَ اللَّهُ امْرَأً جَعَلَ لِنَفْسِهِ خِطَامًا وَزِمَامًا؛ فَقَادَهَا بِخِطَامِهَا إِلَى طَاعَةِ اللَّهِ، وَصَرَفَهَا بِزِمَامِهَا عَنْ مَعْصِيَةِ اللَّهِ، فَإِنَّ الصَّبْرَ عَنْ مَحَارِمِ اللَّهِ أَيْسَرُ مِنَ الصَّبْرِ عَلَى عَذَابِهِ".

It was preserved from the speeches of Al-Hajjaj: "Restrain these souls; for they are avidly looking for all sorts of evil. May Allah have mercy on a man who puts a harness and rein on his soul; he leads it with its harness to the obedience of Allah and diverts it with its rein from the disobedience of Allah, for patience from the prohibitions of Allah is easier than patience upon His punishment."

قُلْتُ: وَالنَّفْسُ فِيهَا قُوَّتَانِ: قُوَّةُ الْإِقْدَامِ، وَقُوَّةُ الْإِحْجَامِ، فَحَقِيقَةُ الصَّبْرِ أَنْ يَجْعَلَ قُوَّةَ الْإِقْدَامِ مَصْرُوفَةً إِلَى مَا يَنْفَعُهُ، وَقُوَّةَ الْإِحْجَامِ إِمْسَاكًا عَمَّا يَضُرُّهُ.

I say: The self has two strengths: the strength of advancing and withholding. The reality of patience is to direct the strength

---

[65] *'Idat al-Ṣābirīn*, chapter 2.

of advancing towards what benefits him and the strength of hesitation to withhold from what harms him.

وَمِنَ النَّاسِ مَنْ يَكُونُ صَبْرُهُ عَلَى فِعْلِ مَا يُنْتَفَعُ بِهِ وَثَبَاتُهُ عَلَيْهِ أَقْوَى مِنْ صَبْرِهِ عَمَّا يَضُرُّهُ، فَيَصْبِرُ عَلَى مَشَقَّةِ الطَّاعَةِ، وَلَا صَبْرَ لَهُ عَنْ دَاعِي هَوَاهُ إِلَى ارْتِكَابِ مَا نُهِيَ عَنْهُ.

And there are some whose patience to do what benefits him and to be steadfast upon it is stronger than his patience from what harms him. Thus, he is patient with the hardship of obedience but has no patience to resist his desire to commit what is prohibited.

وَمِنْهُمْ مَنْ تَكُونُ قُوَّةُ صَبْرِهِ عَنِ الْمُخَالَفَاتِ أَقْوَى مِنْ صَبْرِهِ عَلَى مَشَقَّةِ الطَّاعَاتِ.

And there are those whose strength of patience from committing violations is stronger than their patience with the hardship of obedience.

وَمِنْهُمْ مَنْ لَا صَبْرَ لَهُ عَلَى هَذَا وَلَا عَلَى هَذَا.

And there are those who have no patience for either.

وَأَفْضَلُ النَّاسِ أَصْبَرُهُمْ عَلَى النَّوْعَيْنِ؛ فَكَثِيرٌ مِنَ النَّاسِ يَصْبِرُ عَلَى مُكَابَدَةِ قِيَامِ اللَّيْلِ فِي الْحَرِّ وَالْبَرْدِ وَعَلَى مَشَقَّةِ الصِّيَامِ، وَلَا يَصْبِرُ عَنْ نَظْرَةٍ مُحَرَّمَةٍ.

And the best of people have the most patience in both types; many are patient in enduring standing for the night prayer in heat and cold and enduring the hardship of fasting, but they cannot resist a forbidden look.

وَكَثِيرٌ مِنَ النَّاسِ يَصْبِرُ عَنَ النَّظَرِ، وَعَنَ الِالْتِفَاتِ إِلَى الصُّوَرِ، وَلَا صَبْرَ لَهُ عَلَى الْأَمْرِ بِالْمَعْرُوفِ وَالنَّهْيِ عَنِ الْمُنْكَرِ وَجِهَادِ الْكُفَّارِ وَالْمُنَافِقِينَ، بَلْ هُوَ أَضْعَفُ شَيْءٍ عَنْ هَذَا وَأَعْجَزُهُ.

And many people resist looking at and being distracted by (impermissible) images but have no patience for commanding good, forbidding evil, and fighting disbelievers and hypocrites. Indeed, he is the weakest in this regard and the most helpless.

وَأَكْثَرُهُمْ لَا صَبْرَ لَهُ عَلَى وَاحِدٍ مِنَ النَّوْعَيْنِ، وَأَقَلُّهُمْ أَصْبَرُهُمْ فِي الْمَوْضَعَيْنِ.

Most of them have no patience for either type, and the fewest are those who are most patient in both situations.

وَقِيلَ: "الصَّبْرُ: ثَبَاتُ بَاعِثِ الْعَقْلِ وَالدِّينِ فِي مُقَابَلَةِ بَاعِثِ الشَّهْوَةِ وَالطَّبَعِ ".

And it is said: "*Patience is the steadiness of the drive of reason and religion in the face of the drive of one's lust and nature.*"

وَمَعْنَى هَذَا: أَنَّ الطَّبَعَ يَتَقَاضَى مَا يُحِبُّ، وَبَاعِثُ الْعَقْلِ وَالدِّينِ يَمْنَعُ مِنْهُ، وَالْحَرْبُ قَائِمَةٌ بَيْنَهُمَا وَهِيَ سِجَالٌ، وَمُعَرَكَةُ هَذِهِ الْحَرْبِ قَلْبُ الْعَبْدِ. وَالصَّبْرُ: الشُّجَاعَةُ وَالثَّبَاتُ.

The meaning of this is: that one's nature demands what it likes, and the drive of reason and religion prevents it, and the war is ongoing between them, and its victors alternate, and the battlefield of this war is the servant's heart. And patience is courage and steadfastness."

## "DON'T LEAVE ME TO MY SELF FOR A MOMENT!"

Ibn al Qayyim (رَحِمَهُ ٱللَّهُ) said:[66]

"وَقَدْ أَجْمَعَ الْعَارِفُونَ بِاللَّهِ أَنَّ التَّوْفِيقَ: أَنْ لَا يَكِلَكَ اللَّهُ إِلَى نَفْسِكَ، وَالْخِذْلَانَ: أَنْ يُخَلِّيَ بَيْنَكَ وَبَيْنَهَا، فَالْعَبِيدُ مُتَقَلِّبُونَ بَيْنَ تَوْفِيقِهِ وَخِذْلَانِهِ،

"And the knowers of Allah unanimously agree that divine guidance to success (*tawfiq*) means Allah does not leave you to your own devices, while divine forsaking (*khidhlan*) is when He leaves you alone with your self. Thus, the servants alternate between His guidance and forsaking.

بَلِ الْعَبْدُ فِي السَّاعَةِ الْوَاحِدَةِ يَنَالُ نَصِيبَهُ مِنْ هَذَا وَهَذَا، فَيُطِيعُهُ وَيُرْضِيهِ وَيَذْكُرُهُ وَيَشْكُرُهُ بِتَوْفِيقِهِ لَهُ، ثُمَّ يَعْصِيهِ وَيُخَالِفُهُ وَيُسْخِطُهُ وَيَغْفُلُ عَنْهُ بِخِذْلَانِهِ لَهُ،

In fact, in the same hour, a servant gets a share of both; he obeys, pleases, remembers, and thanks Him due to His guidance, then disobeys, opposes, displeases, and forgets Him due to His disappointment.

فَهُوَ دَائِرٌ بَيْنَ تَوْفِيقِهِ وَخِذْلَانِهِ، فَإِنْ وَفَّقَهُ فَبِفَضْلِهِ وَرَحْمَتِهِ، وَإِنْ خَذَلَهُ فَبِعَدْلِهِ وَحِكْمَتِهِ، وَهُوَ الْمَحْمُودُ فِي هَذَا وَهَذَا، لَهُ أَتَمُّ حَمْدٍ وَأَكْمَلُهُ، وَلَمْ يَمْنَعِ الْعَبْدَ شَيْئًا هُوَ لَهُ، وَإِنَّمَا مَنَعَهُ مَا هُوَ مُجَرَّدُ فَضْلِهِ وَعَطَائِهِ، وَهُوَ أَعْلَمُ حَيْثُ يَضَعُهُ وَأَيْنَ يَجْعَلُهُ.

So he constantly oscillates between His guidance and His forsaking. If He guides, it's by His grace and mercy; if He forsakes, it's by His justice and wisdom. He (سُبْحَانَهُۥ وَتَعَالَىٰ) is praiseworthy in both scenarios. He deserves the utmost and most complete praise. Nothing that belongs to the servant is withheld

---

[66] al Madārij 2/25.

from him. What is withheld is solely by His grace and bounty. He is the most knowledgeable about where and how to bestow it.

فَمَتَى شَهِدَ الْعَبْدُ هَذَا الْمَشْهَدَ وَأَعْطَاهُ حَقَّهُ، عَلِمَ ضَرُورَتَهُ وَفَاقَتَهُ إِلَى التَّوْفِيقِ كُلَّ نَفَسٍ وَكُلَّ لَحْظَةٍ وَطَرْفَةِ عَيْنٍ، وَأَنَّ إِيمَانَهُ وَتَوْحِيدَهُ مُمْسَكٌ بِيَدِ غَيْرِهِ، لَوْ تَخَلَّى عَنْهُ طَرْفَةَ عَيْنٍ لَثُلَّ عَرْشُهُ وَلَخَرَّتْ سَمَاءُ إِيمَانِهِ عَلَى الْأَرْضِ، وَأَنَّ الْمُمْسِكَ لَهُ مَنْ يُمْسِكُ السَّمَاءَ أَنْ تَقَعَ عَلَى الْأَرْضِ إِلَّا بِإِذْنِهِ،

When the servant witnesses this perspective and gives it its due, he realizes his absolute need and dependency on Allah's guidance at every breath, every moment, and every blink. His faith and monotheism are held by the Hand of another, if he neglects it for the blink of an eye, his throne will collapse, and the sky of his faith will fall to the earth. The One who holds it is the One who keeps the sky from falling on the earth except by His permission.

فَهِجِّيرَى قَلْبِهِ وَدَأْبُ لِسَانِهِ: **يَا مُقَلِّبَ الْقُلُوبِ ثَبِّتْ قَلْبِي عَلَى دِينِكَ**، يَا مُصَرِّفَ الْقُلُوبِ صَرِّفْ قَلْبِي إِلَى طَاعَتِكَ، وَدُعَاءُهُ: **يَا حَيُّ يَا قَيُّومُ، يَا بَدِيعَ السَّمَاوَاتِ وَالْأَرْضِ، يَا ذَا الْجَلَالِ وَالْإِكْرَامِ، لَا إِلَهَ إِلَّا أَنْتَ، بِرَحْمَتِكَ أَسْتَغِيثُ، أَصْلِحْ لِي شَأْنِي كُلَّهُ وَلَا تُكَلِّنِي إِلَى نَفْسِي طَرْفَةَ عَيْنٍ وَلَا إِلَى أَحَدٍ مِنْ خَلْقِكَ**."

So, his heart's constant state and tongue's habit becomes: '**O controller of hearts, stabilize my heart on Your religion. O director of hearts, direct my heart to Your obedience**'. And his invocation is: '**O the Living, the Sustainer, O Originator of the heavens and the earth, O Possessor of majesty and honor, there is no deity except You. I seek refuge in Your mercy. Fix all my affairs, and do not leave me to myself for the blink of an eye, or to any of Your creatures**'.

فَفِي هَذَا الْمَشْهَدِ يَشْهَدُ تَوْفِيقَ اللَّهِ وَخِذْلَانَهُ، كَمَا يَشْهَدُ رُبُوبِيَّتَهُ وَخَلْقَهُ، فَيَسْأَلُهُ تَوْفِيقَهُ مَسْأَلَةَ الْمُضْطَرِّ، وَيَعُوذُ بِهِ مِنْ خِذْلَانِهِ عِيَاذَ الْمَلْهُوفِ، وَيُلْقِي

نَفْسَهُ بَيْنَ يَدَيْهِ، طَرِيحًا بِبَابِهِ مُسْتَسْلِمًا لَهُ، نَاكِسَ الرَّأْسِ بَيْنَ يَدَيْهِ، خَاضِعًا ذَلِيلًا مُسْتَكِينًا، لَا يَمْلِكُ لِنَفْسِهِ ضُرًّا وَلَا نَفْعًا وَلَا مَوْتًا وَلَا حَيَاةً وَنُشُورًا

In this state of observation, he witnesses Allah's guidance to success and His forsaking, as well as His Lordship and His creation. He asks for His guidance to succeed as someone in desperate need would, and he seeks refuge in Him from His forsaking as someone in distress would. He throws himself in front of Him, humbly submitting himself to Him, lowering his head before Him, submitting, feeling helpless, not possessing the power to bring about harm or benefit, death or life, resurrection or oblivion.

وَالتَّوْفِيقُ إِرَادَةُ اللَّهِ مِنْ نَفْسِهِ أَنْ يَفْعَلَ بِعَبْدِهِ مَا يُصْلِحُ بِهِ الْعَبْدَ، بِأَنْ يَجْعَلَهُ قَادِرًا عَلَى فِعْلِ مَا يُرْضِيهِ، مُرِيدًا لَهُ، مُحِبًّا لَهُ، مُؤْثِرًا لَهُ عَلَى غَيْرِهِ، وَيُبَغِّضَ إِلَيْهِ مَا يُسْخِطُهُ، وَيُكَرِّهَهُ إِلَيْهِ، وَهَذَا مُجَرَّدُ فِعْلِهِ، وَالْعَبْدُ مَحَلٌّ لَهُ،

Divine guidance to success (*al-tawfīq*) is the will of Allah, from Himself, to act with His servant in a manner that rectifies the servant by enabling him to do what pleases Him, desiring it, loving it, and preferring it over other things. He also makes what displeases Him and what He hates repugnant to him. This is solely His action, and the servant is the recipient.

قَالَ تَعَالَى {**وَلَكِنَّ اللَّهَ حَبَّبَ إِلَيْكُمُ الْإِيمَانَ وَزَيَّنَهُ فِي قُلُوبِكُمْ وَكَرَّهَ إِلَيْكُمُ الْكُفْرَ وَالْفُسُوقَ وَالْعِصْيَانَ أُولَئِكَ هُمُ الرَّاشِدُونَ - فَضْلًا مِنَ اللَّهِ وَنِعْمَةً وَاللَّهُ عَلِيمٌ حَكِيمٌ**} فَهُوَ سُبْحَانَهُ عَلِيمٌ بِمَنْ يَصْلُحُ لِهَذَا الْفَضْلِ وَمَنْ لَا يَصْلُحُ لَهُ، حَكِيمٌ يَضَعُهُ فِي مَوَاضِعِهِ وَعِنْدَ أَهْلِهِ، لَا يَمْنَعُهُ أَهْلَهُ، وَلَا يَضَعُهُ عِنْدَ غَيْرِ أَهْلِهِ.

Allah the Exalted said: "**But Allah has endeared the Faith to you, and has beautified it in your hearts, and has made disbelief, wickedness, and disobedience hateful unto you. Such are they who are rightly guided. It is a bounty and a**

**grace from Allah, and Allah is All-Knowing, All-Wise."**[67] He (سُبْحَانَهُ وَتَعَالَىٰ) knows who is suitable for this grace and who is not, and with wisdom, He gives it to those who deserve it and does not give it to those who don't.

وذَكَر هذا عقيب قوله: {**وَاعْلَمُوا أَنَّ فِيكُمْ رَسُولَ اللَّهِ لَوْ يُطِيعُكُمْ فِي كَثِيرٍ مِنَ الْأَمْرِ لَعَنِتُّمْ**}، ثمَّ جاء به بحرف الاستدراك فقال: {**وَلَكِنَّ اللَّهَ حَبَّبَ إِلَيْكُمُ الْإِيمَانَ**}. يَقُول سُبْحَانَهُ: لَمْ تَكُنْ مُحَبَّتُكُمْ لِلْإِيمَانِ وَإِرَادَتُهُ وَتَزْيِينُهُ فِي قُلُوبِكُم مِنْكُمْ، وَلَكِنَّ اللَّهَ هُوَ الَّذِي جَعَلَهُ فِي قُلُوبِكُمْ كَذَٰلِكَ، فَآثَرْتُمُوهُ وَرَضِيتُمُوهُ،

This was mentioned after His saying: "**And know that among you is Allah's Messenger. If he were to obey you in much of the matter, you would be in difficulty**." Then He used the term of remediation (i.e., لَـٰكِنْ: however) and said: "**However, Allah has endeared the Faith to you.**" So He (سُبْحَانَهُ وَتَعَالَىٰ) is saying: your love for faith, your desire for it, and the beautification of it in your hearts is not from you, but Allah is the One who made it such in your hearts. Thus, you preferred it and were pleased with it.

فَكَذَٰلِكَ لَا تُقَدِّمُوا بَيْنَ يَدَيِ اللَّهِ وَرَسُولِهِ، وَلَا تَقُولُوا حَتَّىٰ يَقُولَ، وَلَا تَفْعَلُوا حَتَّىٰ يَأْمُرَ، فَالَّذِي حَبَّبَ إِلَيْكُمُ الْإِيمَانَ أَعْلَمُ بِمَصَالِحِ عِبَادِهِ وَمَا يُصْلِحُهُم مِنْكُمْ، وَأَنْتُم فَلَوْلَا تَوْفِيقُهُ لَكُمْ لَمَا أَذْعَنَتْ نُفُوسُكُمْ لِلْإِيمَانِ، فَلَمْ يَكُنِ الْإِيمَانُ بِمَشُورَتِكُم وَتَوْفِيقِ أَنْفُسِكُمْ، وَلَا تَقَدَّمْتُمْ بِهِ إِلَيْهَا،

Similarly, you must not put yourselves forward before Allah and His Messenger, do not speak until he speaks, and do not act until he commands. The One who made faith beloved to you knows better what benefits His servants and what makes them upright than you do. If it weren't for His guidance, your souls would not have complied with faith. You didn't have faith by

---

[67] Al-Hujurat: 7-8.

your own consulted choice or through your own guidance, and you did not bring it to yourselves.

فَنُفُوسُكُمْ تَقْصُرُ وَتَعْجِزُ عَنْ ذٰلِكَ وَلَا تَبْلُغُهُ، فَلَوْ أَطَاعَكُمْ رَسُولِي فِي كَثِيرٍ مِمَّا تُرِيدُونَ لَشَقَّ عَلَيْكُمْ ذٰلِكَ وَلَهَلَكْتُمْ وَفَسَدَتْ مَصَالِحُكُمْ وَأَنْتُمْ لَا تَشْعُرُونَ،

Your souls fall short and are incapable of doing that and cannot reach it. If my Messenger obeyed you in much of what you want, that would be difficult for you, and you would be destroyed, and your affairs would be corrupted while you are not aware.

وَلَا تَظُنُّوا أَنَّ نُفُوسَكُمْ تُرِيدُ بِكُمُ الرُّشْدَ وَالصَّلَاحَ كَمَا أَرَدْتُمُ الْإِيمَانَ، فَلَوْلَا أَنِّي حَبَّبْتُهُ إِلَيْكُمْ وَزَيَّنْتُهُ فِي قُلُوبِكُمْ وَكَرَّهْتُ إِلَيْكُمْ ضِدَّهُ لَمَا وَقَعَ مِنْكُمْ وَلَا سَمَحَتْ بِهِ نُفُوسُكُمْ.

And do not think that your souls want what is best and suitable for you, as you wanted faith. If it weren't for the fact that I made it beloved to you, beautified it in your hearts, and made its opposite repugnant to you, you would not have accepted it, and your souls would not have allowed it.

وَقَدْ ضُرِبَ لِلتَّوْفِيقِ وَالْخِذْلَانِ مَثَلُ مَلِكٍ أَرْسَلَ إِلَى أَهْلِ بَلْدَةٍ مِنْ بِلَادِهِ رَسُولًا، وَكَتَبَ مَعَهُ كِتَابًا يُعَلِّمُهُمْ أَنَّ الْعَدُوَّ مُصَبِّحُهُمْ عَنْ قَرِيبٍ وَمُجْتَاحُهُمْ وَمُخَرِّبُ الْبَلَدِ وَمُهْلِكُ مَنْ فِيهَا،

A parable of divine guidance and abandonment is like a king who sent a messenger to a town of his land. He wrote a letter with him to inform them that an enemy will invade them soon, will destroy the town and kill those who are in it.

وَأَرْسَلَ إِلَيْهِمْ أَمْوَالًا وَمَرَاكِبَ وَزَادًا وَعُدَّةً وَأَدِلَّةً، وَقَالَ: ارْتَحِلُوا إِلَيَّ مَعَ هَؤُلَاءِ الْأَدِلَّةِ وَقَدْ أَرْسَلْتُ إِلَيْكُمْ جَمِيعَ مَا تَحْتَاجُونَ إِلَيْهِ،

He sent them money, vehicles, supplies, and guides and said: Travel to me with these guides, and I have sent you everything you need.

ثُمَّ قَالَ لِجَمَاعَةٍ مِنْ مَمَالِيكِهِ: اذْهَبُوا إِلَى فُلَانٍ فَخُذُوا بِيَدِهِ وَاحْمِلُوهُ وَلَا تَذَرُوهُ يَقْعُدُ، وَاذْهَبُوا إِلَى فُلَانٍ كَذَلِكَ وَإِلَى فُلَانٍ، وَذَرُوا مَنْ عَدَاهُمْ فَإِنَّهُمْ لَا يَصْلُحُونَ أَنْ يَسَاكِنُونِي فِي بَلَدِي،

Then he said to a group of his subjects: Go to so and so, take his hand, carry him, and do not let him sit. Do the same to another and another, and leave the rest as they are not fit to live with me in my land.

فَذَهَبَ خَوَاصُّ مَمَالِيكِهِ إِلَى مَنْ أُمِرُوا بِحَمْلِهِمْ، فَلَمْ يَتْرُكُوهُمْ يَقَرُّونَ، بَلْ حَمَلُوهُمْ حَمْلًا، وَسَاقُوهُمْ سَوْقًا إِلَى الْمَلِكِ،

The king's special slaves went to those they were ordered to carry, and they did not let them stay but carried them and drove them to the king.

فَاجْتَاحَ الْعَدُوُّ مَنْ بَقِيَ فِي الْمَدِينَةِ وَقَتَلَهُمْ، وَأُسِرَ مَنْ أُسِرَ.

The enemy invaded those who remained in the city, killed them, and took captive those he captured.

فَهَلْ يُعَدُّ الْمَلِكُ ظَالِمًا لِهَؤُلَاءِ، أَمْ عَادِلًا فِيهِمْ؟ نَعَمْ خَصَّ أُولَئِكَ بِإِحْسَانِهِ وَعِنَايَتِهِ وَحَرَمَهَا مَنْ عَدَاهُمْ، إِذْ لَا يَجِبُ عَلَيْهِ التَّسْوِيَةُ بَيْنَهُمْ فِي فَضْلِهِ وَإِكْرَامِهِ، بَلْ ذَلِكَ فَضْلُهُ يُؤْتِيهِ مَنْ يَشَاءُ

Was the king unjust to these people or was he just? Yes, he treated those with kindness and care and withheld it from the others, because he is not obliged to treat them equally in terms of his grace and honor. Rather, this is his grace, he gives it to whom he wishes."

Elsewhere, Imām Ibn al Qayyim (رَحِمَهُ ٱللَّهُ) elaborates on the reality of divine guidance (*al-tawfīq*) and Allah's forsaking and abandonment (*al khidhlān*), saying:[68]

"وَأَمَّا الْخِذْلَانُ، فَقَالَ تَعَالَى: {**إِن يَنصُرْكُمُ اللَّهُ فَلَا غَالِبَ لَكُمْ وَإِن يَخْذُلْكُمْ فَمَن ذَا الَّذِي يَنصُرُكُم مِن بَعْدِهِ**}، وَأَصْلُ الْخِذْلَانِ: التَّرْكُ وَالتَّخْلِيَةُ، وَيُقَالُ لِلْبَقَرَةِ وَالشَّاةِ إِذَا تَخَلَّفَتْ مَعَ وَلَدِهَا فِي الْمَرْعَى، وَتَرَكَتْ صَوَاحِبَاتِهَا: خَذُولٌ.

As for abandonment, Allah (سُبْحَانَهُ وَتَعَالَىٰ) says: "**If Allah helps you, none can overcome you: If He forsakes you, who is there, after that, that can help you?**"[69] The root of 'abandonment' comes from leaving and deserting. It is said of a cow or a sheep that lags with her calf in the pasture, leaving her companions, that she is 'abandoned' — "*khathūl.*"

قَالَ مُحَمَّدُ بْنُ إِسْحَاقَ فِي هَذِهِ الْآيَةِ: "إِن يَنصُرْكَ اللَّهُ فَلَا غَالِبَ لَكَ مِنَ النَّاسِ، وَلَنْ يَضُرَّكَ خِذْلَانُ مَنْ خَذَلَكَ، وَإِن يَخْذُلْكَ فَلَنْ يَنصُرَكَ النَّاسُ، أَيْ: لَا تَتْرُكْ أَمْرِي لِلنَّاسِ، وَارْفَضِ النَّاسَ لِأَمْرِي".

Muhammad Ibn Ishaq said regarding this verse, "If Allah supports you, no one among people can overcome you, and the abandonment of anyone who abandons you will not harm you. But if He abandons you, no one among people can support you," which means, "Do not leave my affairs to people, and prevent people from controlling my affairs."

فَالْخِذْلَانُ أَنْ يُخَلِّيَ اللَّهُ تَعَالَى بَيْنَ الْعَبْدِ وَبَيْنَ نَفْسِهِ وَيَكِلَهُ إِلَيْهَا، وَالتَّوْفِيقُ ضِدُّهُ: أَنْ لَا يَدَعَهُ وَنَفْسَهُ وَلَا يَكِلَهُ إِلَيْهَا، بَلْ يَصْنَعُ لَهُ وَيَلْطُفُ بِهِ، وَيُعِينُهُ وَيَدْفَعُ عَنْهُ، وَيَكْلَؤُهُ كَلَاءَةَ الْوَالِدِ الشَّفِيقِ لِلْوَلَدِ الْعَاجِزِ عَنْ نَفْسِهِ، فَمَنْ خَلَّى بَيْنَهُ وَبَيْنَ نَفْسِهِ، فَقَدْ هَلَكَ كُلَّ الْهَلَاكِ.

[68] Shifā al 'Alīl (1/331-333).

[69] Al-Imran: 160.

Abandonment is when Allah leaves a servant alone with his own self and relies on it. In contrast, success is when He does not leave him to himself but instead creates for him, shows kindness, assists, defends, and looks after him, like a caring father takes care of a child who cannot fend for himself. Whoever is left alone with himself is entirely ruined.

وَلِهَذَا كَانَ مِنْ دُعَائِهِ صَلَّى اللَّهُ عَلَيْهِ وَسَلَّمَ: **"يَا حَيُّ، يَا قَيُّومُ، يَا بَدِيعَ السَّمَاوَاتِ وَالْأَرْضِ، يَا ذَا الْجَلَالِ وَالْإِكْرَامِ، لَا إِلَهَ إِلَّا أَنْتَ، بِرَحْمَتِكَ أَسْتَغِيثُ، أَصْلِحْ لِي شَأْنِي كُلَّهُ، وَلَا تَكِلْنِي إِلَى نَفْسِي طَرْفَةَ عَيْنٍ، وَلَا إِلَى أَحَدٍ مِنْ خَلْقِكَ"**.

For this reason, one of His supplications (صَلَّى ٱللَّهُ عَلَيْهِ وَسَلَّمَ) was: **"O Living, O Sustainer, O Originator of the heavens and the earth, O Possessor of majesty and honor, there is no god but You, I seek help through Your mercy, put right all my affairs, and do not leave me to myself for the blink of an eye, nor to any of Your creation."**[70]

فَالْعَبْدُ مَطْرُوحٌ بَيْنَ اللَّهِ وَبَيْنَ عَدُوِّهِ إِبْلِيسَ، فَإِنْ تَوَلَّاهُ اللَّهُ لَمْ يَظْفَرْ بِهِ عَدُوُّهُ، وَإِنْ خَذَلَهُ وَأَعْرَضَ عَنْهُ افْتَرَسَهُ الشَّيْطَانُ كَمَا يَفْتَرِسُ الذِّئْبُ الشَّاةَ إِذَا خَلَّى الرَّاعِي بَيْنَهُ وَبَيْنَهَا، فَالشَّيْطَانُ ذِئْبُ الْإِنْسَانِ.

The servant is left between Allah and his enemy, Iblīs. If Allah takes care of him, his enemy will not conquer him. But if He abandons and turns away from him, *Shayṭān* will prey on him as a wolf preys on a sheep when the shepherd leaves it alone. Thus, *Shayṭān* is like a wolf to a human.

فَإِنْ قِيلَ: فَمَا ذَنْبُ الشَّاةِ إِذَا خَلَّى الرَّاعِي بَيْنَ الذِّئْبِ وَبَيْنَهَا، وَهَلْ يُمْكِنُهَا أَنْ تَقْوَى عَلَى الذِّئْبِ وَتَنْجُو مِنْهُ؟

---

[70] Reported by al-Nasā'i, al Bazzār and al Ḥākim, and graded ḥasan by al Albānī (*Ṣaḥīḥ al-Targhīb wal-Tarhīb* [661]), with the wording:

يا حيُّ يا قيومُ برحمتِكَ أستغيثُ، أصلِحْ لي شأنِيَ كلَّه، ولا تَكِلْني إلى نفسي طَرفةَ عينٍ

**"O Living, O Sustainer, I seek help through Your mercy, put right all my affairs, and do not leave me to myself for the blink of an eye."**

If asked: What is the sheep's fault when the shepherd leaves it between the wolf and itself, and can it resist the wolf and escape from it?

قِيلَ: لَعَمْرُ اللَّهِ، إِنَّ الشَّيْطَانَ ذِئْبُ الْإِنْسَانِ كَمَا قَالَهُ الصَّادِقُ الْمَصْدُوقُ، **وَلَكِنْ لَمْ يَجْعَلِ اللَّهُ لِهَذَا الذِّئْبِ اللَّعِينِ عَلَى هَذِهِ الشَّاةِ سُلْطَانًا مَعَ ضَعْفِهَا،** فَإِذَا أَعْطَتْ بِيَدِهَا، وَسَالَمَتْ الذِّئْبَ، وَدَعَاهَا فَلَبَّتْ دَعْوَتَهُ، وَأَجَابَتْ أَمْرَهُ وَلَمْ تَتَخَلَّفْ، بَلْ أَقْبَلَتْ نَحْوَهُ سَرِيعَةً مُطِيعَةً، وَفَارَقَتْ حَمَى الرَّاعِي الَّذِي لَيْسَ لِلذِّئَابِ عَلَيْهِ سَبِيلٌ، وَدَخَلَتْ فِي مَحَلِّ الذِّئَابِ الَّذِي مَنْ دَخَلَهُ كَانَ صَيْدًا لَهُمْ، فَهَلْ الذَّنْبُ كُلُّ الذَّنْبِ إِلَّا لِلشَّاةِ،

The answer is: By Allah, the devil is a wolf to man, as said by the truthful and trustworthy one (i.e., the Prophet ﷺ). **However, Allah has not given this cursed wolf (Shayṭān) authority over this weak sheep.** If the sheep willingly gives itself to the wolf, makes peace with it, responds to its call, obeys its command without any resistance, quickly runs towards it, leaves the protection of the shepherd who is invincible to the wolves, and enters the territory of the wolves — where anyone who enters becomes their prey — then isn't the entirety of the blame on the sheep?

فَكَيْفَ وَالرَّاعِي يُحَذِّرُهَا، وَيُخَوِّفُهَا وَيُنْذِرُهَا، وَقَدْ أَرَاهَا مَصَارِعَ الشَّاءِ الَّتِي انْفَرَدَتْ عَنِ الرَّاعِي، وَدَخَلَتْ وَادِي الذِّئَابِ.

How else could it be when the shepherd has warned, frightened, admonished, and showed it the demise of other sheep who separated from the shepherd and entered the valley of the wolves?

قَالَ أَحْمَدُ بْنُ مَرْوَانَ الْمَالِكِيُّ فِي كِتَابِ "الْمُجَالَسَةِ": "سَمِعْتُ ابْنَ أَبِي الدُّنْيَا يَقُولُ: إِنَّ لِلَّهِ سُبْحَانَهُ مِنَ الْعُلُومِ مَا لَا يُحْصَى، يُعْطِي كُلَّ وَاحِدٍ مِنْ ذَلِكَ مَا لَا يُعْطِي غَيْرَهُ.

Ahmad bin Marwan al-Maliki narrated in the book "*Al-Mujālasah*" that he heard Ibn Abi Dunya say: "Allah (سُبْحَانَهُ وَتَعَالَىٰ) has unlimited knowledge. He gives each one something that He does not give to others.

لَقَدْ حَدَّثَنَا أَبُو عَبْدِ اللَّهِ أَحْمَدُ بْنُ مُحَمَّدِ بْنِ سَعِيدٍ الطَّائِيُّ، ثَنَا عَبْدُ اللَّهِ بْنُ بَكْرٍ السَّهْمِيُّ، عَنْ أَبِيهِ: أَنَّ قَوْمًا كَانُوا فِي سَفَرٍ، فَكَانَ فِيهِمْ رَجُلٌ يَمُرُّ الطَّائِرُ فَيَقُولُ: أَتَدْرُونَ مَا تَقُولُ هَذِهِ؟ فَيَقُولُونَ: لَا. فَيَقُولُ: تَقُولُ كَذَا وَكَذَا. فَيُحَيِّلُنَا عَلَى شَيْءٍ لَا نَدْرِي أَصَادِقٌ هُوَ أَمْ كَاذِبٌ.

Abu Abdullah Ahmad bin Muhammad bin Said al-Tai narrated to us from Abdullah bin Bakr al-Sahmi, from his father, about a group of people on a journey. Among them was a man who would interpret the sounds of the birds, and he would say: "Do you know what this bird is saying?" They would say: "No." Then he would tell them what it was saying, and we were uncertain whether he was telling the truth or lying.

إِلَى أَنَّ مَرُّوا عَلَى غَنَمٍ وَفِيهَا شَاةٌ قَدْ تَخَلَّفَتْ عَلَى سَخْلَةٍ لَهَا، فَجَعَلَتْ تَحْنُو عُنُقَهَا إِلَيْهَا وَتَثْغُو، فَقَالَ: أَتَدْرُونَ مَا تَقُولُ هَذِهِ الشَّاةُ؟ قُلْنَا: لَا. قَالَ: تَقُولُ لِلسَّخْلَةِ: الْحَقِي، لَا يَأْكُلُكَ الذِّئْبُ كَمَا أَكَلَ أَخَاكَ عَامَ أَوَّلَ فِي هَذَا الْمَكَانِ. قَالَ: فَانْتَهَيْنَا إِلَى الرَّاعِي، فَقُلْنَا لَهُ: وَلَدَتْ هَذِهِ الشَّاةُ قَبْلَ عَامِكَ هَذَا؟ قَالَ: نَعَمْ، وَلَدَتْ سَخْلَةً عَامَ أَوَّلَ، فَأَكَلَهَا الذِّئْبُ بِهَذَا الْمَكَانِ.

Once, they passed by a flock of sheep, among which was a sheep lagging, caring for its lamb. The sheep was arching its neck towards the lamb and bleating. The man asked, "Do you know what this sheep is saying?" They replied, "No." He said, "It's telling the lamb, 'Follow me, so the wolf won't eat you, just as it ate your brother last year at this place.'" When they reached the shepherd, they asked him, "Did this sheep give birth to a lamb last year?" He replied, "Yes, she gave birth to a lamb last year, and a wolf ate it in this place."

[Ibn al Qayyim comments on this story:]

فَهَذِهِ شَاةٌ قَدْ حَذَّرَتْ سَخْلَتَهَا مِنَ الذِّئْبِ مَرَّةً فَحَذَرَتْ، وَقَدْ حَذَّرَ اللَّهُ سُبْحَانَهُ ابْنَ آدَمَ مَنْ ذِئْبِهِ مَرَّةً بَعْدَ مَرَّةٍ، وَهُوَ يَأْبَى إِلَّا أَنْ يَسْتَجِيبَ لَهُ إِذَا دَعَاهُ، وَيَبِيتُ مَعَهُ وَيُصْبِحُ، {**وَقَالَ الشَّيْطَانُ لَمَّا قُضِيَ الْأَمْرُ إِنَّ اللَّهَ وَعَدَكُمْ وَعْدَ الْحَقِّ وَوَعَدْتُكُمْ فَأَخْلَفْتُكُمْ وَمَا كَانَ لِي عَلَيْكُمْ مِنْ سُلْطَانٍ إِلَّا أَنْ دَعَوْتُكُمْ فَاسْتَجَبْتُمْ لِي فَلَا تَلُومُونِي وَلُومُوا أَنْفُسَكُمْ مَا أَنَا بِمُصْرِخِكُمْ وَمَا أَنْتُمْ بِمُصْرِخِيَّ إِنِّي كَفَرْتُ أَشْرَكْتُمُونِ مِنْ قَبْلُ إِنَّ الظَّالِمِينَ لَهُمْ عَذَابٌ**}.

So, here is a sheep warning its lamb about the wolf one time, which then heeded her warning. Allah has also warned the son of Adam about his wolf (*Shayṭān*) time and time again, but he refuses to do anything but respond to *Shayṭān* when he calls him, spending both his night and day with him. And *Shayṭān* said when the matter was decided, "**Indeed, Allah had promised you the promise of truth. And I promised you, but I betrayed you. I had no authority over you except that I invited you, and you responded to me. So do not blame me, but blame yourselves. I cannot come to your aid, nor can you come to mine. Indeed, I deny your association of me (with Allah) before. Indeed, for the wrongdoers is a painful punishment.**"[71]

71

## THE INSISTENT SELF EMPOWERS SHAYTĀN

Anas b. Mālik (رَضِيَ ٱللَّهُ عَنْهُ) reported from Allah's Messenger (صَلَّى ٱللَّهُ عَلَيْهِ وَسَلَّمَ) that he said:[72]

«لَمَّا صَوَّرَ اللهُ (عَزَّوَجَلَّ) آدَمَ (عَلَيْهِ ٱلسَّلَامُ) فِي الْجَنَّةِ تَرَكَهُ مَا شَاءَ أَنْ يَتْرُكَهُ، فَجَعَلَ إِبْلِيسُ يُطِيفُ بِهِ يَنْظُرُ إِلَيْهِ، فَلَمَّا رَآهُ أَجْوَفَ قال ظَفِرْتُ به خَلْقٌ لَا يَتَمَالَكُ».

**"When Allah created Adam in Paradise, it made Iblis (Satan) circulate around him. When Iblis saw that Adam was hollow, he said: 'I have mastered him; a creation that cannot control itself.'"**

Despite Iblīs identifying humankind's greatest vulnerability before Adam even had a soul in his body, Allah (جَلَّ وَعَلَا) did not cede any authority to Iblīs over the children of Adam except in proportion to the authority they cede to him over themselves. Allah (عَزَّوَجَلَّ) said:[73]

{إِنَّ عِبَادِي لَيْسَ لَكَ عَلَيْهِمْ سُلْطَانٌ}.

**"Indeed, My honored servants, you have no authority over them."**

---

Ibn al Qayyim (رَحِمَهُ ٱللَّهُ) explains how the threat posed by Shayṭān is greater than that of the inner-self. He says:[74]

[72] Reported by Aḥmad and Muslim. See *al-Ṣaḥīḥah* by al Albānī (2158).

[73] al Ḥijr: 42.

[74] *Ighāthah al-Lahfān*, chapter 12.

"وَمَن تَأَمَّلَ الْقُرْآنَ وَالسُّنَّةَ وَجَدَ اعْتِنَاءَهُمَا بِذِكْرِ الشَّيْطَانِ وَكَيْدِهِ وَمُحَارَبَتِهِ أَكْثَرَ مِنْ ذِكْرِ النَّفْسِ؛ فَإِنَّ النَّفْسَ الْمَذْمُومَةَ ذُكِرَتْ فِي قَوْلِهِ: {**إِنَّ النَّفْسَ لَأَمَّارَةٌ بِالسُّوءِ**}، وَاللَّوَّامَةُ فِي قَوْلِهِ: {**وَلَا أُقْسِمُ بِالنَّفْسِ اللَّوَّامَةِ**}، وَذُكِرَتِ النَّفْسُ الْمَذْمُومَةُ فِي قَوْلِهِ: {**وَنَهَى النَّفْسَ عَنِ الْهَوَى**}،

"Whoever reflects on the Quran and the Sunnah will find that they both pay more attention to mentioning Satan, his deceit, and fighting against him, more than they mention the self. Indeed, the blameworthy self is mentioned in the verse: **'Indeed, the self is inclined to evil.'**[75] And the reproachful self is mentioned in the verse: **'And I do not swear by the reproachful soul.'**[76] and the blameworthy self is mentioned in the verse: **'And he restrained himself from desires.'**[77]

وَأَمَّا الشَّيْطَانُ فَذُكِرَ فِي عِدَّةِ مَوَاضِعَ، وَأُفْرِدَتْ لَهُ سُورَةٌ تَامَّةٌ، فَتَحْذِيرُ الرَّبِّ تَعَالَى لِعِبَادِهِ مِنْهُ جَاءَ أَكْثَرَ مِنْ تَحْذِيرِهِ مِنَ النَّفْسِ،

But *Shayṭān* is mentioned in several places, and an entire *Surah* is devoted to him.[78] Thus, the warning of the Lord to His servants against *Shayṭān* came more than His warning against the self.

وَهَذَا هُوَ الَّذِي لَا يَنْبَغِي غَيْرُهُ؛ فَإِنَّ شَرَّ النَّفْسِ وَفَسَادَهَا يَنْشَأُ مِنْ وَسْوَسَتِهِ، فَهِيَ مَرْكَبُهُ، وَمَوْضِعُ شَرِّهِ، وَمَحَلُّ طَاعَتِهَا،

This is what is appropriate, as the evil of the self and its corruption arises from his whispering, it is his vessel, the place of his evil, and the location of his obedience.

[75] Yusuf: 53.

[76] Al-Qiyama: 2.

[77] Al-Nazi'āt: 40.

[78] Meaning *Surah al-Nās*.

وَقَدْ أَمَرَ اللَّهُ سُبْحَانَهُ بِالاسْتِعَاذَةِ مِنْهُ عِنْدَ قِرَاءَةِ الْقُرْآنِ وَغَيْرِ ذَلِكَ، وَهَذَا لِشِدَّةِ الْحَاجَةِ إِلَى التَّعَوُّذِ مِنْهُ، وَلَمْ يَأْمُرْ بِالاسْتِعَاذَةِ مِنَ النَّفْسِ فِي مَوْضِعٍ وَاحِدٍ، وَإِنَّمَا جَاءَتِ الاسْتِعَاذَةُ مِنْ شَرِّهَا فِي خُطْبَةِ الْحَاجَةِ فِي قَوْلِهِ: «**وَنَعُوذُ بِاللَّهِ مِنْ شُرُورِ أَنْفُسِنَا وَمِنْ سَيِّئَاتِ أَعْمَالِنَا**»، كَمَا تَقَدَّمَ ذَلِكَ فِي الْبَابِ الَّذِي قَبْلَهُ

Allah has commanded us to seek refuge from him when reading the Quran and otherwise due to the great need to seek refuge from him. He did not command to seek refuge from the self in one place. Still, the refuge from its evil came in the sermon of need in his saying (صَلَّىٱللَّهُعَلَيْهِوَسَلَّمَ): '**And we seek refuge in Allah from the evils of ourselves and our bad deeds,**' as was previously mentioned in the preceding chapter.

وَقَدْ جَمَعَ النَّبِيُّ صَلَّى اللَّهُ عَلَيْهِ وَسَلَّمَ بَيْنَ الاسْتِعَاذَةِ مِنَ الْأَمْرَيْنِ؛ فِي الْحَدِيثِ الَّذِي رَوَاهُ التِّرْمِذِيُّ وَصَحَّحَهُ، عَنْ أَبِي هُرَيْرَةَ: أَنَّ أَبَا بَكْرٍ الصِّدِّيقَ رَضِيَ اللَّهُ عَنْهُ قَالَ: يَا رَسُولَ اللَّهِ! عَلِّمْنِي شَيْئًا أَقُولُهُ إِذَا أَصْبَحْتُ وَإِذَا أَمْسَيْتُ؟ قَالَ: «**قُلْ: اللَّهُمَّ عَالِمَ الْغَيْبِ وَالشَّهَادَةِ! فَاطِرَ السَّمَاوَاتِ وَالْأَرْضِ! رَبَّ كُلِّ شَيْءٍ وَمَلِيكَهُ! أَشْهَدُ أَنْ لَا إِلَهَ إِلَّا أَنْتَ؛ أَعُوذُ بِكَ مِنْ شَرِّ نَفْسِي، وَمِنْ شَرِّ الشَّيْطَانِ وَشَرَكِهِ، وَأَنْ أَقْتَرِفَ عَلَى نَفْسِي سُوءًا، أَوْ أَجُرَّهُ إِلَى مُسْلِمٍ. قُلْهُ إِذَا أَصْبَحْتَ، وَإِذَا أَمْسَيْتَ، وَإِذَا أَخَذْتَ مَضْجَعَكَ**».

The Prophet (صَلَّىٱللَّهُعَلَيْهِوَسَلَّمَ) combined seeking refuge from the two matters; in the hadith narrated by Al-Tirmidhi (d. 279 AH رَحِمَهُٱللَّهُ) and authenticated by him, from Abu Hurayra (رَضِيَٱللَّهُعَنْهُ): that Abu Bakr Al-Siddiq (رَضِيَٱللَّهُعَنْهُ) said: 'O Messenger of Allah! Teach me something to say when I wake up and when I enter the evening?' He said: '**Say: O Allah, knower of the unseen and the witnessed, creator of the heavens and the earth, Lord of everything and its King, I bear witness that there is no god but You; I seek refuge in You from the evil of my soul, and from the evil of Shayṭān and his partnership, and that I commit evil against myself, or drag it to a Muslim. Say it**

**when you wake up, when you enter the evening, and when you take to your bed.'**

فَقَدْ تَضَمَّنَ هَذَا الْحَدِيثِ الشَّرِيفِ الِاسْتِعَاذَةَ مِنَ الشَّرِّ وَأَسْبَابِهِ وَغَايَتِهِ: فَإِنَّ الشَّرَّ كُلَّهُ إِمَا أَنْ يَصْدُرَ مِنَ النَّفْسِ أَوْ مِنَ الشَّيْطَانِ، وَغَايَتُهُ: إِمَا أَنْ تَعُودَ عَلَى الْعَامِلِ، أَوْ عَلَى أَخِيهِ الْمُسْلِمِ، فَتَضَمَّنَ الْحَدِيثُ مَصَدَّرَيِ الشَّرِّ اللَّذَيْنِ يَصْدُرُ عَنْهُمَا، وَغَايَتَيْهِ اللَّتَيْنِ يَصِلُ إِلَيْهِمَا.

This noble Hadith includes seeking refuge from evil, its causes and its ultimate end: for all evil either comes from the self or from Satan, and its ultimate end: either it falls back on the doer or on his Muslim brother, so the Hadith included the two sources of evil that it emanates from and the two ends that it reaches."

## SHAYTĀN HAS NO AUTHORITY OVER THE BELIEVER

Allah (سُبْحَانَهُ وَتَعَالَىٰ) said:

{إِنَّهُ لَيْسَ لَهُ سُلْطَانٌ عَلَى الَّذِينَ آمَنُوا وَعَلَىٰ رَبِّهِمْ يَتَوَكَّلُونَ ﴿٩٩﴾}

**"Indeed, He has no authority over those who have believed and rely upon their Lord."**[79]

Ibn al Qayyim (رَحِمَهُ ٱللَّهُ) explains what is meant by Shayṭān having no authority over the righteous believers:[80]

"قَالَ مُجَاهِدٌ، وَعِكْرَمَةُ، وَالْمُفَسِّرُونَ: لَيْسَ لَهُ حُجَّةٌ.

"Mujahid, Ikrimah, and the scholars of *Tafsīr* said: "He has no argument against them."

وَالصَّوَابُ أَنْ يُقَالَ: لَيْسَ لَهُ طَرِيقٌ يَتَسَلَّطُ بِهِ عَلَيْهِمْ لَا مِنْ جِهَةِ الْحُجَّةِ، وَلَا مِنْ جِهَةِ الْقُدْرَةِ، فَالْقُدْرَةُ دَاخِلَةٌ فِي مُسَمَّى السُّلْطَانِ، وَإِنَّمَا سُمِّيَتْ الْحُجَّةُ سُلْطَانًا؛ لِأَنَّ صَاحِبَهَا يَتَسَلَّطُ بِهَا تَسَلُّطَ صَاحِبِ الْقُدْرَةِ بِيَدِهِ، وَقَدْ أَخْبَرَ سُبْحَانَهُ أَنَّهُ لَا سُلْطَانَ لِعَدُوِّهِ عَلَى عِبَادِهِ الْمُخْلِصِينَ الْمُتَوَكِّلِينَ،

The correct interpretation is that it means: He has no means by which he can exercise authority over them, neither through argument nor through power. Power is included in the term authority, and the term argument has been referred to as authority because its possessor exercises authority with it, just as the one who possesses power exercises authority with his hand. Allah (سُبْحَانَهُ وَتَعَالَىٰ) has informed that the enemy has no authority over His sincere servants who rely on Him.

---

79 Al-Naḥl 16:99.

80 *Ighātha al-Lahfān*, Chapter 12.

فَقَالَ فِي سُورَةِ الْحِجْرِ: {قَالَ رَبِّ بِمَا أَغْوَيْتَنِي لَأُزَيِّنَنَّ لَهُمْ فِي الْأَرْضِ وَلَأُغْوِيَنَّهُمْ أَجْمَعِينَ (39) إِلَّا عِبَادَكَ مِنْهُمُ الْمُخْلَصِينَ (40) قَالَ هَذَا صِرَاطٌ عَلَيَّ مُسْتَقِيمٌ (41) إِنَّ عِبَادِي لَيْسَ لَكَ عَلَيْهِمْ سُلْطَانٌ إِلَّا مَنِ اتَّبَعَكَ مِنَ الْغَاوِينَ}.

In *Surah Al-Hijr*, Allah says: "**He said, 'My Lord, because You have put me in error, I will surely make [disobedience] attractive to them on earth, and I will mislead them all (39). Except, among them, Your chosen servants (40).' [Allah] said, 'This is a path [of return] to Me [that is] straight. (41) Indeed, My servants - no authority will you have over them, except those who follow you of the deviators (42).'**"[81]

وقال في سورة النحل: {إِنَّهُ لَيْسَ لَهُ سُلْطَانٌ عَلَى الَّذِينَ آمَنُوا وَعَلَى رَبِّهِمْ يَتَوَكَّلُونَ (99) إِنَّمَا سُلْطَانُهُ عَلَى الَّذِينَ يَتَوَلَّوْنَهُ وَالَّذِينَ هُمْ بِهِ مُشْرِكُونَ} [النحل: 99، 100].

And in *Surah An-Nahl*, Allah says: "**Indeed, He has no authority over those who have believed and rely upon their Lord (99). His authority is only over those who take Him as an ally and those who associate others (in worship) with Him.**"[82]

فَتَضَمَّنَ ذَلِكَ أَمْرَيْنِ:

This includes two matters:

أَحَدُهُمَا: نَفْيُ سُلْطَانِهِ وَإِبْطَالُهُ عَلَى أَهْلِ التَّوْحِيدِ وَالْإِخْلَاصِ.

Firstly, the negation of his authority and its invalidation over the people of monotheism and sincerity.

وَالثَّانِي: إِثْبَاتُ سُلْطَانِهِ عَلَى أَهْلِ الشِّرْكِ وَعَلَى مَنْ تَوَلَّاهُ.

---

[81] al-Ḥijr 15:39-42

[82] al-Naḥl: 99-100.

Secondly, the affirmation of his authority over the polytheists and those who take him as an ally.

وَلَمَّا عَلِمَ عَدُوُّ اللَّهِ أَنَّ اللَّهَ لَا يُسَلِّطُهُ عَلَى أَهْلِ التَّوْحِيدِ وَالْإِخْلَاصِ قَالَ: {فَبِعِزَّتِكَ لَأُغْوِيَنَّهُمْ أَجْمَعِينَ (82) إِلَّا عِبَادَكَ مِنْهُمُ الْمُخْلَصِينَ}.

When the enemy of Allah knew that Allah would not grant him authority over the people of monotheism and sincerity, he said: **"So, by Your might, I will surely mislead them all. Except Your chosen servants among them."**[83]

فَعَلِمَ عَدُوُّ اللَّهِ أَنَّ مَنْ اعْتَصَمَ بِاللَّهِ، وَأَخْلَصَ لَهُ، وَتَوَكَّلَ عَلَيْهِ لَا يَقْدِرُ عَلَى إِغْوَائِهِ وَإِضْلَالِهِ، وَإِنَّمَا يَكُونُ لَهُ السُّلْطَانُ عَلَى مَنْ تَوَلَّاهُ وَأَشْرَكَ مَعَ اللَّهِ، فَهَؤُلَاءِ رَعِيَّتُهُ، وَهُوَ وَلِيُّهُمْ وَسُلْطَانُهُمْ وَمُتَبَّعُهُمْ...

Thus, the enemy of Allah knew that whoever holds fast to Allah, sincerely worships Him, and relies upon Him cannot be seduced or misguided by *Shayṭān*. Rather, *Shayṭān* only has authority over those who follow him and associate partners with Allah. These are his subjects, and he is their guardian, authority, and leader."

---

Ibn al Qayyim (رَحِمَهُ ٱللَّهُ) concludes by further explaining what is meant by this authority:[84]

"...فَهَذَا مِنَ السُّلْطَانِ الَّذِي لَهُ عَلَى أَوْلِيَائِهِ وَأَهْلِ الشِّرْكِ، وَلَكِنْ لَيْسَ لَهُ عَلَى ذَلِكَ سُلْطَانُ حُجَّةٍ وَبُرْهَانٍ، وَإِنَّمَا اسْتَجَابُوا لَهُ بِمُجَرَّدِ دَعْوَتِهِ إِيَّاهُمْ، لَمَّا وَافَقَتْ أَهْوَاءَهُمْ وَأَغْرَاضَهُمْ،

This is from the authority that he has over his allies and the polytheists, but he does not have any authoritative argument or

---

[83] Ṣād 38:82-83.

[84] *Ighāthah al-Lahfān*, chapter 12.

evidence in that regard. Rather, they responded to him simply because his call aligned with their desires and objectives.

فَهُمُ الَّذِينَ أَعَانُوا عَلَى أَنْفُسِهِمْ، وَمَكَّنُوا عَدُوَّهُمْ مِنْ سُلْطَانِهِ عَلَيْهِمْ بِمُوَافَقَتِهِ وَمُتَابَعَتِهِ، فَلَمَّا أَعْطَوْا بِأَيْدِيهِمْ وَاسْتَأْسَرُوا لَهُ سُلِّطَ عَلَيْهِمْ عُقُوبَةً لَهُمْ!

They are the ones who aided against their own selves and allowed their enemy to have authority over them by agreeing with him and following him. So when they gave it up with their own hands and willingly submitted to him, they subjected themselves to his being unleashed against them as a punishment.

وَبِهَذَا يَظْهَرُ مَعْنَى قَوْلِهِ سُبْحَانَهُ: {**وَلَنْ يَجْعَلَ اللَّهُ لِلْكَافِرِينَ عَلَى الْمُؤْمِنِينَ سَبِيلًا**}، فَالْآيَةُ عَلَى عُمُومِهَا وَظَاهِرِهَا، وَإِنَّمَا الْمُؤْمِنُونَ يَصْدُرُ مِنْهُمْ مِنَ الْمَعْصِيَةِ وَالْمُخَالَفَةِ الَّتِي تُضَادُّ الْإِيمَانَ مَا يَصِيرُ بِهِ لِلْكَافِرِينَ عَلَيْهِمْ سَبِيلٌ، بِحَسَبِ تِلْكَ الْمُخَالَفَةِ، فَهُمُ الَّذِينَ تَسَبَّبُوا إِلَى جَعْلِ السَّبِيلِ عَلَيْهِمْ، كَمَا تَسَبَّبُوا إِلَيْهِ يَوْمَ أُحُدٍ بِمَعْصِيَةِ الرَّسُولِ وَمُخَالَفَتِهِ.

Thus, the meaning of Allah's statement is evident: "**And never will Allah give the disbelievers over the believers a way [to overcome them].**"[85] The verse is intended in its generality and apparent meaning, showing that the believers, when they commit acts of disobedience and opposition that contradict faith, make a way for the disbelievers to prevail over them according to those acts of opposition. They are the ones who caused the way to be established against themselves, just as they caused it to happen on the Day of Uhud by disobeying the Messenger and opposing him.

وَاللَّهُ سُبْحَانَهُ لَمْ يَجْعَلْ لِلشَّيْطَانِ عَلَى الْعَبْدِ سُلْطَانًا حَتَّى جَعَلَ لَهُ الْعَبْدُ سَبِيلًا إِلَيْهِ؛ بِطَاعَتِهِ وَالشِّرْكِ بِهِ، فَجَعَلَ اللَّهُ حِينَئِذٍ لَهُ عَلَيْهِ تَسَلُّطًا وَقَهْرًا، فَمَنْ وَجَدَ خَيْرًا فَلْيَحْمَدِ اللَّهَ، وَمَنْ وَجَدَ غَيْرَ ذَلِكَ فَلَا يَلُومَنَّ إِلَّا نَفْسَهُ.

---

[85] Al-Nisā' 4:141.

Allah, the Exalted, has not given *Shayṭān* any authority over the servant until the servant himself provides a way for *Shayṭān* through obedience to him and associating partners with Allah. At that point, Allah grants *Shayṭān* authority and dominance over the servant. So whoever finds goodness, let them thank Allah, and whoever finds otherwise, let them blame none but themselves.

فَالتَّوْحِيدُ وَالتَّوَكُّلُ وَالْإِخْلَاصُ يَمْنَعُ سُلْطَانَهُ، وَالشِّرْكُ وَفُرُوعُهُ يُوجِبُ سُلْطَانَهُ، وَالْجَمِيعُ بِقَضَاءِ مَنْ أَزِمَّةِ الْأُمُورِ بِيَدَيْهِ، وَمَرَدُّهَا إِلَيْهِ، وَلَهُ الْحُجَّةُ الْبَالِغَةُ، وَلَوْ شَاءَ لَجَعَلَ النَّاسَ أُمَّةً وَاحِدَةً، لَكِنْ أَبَتْ حِكْمَتُهُ وَحَمْدُهُ وَمَلَكُهُ إِلَّا ذَلِكَ.: {**فَلِلَّهِ الْحَمْدُ رَبِّ السَّمَاوَاتِ وَرَبِّ الْأَرْضِ رَبِّ الْعَالَمِينَ (36) وَلَهُ الْكِبْرِيَاءُ فِي السَّمَاوَاتِ وَالْأَرْضِ وَهُوَ الْعَزِيزُ الْحَكِيمُ**}

*Tawḥīd* (monotheism), reliance on Allah, and sincerity prevent his authority, while *shirk* (associating partners with Allah) and its branches necessitate his authority. All of that happens by the predestining of He in whose hands is the authority of all matters, and to whom everything ultimately refers. Allah has the ultimate and decisive argument, and if He willed, He could have made the people one nation. However, His wisdom, praise, and sovereignty deny that any but that should be the case: "**So, to Allah belongs [all] praise, Lord of the heavens and Lord of the earth, Lord of the worlds (36). And to Him belongs [all] grandeur within the heavens and the earth, and He is the Exalted in Might, the Wise.**"[86]

[86] Al Jāthiyah 45:36-37.

## SHAYTĀN'S 3 POINTS OF ATTACK

Ibn al Qayyim (رَحِمَهُ ٱللَّهُ) explains the main avenues by which the *Shayṭān* attacks mankind. He said:[87]

"وَلَمَّا عَلِمَ عَدُوُّ اللَّهِ إِبْلِيسُ أَنَّ اللهَ تَعَالَى لَا يُسْلِم عِبَادَهُ إِلَيْهِ، وَلَا يُسَلِّطُه عَلَيْهِمْ قال: {**فَبِعِزَّتِكَ لَأُغْوِيَنَّهُمْ أَجْمَعِينَ** (82) **إِلَّا عِبَادَكَ مِنْهُمُ الْمُخْلَصِينَ** (83)}. قال الله تعالى: {**وَلَقَدْ صَدَّقَ عَلَيْهِمْ إِبْلِيسُ ظَنَّهُ فَاتَّبَعُوهُ إِلَّا فَرِيقًا مِنَ الْمُؤْمِنِينَ** (20) **وَمَا كَانَ لَهُ عَلَيْهِمْ مِنْ سُلْطَانٍ إِلَّا لِنَعْلَمَ مَنْ يُؤْمِنُ بِالْآخِرَةِ مِمَّنْ هُوَ مِنْهَا فِي شَكٍّ**}

"When the enemy of Allah, Iblis (Satan), knew that Allah (سُبۡحَانَهُۥ وَتَعَالَىٰ) does not surrender His servants to him and does not give him authority over them, he said: "**By your might, I will surely mislead them all. Except, among them, Your chosen servants.**"[88] Allah, the Exalted said: "**And indeed Iblīs (Satan) did prove true his thought about them, and they followed him, all except a group of true believers (in the Oneness of Allah). And he had over them no authority, but [it was decreed] to distinguish who believes in the Hereafter from who is thereof in doubt.**"[89]

فَلَمْ يَجْعَلْ لِعَدُوِّهِ سُلْطَانًا عَلَى عِبَادِهِ الْمُؤْمِنِينَ؛ فَإِنَّهُمْ فِي حِرْزِهِ وَكَلَاءَتِهِ، وَحِفْظِهِ، وَتَحْتَ كَنَفِهِ، وَإِنْ اغْتَالَ عَدُوُّهُ أَحَدَهُمْ كَمَا يَغْتَالُ اللِّصُّ الرَّجُلَ الْغَافِلَ، فَهَذَا لَابُدَّ مِنْهُ؛ **لِأَنَّ الْعَبْدَ قَدْ بُلِيَ بِالْغَفْلَةِ وَالشَّهْوَةِ وَالْغَضَبِ.**

So, He did not grant His enemy authority over His believing servants; they are under His protection, stewardship, preservation, and under His wing. If his enemy strikes one of them as a thief

[87] *al Wābil al-Ṣayyib*, p. 8.

[88] Ṣād: 82, 83.

[89] Saba: 20, 21.

strikes a heedless man, this is inevitable; **because the servant is afflicted with heedlessness, desire, and anger.**

وَدُخُولُهُ عَلَى الْعَبْدِ مِنْ هَذِهِ الْأَبْوَابِ الثَّلَاثَةِ، وَلَوِ احْتَرَزَ الْعَبْدُ مَا احْتَرَزَ، فَلَا بُدَّ لَهُ مِنْ غَفْلَةٍ، وَلَا بُدَّ لَهُ مِنْ شَهْوَةٍ، وَلَا بُدَّ لَهُ مِنْ غَضَبٍ، وَقَدْ كَانَ آدَمُ أَبُو الْبَشَرِ صَلَّى اللَّهُ عَلَيْهِ وَسَلَّمَ مِنْ أَحْلَمِ الْخَلْقِ، وَأَرْجَحِهِمْ عَقْلًا، وَأَثْبَتِهِمْ، وَمَعَ هَذَا فَلَمْ يَزَلْ بِهِ عَدُوُّ اللَّهِ حَتَّى أَوْقَعَهُ فِيمَا أَوْقَعَهُ فِيهِ، فَمَا الظَّنُّ بِفَرَاشَةِ الْحِلْمِ، وَمَنْ عَقْلُهُ فِي جَنْبِ عَقْلِ أَبِيهِ كَتَفْلَةٍ فِي بَحْرٍ؟!

The enemy's point of entry upon the servant is from these three doors, even if the servant takes precautions, the servant is inevitably **prone to negligence, desires, and anger**. Adam, the father of all humans (عَلَيْهِ ٱلصَّلَاةُ وَٱلسَّلَامُ), was among the most forbearing of creation, the most rational and steadfast, and yet the enemy of Allah persistently targeted him until he fell into what he fell into. So, what is to be thought of someone with forbearance like a butterfly, whose intellect — compared to his forefather's — is like a droplet in the sea?!

وَلَكِنَّ عَدُوَّ اللَّهِ لَا يَخْلُصُ إِلَى الْمُؤْمِنِ إِلَّا غِيلَةً عَلَى غِرَّةٍ وَغَفْلَةٍ، فَيُوقِعُهُ، وَيَظُنُّ أَنَّهُ لَا يَسْتَقِيلُ رَبَّهُ عَزَّ وَجَلَّ بَعْدَهَا، وَأَنَّ تِلْكَ الْوَاقِعَةَ قَدِ اجْتَاحَتْهُ وَأَهْلَكَتْهُ، وَفَضْلُ اللَّهِ تَعَالَى وَرَحْمَتُهُ وَعَفْوُهُ وَمَغْفِرَتُهُ مِنْ وَرَاءِ ذَلِكَ كُلِّهِ.

However, the enemy of Allah does not reach the believer except by stealthily attacking suddenly during moments of carelessness, causing him to stumble. The enemy believes the believer will not seek his Lord's pardon after this, thinking that this incident has overwhelmed and destroyed him. But Allah's grace, mercy, forgiveness, and pardon are behind all of this.

فَإِذَا أَرَادَ اللَّهُ بِعَبْدِهِ خَيْرًا فَتَحَ لَهُ بَابًا مِنْ أَبْوَابِ التَّوْبَةِ، وَالنَّدَمِ، وَالِانْكِسَارِ، وَالذُّلِّ، وَالِافْتِقَارِ، وَالِاسْتِغَاثَةِ بِهِ، وَصِدْقِ اللَّجَأِ إِلَيْهِ، وَدَوَامِ التَّضَرُّعِ، وَالدُّعَاءِ، وَالتَّقَرُّبِ إِلَيْهِ بِمَا أَمْكَنَ مِنَ الْحَسَنَاتِ — مَا تَكُونُ تِلْكَ السَّيِّئَةُ بِهِ سَبَبَ رَحْمَتِهِ،

"

If Allah wishes good for His servant, He opens for him a door of repentance, regret, humility, brokenness, neediness, calling upon Him, sincerely seeking refuge in Him, continuous supplication, prayer, and getting closer to Him with as many good deeds as possible - to such an extent that the sin itself can become a cause of His mercy."

---

Elsewhere, he (رَحِمَهُ ٱللَّهُ) writes:[90]

"كُلّ ذِي لُبٍّ يَعْلَمُ أَنَّهُ لَا طَرِيقَ لِلشَّيْطَانِ عَلَيْهِ إِلَّا مِنْ ثَلَاثِ جِهَاتٍ:

"Every discerning person knows that there are only three ways for *Shayṭān* to approach him:

أَحَدُهَا: التَّزَيُّدُ وَالْإِسْرَافُ، فَيَزِيدُ عَلَى قَدْرِ الْحَاجَّةِ، فَتَصِيرُ فَضْلَةً، وَهِيَ حَظُّ الشَّيْطَانِ وَمَدْخَلُهُ إِلَى الْقَلْبِ. وَطَرِيقُ الِاحْتِرَازِ مِنْهُ الِاحْتِرَازُ مِنْ إِعْطَاءِ النَّفْسِ تَمَامَ مَطْلُوبِهَا مِنْ غِذَاءٍ أَوْ نَوْمٍ أَوْ لَذَّةٍ أَوْ رَاحَةٍ؛ فَمَتَى أَغْلَقْتَ هَذَا الْبَابَ حَصَلَ الْأَمَانُ مِنْ دُخُولِ الْعَدُوِّ مِنْهُ.

The first: Excess and extravagance, where one exceeds the necessary limits, leading to indulgence and becoming vulnerable to the influence of Satan. The gateway for *Shayṭān* to enter the heart is through indulgence. The way to guard against this is by exercising caution and refraining from providing the self with excessive food, sleep, pleasure, or comfort. By closing this door, one achieves safety from the enemy's intrusion.

الثَّانِيَةُ: الْغَفْلَةُ؛ فَإِنَّ الذَّاكِرَ فِي حِصْنِ الذِّكْرِ؛ فَمَتَى غَفَلَ فَتَحَ بَابَ الْحِصْنِ، فَوَلَجَهُ الْعَدُوُّ، فَيَعْسُرُ عَلَيْهِ أَوْ يَصْعَبُ إِخْرَاجُهُ.

The second: Heedlessness. The one who remembers Allah is in the fortress of remembrance. But when one becomes

---

[90] al Fawā'id (p. 277).

negligent, the door of the fortress opens, allowing the enemy to enter. It becomes difficult to repel or remove the enemy in such a state.

الثَّالِثَةُ: تَكَلُّفُ مَا لَا يَعْنِيهِ مِنْ جَمِيعِ الْأَشْيَاءِ»

The third: Involvement in matters that do not concern one as it relates to anything."

---

Elsewhere, Ibn al Qayyim elaborates on three kinds on hearts in relation to the onslaught of *Shayṭān*. He writes:[91]

"وَالْقُلُوبُ ثَلَاثَةٌ:

"Hearts are of three kinds:

- قَلْبٌ خَالٍ مِنَ الْإِيمَانِ وَجَمِيعِ الْخَيْرِ، فَذَلِكَ قَلْبٌ مُظْلِمٌ، قَدِ اسْتَرَاحَ الشَّيْطَانُ مِنْ إِلْقَاءِ الْوَسَاوِسِ إِلَيْهِ؛ لِأَنَّهُ قَدْ اتَّخَذَهُ بَيْتًا وَوَطَنًا، وَتَحَكَّمَ فِيهِ بِمَا يُرِيدُ، وَتَمَكَّنَ مِنْهُ غَايَةَ التَّمَكُّنِ.

**The first heart** s devoid of faith and all good; this is a darkened heart. Shayṭān has found ease in casting whisperings into it because he has made it his home and homeland, controls it as he wishes, and has utmost domination over it.

- **القلب الثاني:** قَلْبٌ قَدِ اسْتَنَارَ بِنُورِ الْإِيمَانِ وَأَوْقَدَ فِيهِ مِصْبَاحَهُ، لَكِنَّ عَلَيْهِ ظُلْمَةُ الشَّهَوَاتِ وَعَوَاصِفُ الْأَهْوَاءِ، فَلِلشَّيْطَانِ هُنَاكَ إِقْبَالٌ وَإِدْبَارٌ وَمُجَاوَلَاتٌ وَمَطَامِعٌ،

**The second heart** is enlightened by the light of faith, with its lamp lit within, but the darkness of desires and storms of passions clouds it. Therefore, Shayṭān has a means of approach, retreat, struggles, and aspirations there.

---

[91] *'Idah al-Ṣābirīn.*

- فَالْحَرْبُ دُوَلٌ وَسِجَالٌ، وَتَخْتَلِفُ أَحْوَالُ هَذَا الصِّنْفِ بِالْقِلَّةِ وَالْكَثْرَةِ، فَمِنْهُمْ مَنْ أَوْقَاتُ غَلَبَتِهِ لِعَدُوِّهِ أَكْثَرُ، وَمِنْهُمْ مَنْ أَوْقَاتُ غَلَبَةِ عَدُوِّهِ لَهُ أَكْثَرُ، وَمِنْهُمْ مَنْ هُوَ تَارَةً وَتَارَةً.

The war is ongoing, and its victors alternate. The outcome depends on the frequency of victories or defeats. Some experience more defeats against their enemy, while others alternate between victories and defeats.

- **القلب الثالث**: قَلْبٌ مَحْشُوٌّ بِالْإِيمَانِ، قَدِ اسْتَنَارَ بِنُورِ الْإِيمَانِ، وَانْقَشَعَتْ عَنْهُ حُجُبُ الشَّهَوَاتِ، وَأَقْلَعَتْ عَنْهُ تِلْكَ الظُّلُمَاتُ، فَلِنُورِهِ فِي قَلْبِهِ إِشْرَاقٌ، وَلِذَلِكَ الْإِشْرَاقِ إِيقَادٌ، لَوْ دَنَا مِنْهُ الْوَسْوَاسُ احْتَرَقَ بِهِ، فَهُوَ كَالسَّمَاءِ الَّتِي حُرِسَتْ بِالنُّجُومِ، فَلَوْ دَنَا مِنْهَا الشَّيْطَانُ لِيَتَخَطَّاهَا رُجِمَ فَاحْتَرَقَ.

**The third heart** is filled with faith, illuminated by the light of *emān*, and the veils of desire have been lifted from it, and those darknesses have been removed. The light in his heart shines, and there is a kindled fuel for that radiance. If the whisperer comes near it, he will be burnt. It is like the sky guarded by stars; if *Shayṭān* comes near to cross it, he will be struck by a projectile and burnt.

وَلَيْسَتِ السَّمَاءُ بِأَعْظَمَ حُرْمَةً مِنَ الْمُؤْمِنِ، وَحِرَاسَةُ اللَّهِ تَعَالَى لَهُ أَتَمُّ مِنْ حِرَاسَةِ السَّمَاءِ، وَالسَّمَاءُ مُتَعَبَّدُ الْمَلَائِكَةِ، وَمُسْتَقَرُّ الْوَحْيِ، وَفِيهَا أَنْوَارُ الطَّاعَاتِ،

And the sky is not more sacred than the believer, and Allah's protection for him is more complete than the sky's protection. The sky is the worship place of the angels, the repository of revelation, and it holds the lights of obedience.

وَقَلْبُ الْمُؤْمِنِ مُسْتَقَرُّ التَّوْحِيدِ وَالْمَحَبَّةِ وَالْمَعْرِفَةِ وَالْإِيمَانِ، وَفِيهِ أَنْوَارُهَا، فَهُوَ حَقِيقٌ أَنْ يُحْرَسَ وَيُحْفَظَ مِنْ كَيْدِ الْعَدُوِّ، فَلَا يَنَالُ مِنْهُ شَيْئًا إِلَّا عَلَى غِرَّةٍ وَغَفْلَةٍ خَطْفَةً.

The believer's heart is the repository of monotheism, love, knowledge, and faith and contains its lights. Therefore, it is natural that it should be guarded and preserved from the enemy's plots, so nothing can be taken except in a moment of carelessness or inattention.

وَقَدْ مُثِّلَ ذَلِكَ بِمِثَالٍ حَسَنٍ، وَهُوَ ثَلَاثَةُ بُيُوتٍ:

This has been illustrated with a good example, which is of three houses:

بَيْتٌ لِلْمَلِكِ، فِيهِ كُنُوزُهُ وَذَخَائِرُهُ وَجَوَاهِرُهُ.

A house for the king, which contains his treasures, reserves, and jewels.

وَبَيْتٌ لِلْعَبْدِ، فِيهِ كُنُوزُ الْعَبْدِ وَذَخَائِرُهُ وَجَوَاهِرُهُ، وَلَيْسَ فِيهِ جَوَاهِرُ الْمَلِكِ وَذَخَائِرُهُ.

A house for the servant containing the servant's treasures, reserves, and jewels, but not the king's jewels and reserves.

وَبَيْتٌ خَالٍ صِفْرٌ لَا شَيْءٌ فِيهِ.

And an empty house that contains nothing.

فَجَاءَ اللِّصُّ لِيَسْرِقَ مِنْ أَحَدِ الْبُيُوتِ، فَمِنْ أَيِّهَا يَسْرِقُ؟!

A thief comes to steal from one of the houses. So which one does he steal from?!

فَإِنْ قُلْتَ: مِنَ الْبَيْتِ الْخَالِي، كَانَ مُحَالًا؛ لِأَنَّ الْبَيْتَ الْخَالِي لَيْسَ فِيهِ شَيْءٌ يُسْرَقُ؛ وَلِهَذَا قِيلَ لِابْنِ عَبَّاسٍ رَضِيَ اللَّهُ عَنْهُمَا: إِنَّ الْيَهُودَ تَزْعُمُ أَنَّهَا لَا تُوَسْوَسُ فِي صَلَاتِهَا، فَقَالَ: "وَمَا يَصْنَعُ الشَّيْطَانُ بِالْقَلْبِ الْخَرَابِ؟! "

If you say: from the empty house, it would be impossible; because there is nothing to steal in an empty house. That's why it was said to Ibn Abbas (رَضِيَ اللَّهُ عَنْهُمَا). when the Jews claimed they did not have whisperings (from the devil) in their prayers, he said: "What would the devil do with a ruined heart?!"

وَإِنْ قُلْتَ: يَسْرِقُ مِنْ بَيْتِ الْمَلِكِ، كَانَ ذَلِكَ كَالْمُسْتَحِيلِ الْمُمْتَنِعِ؛ فَإِنَّ عَلَيْهِ مِنَ الْحَرَسِ وَالْيَزَكِ مَا لَا يَسْتَطِيعُ اللِّصُّ الدُّنُوَّ مِنْهُ، كَيْفَ وَحَارِسُهُ الْمَلِكُ بِنَفْسِهِ؟!، وَكَيْفَ يَسْتَطِيعُ اللِّصُّ الدُّنُوَّ مِنْهُ وَحَوْلَهُ مِنَ الْحَرَسِ وَالْجُنْدِ مَا حَوْلَهُ؟!

If you said: "The thief steals from the king's house," it would be impossible. For he has guards and fortifications that the thief cannot approach. How, when the king himself is the guard?! And how can the thief approach it when guards and troops surround it?!

فَلَمْ يَبْقَ لِلِّصِّ إِلَّا الْبَيْتُ الثَّالِثُ، فَهُوَ الَّذِي يَشُنُّ عَلَيْهِ الْغَارَةَ.

So, the only place left for the thief is the third house, so he raids it.

فَلْيَتَأَمَّلِ اللَّبِيبُ هَذَا الْمِثَالَ حَقَّ التَّأَمُّلِ، وَلْيُنْزِلْهُ عَلَى الْقُلُوبِ، فَإِنَّهَا عَلَى مِنْوَالِهِ.

Let the wise contemplate this example properly, and let him apply it to the hearts, for they are in its fashion.

فَقَلْبٌ خَلَا مِنَ الْخَيْرِ كُلِّهِ، وَهُوَ قَلْبُ الْكَافِرِ وَالْمُنَافِقِ، فَذَلِكَ بَيْتُ الشَّيْطَانِ، قَدْ أَحْرَزَهُ لِنَفْسِهِ وَاسْتَوْطَنَهُ، وَاتَّخَذَهُ سَكَنًا وَمُسْتَقَرًّا، فَأَيُّ شَيْءٍ يَسْرِقُ مِنْهُ، وَفِيهِ خَزَائِنُهُ وَذَخَائِرُهُ، وَشُكُوكُهُ وَخَيَالَاتُهُ وَوَسَاوِسُهُ؟!

A heart that is devoid of all good, which is the heart of the disbeliever and the hypocrite, is the house of Satan. He has secured, settled in, and made it his residence and stable. What can he steal from it when his treasures, reserves, doubts, imaginations, and whisperings are in it?!

- وَقَلْبٌ قَدِ امْتَلَأَ مِنْ جَلَالِ اللَّهِ عَزَّ وَجَلَّ وَعَظَمَتِهِ، وَمَحَبَّتِهِ وَمُرَاقَبَتِهِ، وَالْحَيَاءِ مِنْهُ، فَأَيُّ شَيْطَانٍ يَجْتَرِئُ عَلَى هَذَا الْقَلْبِ؟!، وَإِنْ أَرَادَ سَرِقَةَ شَيْءٍ مِنْهُ، فَمَاذَا يَسْرِقُ؟!، وَغَايَتُهُ أَنْ يَظْفَرَ فِي الْأَحَايِينِ مِنْهُ بِخَطْفَةٍ وَنَهْبَةٍ تَحْصُلُ لَهُ عَلَى غِرَّةٍ مِنَ الْعَبْدِ وَغَفْلَةٍ لَابُدَّ لَهُ مِنْهَا؛ إِذْ هُوَ بَشَرٌ، وَأَحْكَامُ الْبَشَرِيَّةِ جَارِيَةٌ عَلَيْهِ مِنَ الْغَفْلَةِ وَالسَّهْوِ، وَالذُّهُولِ وَغَلَبَةِ الطَّبْعِ.

And a heart filled with the majesty of Allah, His greatness, His love, self-supervision, and shyness from Him, which devil would dare approach this heart?! If he intended to steal something from it, what could he steal?! His ultimate goal is to snatch something in moments of the servant's unawareness and inevitable carelessness, as he is a human and the rules of being human apply to him, such as heedlessness, oversight, absent-mindedness, and the dominance of human nature.

...وَقَلْبٌ فِيهِ تَوْحِيدُ اللَّهِ تَعَالَى وَمَعْرِفَتُهُ وَمَحَبَّتُهُ، وَالْإِيمَانُ بِهِ وَالتَّصْدِيقُ بِوَعْدِهِ وَوَعِيدِهِ، وَفِيهِ شَهَوَاتُ النَّفْسِ وَأَخْلَاقُهَا، وَدَوَاعِي الْهَوَى وَالطَّبْعِ.

...And another heart contains singling Allah out, knowing Him, loving Him, believing in Him, and affirming His promise and threat. Yet, it also contains the desires and characteristics of the self and the temptations of passion and human nature.

وَقَلْبٌ بَيْنَ هَذَيْنِ الدَّاعِيَيْنِ، فَمَرَّةً يَمِيلُ بِقَلْبِهِ دَاعِي الْإِيمَانِ وَالْمَعْرِفَةِ، وَالْمَحَبَّةِ لِلَّهِ تَعَالَى وَإِرَادَتِهِ وَحْدَهُ، وَمَرَّةً يَمِيلُ بِقَلْبِهِ دَاعِي الْهَوَى وَالشَّيْطَانِ وَالطِّبَاعِ، فَهَذَا الْقَلْبُ لِلشَّيْطَانِ فِيهِ مُطْمَعٌ، وَلَهُ مِنْهُ مَنَازِلَاتٌ وَوَقَائِعُ، وَيُعْطِي اللَّهُ النَّصْرَ لِمَنْ يَشَاءُ {وَمَا النَّصْرُ إِلَّا مِنْ عِنْدِ اللَّهِ الْعَزِيزِ الْحَكِيمِ (126) } [آل عمران: 126].

And a heart between these two callers, sometimes, the call of faith, knowledge, and love for Allah, and sincerely intending Him, sways the heart. At other times, the call of passion, *Shayṭān*, and nature sway it. This heart is a potential ground for *Shayṭān*, and encounters and battles with him exist. And Allah grants victory to whom He wills, "And victory is not but from Allah, the Mighty, the Wise." (Ali 'Imran: 126).

وَهَذَا لَا يَتَمَكَّنُ الشَّيْطَانُ مِنْهُ إِلَّا بِمَا عِنْدَهُ مِنْ سِلَاحِهِ، فَيَدْخُلُ الشَّيْطَانُ إِلَيْهِ فَيَجِدُ سِلَاحَهُ عِنْدَهُ فَيَأْخُذُهُ وَيُقَاتِلُهُ بِهِ؛ فَإِنَّ أَسْلِحَتَهُ هِيَ الشَّهَوَاتُ وَالشُّبُهَاتُ، وَالْخَيَالَاتُ وَالْأَمَانِيُّ الْكَاذِبَةُ، وَهِيَ فِي الْقَلْبِ، فَيَدْخُلُ الشَّيْطَانُ فَيَجِدُهَا عِنْدَهُ

فَيَأْخُذُهَا وَيَصُولُ بِهَا عَلَى الْقَلْبِ؛ فَإِنْ كَانَ عِنْدَ الْعَبْدِ عُدَّةٌ عَتِيدَةٌ مِنَ الْإِيمَانِ تُقَاوِمُ تِلْكَ الْعُدَّةِ وَتَزِيدُ عَلَيْهَا، انتَصَفَ مِنَ الشَّيْطَانِ، وَإِلَّا فَالدَّوْلَةُ لِعَدُوِّهِ عَلَيْهِ، وَلَا حَوْلَ وَلَا قُوَّةَ إِلَّا بِاللَّهِ الْعَلِيِّ الْعَظِيمِ.

*Shayṭān* cannot control this heart except with the weapon he possesses. *Shayṭān* enters it and finds his weapon there, takes it and fights with it. Indeed, his weapons are desires, doubts, fantasies, and false hopes in the heart. Shayṭān enters, finds them there, takes them, and assaults the heart with them. If the servant has a strong defense of faith to resist these weapons and exceed them, he can hold off Satan. Otherwise, the control will be to his enemy, and there is no power or strength except with Allah, the High, the Great.

فَإِذَا أَذِنَ الْعَبْدُ لِعَدُوِّهِ، وَفَتَحَ لَهُ بَابَ بَيْتِهِ، وَأَدْخَلَهُ عَلَيْهِ، وَمَكَّنَهُ مِنَ السِّلَاحِ يُقَاتِلُهُ بِهِ، فَهُوَ الْمَلُومُ.

If the servant opens the door of his house to his enemy, allows him in, and arms him with weapons to fight with, he is to blame.

فَنَفْسَكَ لُمْ وَلَا تَلُمِ المَطَايَا ... وَمُتْ كَمَدًا فَلَيْسَ لَكَ اعْتِذَارُ

So blame your own self, do not blame the steeds ... and die in agony for you have no excuse."

## THE STRONG BELIEVER WEARS OUT HIS SHAYTĀN

Abū Hurayrah (رَضِيَٱللَّهُعَنْهُ) reported that Allah's Messenger (صَلَّىٱللَّهُعَلَيْهِوَسَلَّمَ) said:[92]

"إِنَّ الْمُؤْمِنَ لَيُنْضِي شَيَاطِينَهُ، كَمَا يُنْضِي أَحَدُكُمْ بَعِيرَهُ فِي السَّفَرِ".

**"Indeed, the believer exhausts his Shayṭān, just as one of you exhausts his camel during a journey."**

Zayn al-Dīn 'Abd al-Ra'ūf al Munāwī (d. 1031 AH رَحِمَهُٱللَّهُ) beautifully commented on this *hadīth*:[93]

"**إِنَّ الْمُؤْمِنَ يُنْضِي شَيْطَانَهُ**" أَيْ يُهْزِلُهُ وَيَجْعَلُهُ نِضْوًا أَيْ مَهْزُولًا لِكَثْرَةِ إِذْلَالِهِ لَهُ وَجَعْلِهِ أَسِيرًا تَحْتَ قَهْرِهِ وَتَصَرُّفِهِ،

"The phrase "**the believer exhausts his Shayṭān**" means that he weakens him and renders him humiliated, due to the believer's continuous humiliation of Satan, making him a captive under his subjugation and disposal.

وَمَنْ أَعَزَّ سُلْطَانَ اللَّهِ أَعَزَّهُ اللَّهُ وَسَلَّطَهُ عَلَى عَدُوِّهِ ، وَحُكْمُ عَكْسِهِ عَكْسُ حُكْمِهِ

And whoever honors and strengthens Allah's *Sulṭān* (i.e., gives authority to the *emān* in the heart), Allah strengthens and empowers them over their enemy, and the opposite scenario has the opposite ruling.

---

[92] Reported by Ahmad in *al Musnad* and Ibn Abī-l-Dunyā in *Makā'id al-Shayṭān*. Al Albānī grades it hasan in al-Ṣaḥīḥah (3586). He said: this chain of transmission is sound (*hasan*). It contains Ibn Lahī'ah, yet his narrations from Qutaybah b. Sa'īd are authentic.

[93] *Fayḍ al Qadīr Sharḥ al Jāmi' al-Ṣaghīr* (2101).

فَظَهَرَ أَنَّ الْمُؤْمِنَ لَا يَزَالُ يُنْضِي شَيْطَانَهُ (كَمَا يُنْضِي أَحَدُكُمْ بَعِيرَهُ فِي السَّفَرِ) لِأَنَّهُ إِذَا عَرَضَ لِقَلْبِهِ احْتَرَزَ عَنْهُ بِمَعْرِفَةِ رَبِّهِ وَإِذَا اعْتَرَضَ لِنَفْسِهِ وَهِيَ شَهَوَاتُهُ احْتَرَزَ بِذِكْرِ اللَّهِ ، فَهُوَ أَبَدًا يُنْضيهِ ،

It is evident that the believer continues to exhaust his *Shayṭān*, just as one of you exhausts his camel during a journey. When it resists, he restrains it by his knowledge of his Lord, and when it presents itself to his inner-self — which is his passions — he defends himself through the remembrance of Allah. Thus, he always exhausts it.

فَالْبَعِيرُ يَتَجَشَّمُ فِي سَفَرِهِ أَثْقَالَ حَمُولَتِهِ فَيَصِيرُ نِضْوًا لِذَلِكَ، وَشَيْطَانُ الْمُؤْمِنِ يَتَجَشَّمُ أَثْقَالَ غَيظِهِ مِنْهُ لِمَا يَرَاهُ مِنَ الطَّاعَةِ وَالْوَفَاءِ لِلَّهِ، فَوَقَفَ مِنْهُ بِمُزْجَرِ الْكَلْبِ نَاحِيَةً،

The camel, during its journey, carries heavy loads and becomes exhausted as a result. Similarly, the *Shayṭān* of the believer carries the weight of his frustration due to witnessing his obedience and loyalty to Allah. The *Shayṭān* stands off to the side like one scared away by a dog's barking.

وَأَشَارَ بِتَعْبِيرِهِ بِـ "يُنْضِي" دُونَ يُهْلِكُ وَنَحْوِهِ إِلَى أَنَّهُ لَا يَتَخَلَّصُ أَحَدٌ مِنْ شَيْطَانٍ مَا دَامَ حَسًّا

The use of the expression "wears out" as opposed to "destroys" or something similar is an indication that no one can completely rid themselves of *Shayṭān* as long as they are living and feeling.

فَإِنَّهُ لَا يَزَالُ يُجَاهِدُ الْقَلْبَ وَيُنَازِعُهُ ، وَالْعَبْدُ لَا يَزَالُ يُجَاهِدُهُ مُجَاهَدَةً لَا آخِرَ لَهَا إِلَّا الْمَوْتَ ، لَكِنَّ الْمُؤْمِنَ الْكَامِلَ يُقَوَّى عَلَيْهِ وَلَا يَنْقَادُ لَهُ،

[*Shayṭān*] continues to struggle and contend with the heart, and the servant constantly fights against him relentlessly until death. However, the perfected believer is given strength against him and does not succumb to him.

وَمَعَ ذَلِكَ لَا يَسْتَغْنِي قَطُّ عَنِ الْجِهَادِ وَالْمُدَافَعَةِ مَا دَامَ الدَّمُ يَجْرِي فِي بَدَنِهِ، فَإِنَّهُ مَا دَامَ حَيًّا فَأَبْوَابُ الشَّيَاطِينِ مَفْتُوحَةٌ إِلَى قَلْبِهِ لَا تَنْغَلِقُ وَهِيَ: الشَّهْوَةُ وَالْغَضَبُ وَالْحِدَّةُ وَالطَّمَعُ وَالثَّرَاءُ وَغَيْرُهَا،

Nevertheless, they never become complacent and stop their jihad and resistance as long as blood flows through their veins. As long as they are alive, the gates of *Shayṭān* remain open to their hearts and do not close. These gates include desires, anger, harshness, greed, wealth, and other matters.

وَمَهْمَا كَانَ الْبَابُ مَفْتُوحًا وَالْعَدُوُّ غَيْرَ عَاقِلٍ لَمْ يُدْفَعْ إِلَّا بِالْحِرَاسَةِ وَالْمُجَاهَدَةِ

No matter how open the gate and irrational the enemy is, he can only be repelled by vigilance and perseverance.

قَالَ رَجُلٌ لِلْحَسَنِ: يَا أَبَا سَعِيدٍ أَيَنَامُ إِبْلِيسُ؟ فَتَبَسَّمَ وَقَالَ: "لَوْ نَامَ لَوَجَدْنَا رَاحَةً".

A man asked Al-Hasan (رَحِمَهُ ٱللَّهُ), "O Abu Sa'īd, does Iblīs sleep?" He smiled and said, "If he slept, we would find comfort."

فَلَا خَلَاصَ لِلْمُؤْمِنِ مِنْهُ لَكِنَّهُ بِسَبِيلٍ مِنْ دَفْعِهِ وَتَضْعِيفِ قُوَّتِهِ وَذَلِكَ عَلَى قَدْرِ قُوَّةِ إِيمَانِهِ وَمِقْدَارِ إِيقَانِهِ...

There is no escape from him for the believer, however, he works to ward him off and weaken his power. This is done in proportion to the strength of one's faith and the level of one's conviction."

## REMEMBRANCE OF ALLAH IS THE GREATEST WEAPON AGAINST SHAYTĀN

Abū Malik al Ash'arī (رَضِيَٱللَّهُعَنْهُ) reported that Allah's Messenger (صَلَّىٱللَّهُعَلَيْهِوَسَلَّمَ) said[94] that Yaḥyā b. Zakariyā (عَلَيْهِمَاٱلسَّلَامُ) was commanded by Allah (سُبْحَانَهُوَتَعَالَىٰ) to command Banū Isrā'īl with five advices. He gathered them at the Bayt al Maqdis and command them with five advices, the last of which was:

"وَآمُرُكُمْ أَنْ تَذْكُرُوا اللَّهَ تَعَالَى؛ فَإِنَّ مَثَلَ ذَلِكَ مَثَلَ رَجُلٍ خَرَجَ الْعَدُوُّ فِي أَثَرِهِ سِرَاعًا، حَتَّى إِذَا أَتَى عَلَى حِصْنٍ حَصِينٍ، فَأَحْرَزَ نَفْسَهُ مِنْهُمْ، كَذَلِكَ الْعَبْدُ لَا يُحْرِزُ نَفْسَهُ مِنَ الشَّيْطَانِ إِلَّا بِذِكْرِ اللَّهِ".

**"And I command you to remember Allah, the Most High, for verily, its likeness is that of a man who is pursued by enemies, so he hastens until he reaches a fortified fortress and saves himself from them. Likewise, a servant does not save himself from Shayṭān except through the remembrance of Allah."**

Ibn al Qayyim (رَحِمَهُٱللَّهُ) explained this *ḥadīth*, saying:[95]

"فَلَوْ لَمْ يَكُنْ فِي الذِّكْرِ إِلَّا هَذِهِ الْخَصْلَةَ الْوَاحِدَةَ لَكَانَ حَقِيقًا بِالْعَبْدِ أَنْ لَا يَفْتُرَ لِسَانُهُ مِنْ ذِكْرِ اللَّهِ تَعَالَى، وَأَنْ لَا يَزَالَ لَهِجًا بِذِكْرِهِ؛ فَإِنَّهُ لَا يُحْرِزُ نَفْسَهُ مِنْ عَدُوِّهِ إِلَّا بِالذِّكْرِ، وَلَا يَدْخُلُ عَلَيْهِ الْعَدُوُّ إِلَّا مِنْ بَابِ الْغَفْلَةِ،

"If there were no other benefit in remembrance except for this one aspect, it would be sufficient for the servant never to let his tongue cease from the remembrance of Allah and to engage in His remembrance continuously. For it is only through

[94] Al-Tirmidhī. Graded *Ṣaḥīḥ* by al Albānī.

[95] *al Wābil al-Ṣayyib* (p. 83).

remembrance that one safeguards oneself from their enemy. And the enemy can only enter through the door of heedlessness.

فَهُوَ يَرْصُدُهُ، فَإِذَا غَفَلَ وَثَبَ عَلَيْهِ وَافْتَرَسَهُ، وَإِذَا ذَكَرَ اللَّهَ تَعَالَى انْخَنَسَ عَدُوُّ اللَّهِ وَتَصَاغَرَ وَانْقَمَعَ، حَتَّى يَكُونَ كَالْوَصْعِ وَكَالذُّبَابِ، وَلِهَذَا سُمِّيَ الْوَسْوَاسَ الْخَنَّاسُ، أَيْ: يُوَسْوِسُ فِي الصُّدُورِ؛ فَإِذَا ذُكِرَ اللَّهُ تَعَالَى خَنَسَ، أَيْ: كَفَّ وَانْقَبَضَ.

The enemy lies in wait, and when one becomes negligent, they pounce and attack. But when one remembers Allah, the enemy of Allah retreats, diminishes and becomes suppressed until it becomes like a mosquito or a fly. That is why it is called the persistent whisperer and retreater (*al-waswās al-khannās,)* meaning it whispers into the hearts. But when Allah, the Most High, is remembered, it retreats and shrinks, meaning it withdraws and contracts.

وَقَالَ ابْنُ عَبَّاسٍ: "الشَّيْطَانُ جَاثِمٌ عَلَى قَلْبِ ابْنِ آدَمَ، فَإِذَا سَهَا وَغَفَلَ وَسْوَسَ، فَإِذَا ذَكَرَ اللَّهُ تَعَالَى خَنَسَ".

Ibn Abbas said, "Shayṭān sits upon the heart of the son of Adam, and when he becomes negligent and heedless, he whispers. But he retreats when Allah, the Most High, is remembered."

---

The need for this protection is dire. Shaykh al Islām Ibn Taymiyyah (d. 728 AH رَحِمَهُ ٱللَّهُ) succinctly explained the nature of devils and how they differ from other creatures due to their reveling and delighting in evil and inflicting misery. He said:[96]

[96] *Majmū' al Fatāwā* (13/83)

"فَالشَّيَاطِينُ لَهُمْ غَرَضٌ فِيمَا نَهَى اللَّهُ عَنْهُ مِنْ الْكُفْرِ وَالْفُسُوقِ وَالْعِصْيَانِ وَلَهُمْ لَذَّةٌ فِي الشَّرِّ وَالْفِتَنِ يُحِبُّونَ ذَلِكَ وَإِنْ لَمْ يَكُنْ فِيهِ مَنْفَعَةٌ لَهُمْ وَهُمْ يَأْمُرُونَ السَّارِقَ أَنْ يَسْرِقَ وَيَذْهَبُونَ إلَى أَهْلِ الْمَالِ فَيَقُولُونَ: فُلَانٌ سَرَقَ مَتَاعَكُمْ؛

"Devils have an agenda in what Allah has forbidden of disbelief, immorality and disobedience, and they find pleasure in evil and strife. They love this, even if there is no benefit for them in it. They command the thief to steal and then go to the owners of the property and say: 'so-and-so stole your goods.'

وَلِهَذَا يُقَالُ: الْقُوَّةُ الْمَلَكِيَّةُ وَالْبَهِيمِيَّةُ والسبعية والشيطانية

Therefore, it is said: there are four types of power - angelic, animalistic, predatory, and demonic.

فَإِنَّ الْمَلَكِيَّةَ فِيهَا الْعِلْمُ النَّافِعُ وَالْعَمَلُ الصَّالِحُ وَالْبَهِيمِيَّةَ فِيهَا الشَّهَوَاتُ كَالْأَكْلِ وَالشُّرْبِ والسبعية فِيهَا الْغَضَبُ وَهُوَ دَفْعُ الْمُؤْذِي

The angelic power is characterized by beneficial knowledge and righteous deeds. The animalistic power is characterized by desires such as eating and drinking. The predatory power is characterized by anger, which is the defense against harm.

وَأَمَّا الشَّيْطَانِيَّةُ فَشَرٌّ مَحْضٌ لَيْسَ فِيهَا جَلْبُ مَنْفَعَةٍ وَلَا دَفْعُ مَضَرَّةٍ"

As for the demonic power, it is pure evil; it neither brings benefit nor wards off harm."

---

The intelligent believer strengthens his alliance with the angels and protection from devils by remaining obedient and constantly remembering Allah. Ibn al Qayyim (رَحِمَهُ ٱللَّهُ) said:[97]

[97] *al Wābil al-Ṣayyib* (p. 99).

"مَجَالِسُ الذِّكْرِ مَجَالِسُ الْمَلَائِكَةِ، وَمَجَالِسَ اللَّغْوِ وَالْغَفْلَةِ مَجَالِسُ الشَّيَاطِينِ، فَلْيَتَخَيَّرِ الْعَبْدُ أَعْجَبَهُمَا إِلَيْهِ، وَأَوْلَاهُمَا بِهِ؛ فَهُوَ مَعَ أَهْلِهِ فِي الدُّنْيَا وَالْآخِرَةِ"

"The gatherings for remembrance [of Allah] are the gatherings of angels, and the gatherings for idle talk and negligence are the gatherings of devils. So let the servant choose what is more appealing and suitable to him; for he will be with those he aligns with, in this world and the Hereafter."

---

Elsewhere he (رَحِمَهُ ٱللَّهُ) explains the amazing effect of *dhikr* in repelling devils. He says:[98]

"فَذِكْرُ اللَّهِ تَعَالَى يَقْمَعُ الشَّيْطَانَ وَيُؤْلِمُهُ وَيُؤْذِيهِ، كَالسِّيَاطِ وَالْمَقَامِعِ الَّتِي تُؤْذِي مَنْ يُضْرَبُ بِهَا. وَلِهَذَا يَكُونُ شَيْطَانُ الْمُؤْمِنِ هَزِيلًا ضَئِيلًا مُضْنًى مِمَّا يُعَذِّبُهُ الْمُؤْمِنُ وَيَقْمَعُهُ بِهِ مِنْ ذِكْرِ اللَّهِ وَطَاعَتِهِ.

"The remembrance of Allah (سُبْحَانَهُ وَتَعَالَىٰ) suppresses *Shayṭān*, causing him pain and distress, similar to whips and maces that harm those struck with them. That is why the *Shayṭān* of the believer becomes feeble, weak, and tormented by the believer's remembrance of Allah and obedience to Him.

وَفِي أَثَرٍ عَنْ بَعْضِ السَّلَفِ: "**إِنَّ الْمُؤْمِنَ يُنْضِي شَيْطَانَهُ، كَمَا يُنْضِي الرَّجُلُ بَعِيرَهُ فِي السَّفَرِ**"؛ لِأَنَّهُ كُلَّمَا اعْتَرَضَهُ صَبَّ عَلَيْهِ سِيَاطَ الذِّكْرِ وَالتَّوَجُّهِ وَالِاسْتِغْفَارِ وَالطَّاعَةِ، فَشَيْطَانُهُ مَعَهُ فِي عَذَابٍ شَدِيدٍ، لَيْسَ بِمَنْزِلَةِ شَيْطَانِ الْفَاجِرِ الَّذِي هُوَ مَعَهُ فِي رَاحَةٍ وَدَعَةٍ، وَلِهَذَا يَكُونُ قَوِيًّا عَاتِيًا شَدِيدًا.

A narration attributed to some of the early righteous predecessors states, "**Verily, the believer exhausts his Satan, just as a person exhausts his camel during a journey.**" Whenever *Shayṭān* tries to obstruct the believer, the believer responds with

---

[98] *Badāʾi al Fawāʾid* (2/792).

lashes of remembrance, turning towards Allah, seeking forgiveness and obedience. Thus, the believer's *Shayṭān* is with him in severe torment, unlike the *Shayṭān* of the wicked, who is at ease and leisure. Hence, it becomes firm, fierce and intense.

فَمَنْ لَمْ يُعَذِّبْ شَيْطَانَهُ فِي هَذِهِ الدَّارِ بِذِكْرِ اللَّهِ تَعَالَى وَتَوْحِيدِهِ وَاسْتِغْفَارِهِ وَطَاعَتِهِ، عَذَّبَهُ شَيْطَانُهُ فِي الْآخِرَةِ بِعَذَابِ النَّارِ، فَلَا بُدَّ لِكُلِّ أَحَدٍ أَنْ يُعَذِّبَ شَيْطَانَهُ أَوْ يُعَذِّبَهُ شَيْطَانُهُ."

Therefore, whoever does not torment his *Shayṭān* in this worldly life through the remembrance of Allah, singling Him out (with His rights), seeking His forgiveness, and obeying Him, his *Shayṭān* will torment him in the hereafter with the punishment of the Fire. Thus, it is inevitable for everyone to either torment his *Shayṭān* or be tormented by his *Shayṭān*.

وَتَأَمَّلْ حِكْمَةَ الْقُرْآنِ الْكَرِيمِ وَجَلَالَتَهُ كَيْفَ أَوْقَعَ الِاسْتِعَاذَةَ مِنْ شَرِّ الشَّيْطَانِ الْمَوْصُوفِ بِأَنَّهُ الْوَسْوَاسُ الْخَنَّاسُ، الَّذِي يُوَسْوِسُ فِي صُدُورِ النَّاسِ، وَلَمْ يَقُلْ: مِنْ شَرِّ وَسْوَسَتِهِ؛ لِتَعَمَّ الِاسْتِعَاذَةُ شَرَّهُ جَمِيعَهُ، فَإِنَّ قَوْلَهُ: {مِنْ شَرِّ الْوَسْوَاسِ الْخَنَّاسِ} [النَّاسُ: 4]، يَعُمُّ كُلَّ شَرِّهِ،

Reflect upon the wisdom of the Noble Qur'an and its magnificence in how it presented seeking refuge from the evil of *Shayṭān*, who is described as the persistent whisperer and retreater. He whispers into the hearts of people. It did not say, "from the evil of his whispers," so that seeking refuge includes the generality of his evil. Thus, when Allah says, **"from the evil of the persistent whisperer who retreats,"**[99] it generally includes all of his evil.

[99] Al-Nās: 4.

وَوَصَفَهُ بِأَعْظَمِ صِفَاتِهِ وَأَشَدِّهَا شَرًّا، وَأَقْوَاهَا تَأْثِيرًا، وَأَعَمِّهَا فَسَادًا، وَهِيَ الْوَسْوَسَةُ الَّتِي هِيَ مَبَادِئُ الْإِرَادَةِ، فَإِنَّ الْقَلْبَ يَكُونُ فَارِغًا مِنَ الشَّرِّ وَالْمَعْصِيَةِ، فَيُوَسْوِسُ إِلَيْهِ، وَيَخْطُرُ الذَّنْبَ بِبَالِهِ، فَيُصَوِّرُهُ لِنَفْسِهِ وَيُمَنِّيهِ، وَيُشَهِّيهِ

It describes him with his greatest attributes and the most intense and impactful forms of evil: the whispering that is the starting point of one's intention. The heart is initially free from evil and disobedience, then (*Shayṭān)* whispers to it, causing sinful thoughts, beautifying and making them appealing to one's self.

فَيَصِيرُ شَهْوَةً، وَيُزَيِّنُهَا لَهُ وَيُحَسِّنُهَا وَيُخَيِّلُهَا لَهُ فِي خَيَالٍ تَمِيلُ نَفْسُهُ إِلَيْهَا، فَيَصِيرُ إِرَادَةً ثُمَّ لَا يَزَالُ يُمَثِّلُ وَيُخَيِّلُ، وَيُمَنِّي وَيُشَهِّي، وَيُنْسِي عِلْمَهُ بِضَرَرِهَا، وَيَطْوِي عَنْهُ سُوءَ عَاقِبَتِهَا، فَيَحُولُ بَيْنَهُ وَبَيْنَ مَطَالَعَتِهِ، فَلَا يَرَى إِلَّا صُورَةَ الْمَعْصِيَةِ وَالتَّذَاذَهُ بِهَا فَقَطْ وَيَنْسَى مَا وَرَاءَ ذَلِكَ،

It becomes a passionate desire that he continues to make him visualize and imagine, desiring and lusting for it while causing him to forget its harm and overlook its consequences. He blocks the person from investigating it so they see nothing but the image of the sin and indulge in it, while forgetting what lies beyond it.

فَتَصِيرُ الْإِرَادَةُ عَزِيمَةً جَازِمَةً، فَيَشْتَدُّ الْحِرْصُ عَلَيْهَا مِنَ الْقَلْبِ، فَيَبْعَثُ الْجُنُودَ فِي الطَّلَبِ، فَيَبْعَثُ الشَّيْطَانُ مَعَهُمْ مَدَدًا لَهُمْ وَعَوْنًا، فَإِنْ فَتَرُوا حَرَّكَهُمْ، وَإِنْ وَنَوْا أَزْعَجَهُمْ، كَمَا قَالَ تَعَالَى: {أَلَمْ تَرَ أَنَّا أَرْسَلْنَا الشَّيَاطِينَ عَلَى الْكَافِرِينَ تَؤُزُّهُمْ أَزًّا} أَيْ: تُزْعِجُهُمْ إِلَى الْمَعَاصِي: إِزْعَاجًا، كُلَّمَا فَتَرُوا أَوْ وَنَوْا أَزْعَجَتْهُمُ الشَّيَاطِينُ، وَأَزَّتْهُمْ وَأَثَارَتْهُمْ، فَلَا تَزَالُ بِالْعَبْدِ تَقُودُهُ إِلَى الذَّنْبِ وَتَنْظِمُ شَمْلَ الِاجْتِمَاعِ بِأَلْطَفِ حِيلَةٍ، وَأَتَمِّ مَكِيدَةٍ.

The intention becomes a decisive determination, and the heart's keenness for it intensifies. It deploys the troops in pursuit, and the *Shayṭān* sends along with them reinforcement and assistance. He spurs them on if they falter, and if they slacken, he agitates them. As Allah (سُبْحَانَهُ وَتَعَالَى) said, **'Have you not seen that We have sent the devils upon the disbelievers, inciting them to evil with constant incitement?'.**[100] Meaning the devils are annoying them to commit sins, causing disturbance whenever they falter or slacken. The devils continually agitate, provoke, and stir them up. They incessantly lead the servant towards sin, coordinating the assembly with the most subtle scheme and total plot.

قَدْ رَضِيَ لِنَفْسِهِ بِالْقِيَادَةِ لِفَجَرَةِ بَنِي آدَمَ، وَهُوَ الَّذِي اسْتَكْبَرَ وَأَبَى أَنْ يَسْجُدَ لِأَبِيهِمْ. فَلَا بِتِلْكَ النَّخْوَةِ وَالْكِبْرِ، وَلَا بِرِضَاهُ أَنْ يَصِيرَ قَوَّادًا لِكُلِّ مَنْ عَصَى اللَّهَ! كَمَا قَالَ بَعْضُهُمْ:

*Shayṭān* was contented to become the leader of the wicked from the children of Adam, yet he had arrogantly refused to prostrate to their father. Neither his pride and arrogance, nor his satisfaction in becoming the pimp of all those who disobey Allah is admirable. As some have said:[101]

عَجِبْتُ مِنْ إِبْلِيسَ فِي تِيهِهِ ... وَقُبْحِ مَا أَظْهَرَ مِنْ نَخْوَتِهْ

I marveled at Iblis in his confusion…And the hideousness of the arrogance that he displayed

تَاهَ عَلَى آدَمَ فِي سَجْدَةٍ ... وَصَارَ قَوَّادًا لِذُرِّيَّتِهْ

He became lost in prostration before Adam…And became a pimp for his progeny

فَأَصْلُ كُلِّ مَعْصِيَةٍ وَبَلَاءٍ إِنَّمَا هُوَ الْوَسْوَسَةُ، فَلِهَذَا وَصَفَهُ بِهَا لِتَكُونَ الِاسْتِعَاذَةُ مِنْ شَرِّهَا أَهَمَّ مِنْ كُلِّ مُسْتَعَاذٍ مِنْهُ، وَإِلَّا فَشَرُّهُ بِغَيْرِ الْوَسْوَسَةِ حَاصِلٌ أَيْضًا."

[100] Maryam 83.

[101] These verses of poetry are from the famous poet Abū Nawwās (d. 198 AH رَحِمَهُ اللَّهُ).

Thus, every sin and affliction is ultimately rooted in whispering. That is why Allah described seeking refuge from it as more important than seeking refuge from anything else. Otherwise, his evil would also be achieved without whispering."

## THE MAIN CATEGORIES OF EVIL THAT SHAYTĀN INVITES TO

Ibn al Qayyim (رَحِمَهُ ٱللَّهُ) discusses at length many types of evil that Shayṭān entices people to and then summarizes the main overarching categories, saying:[102]

فَإِذَا كَانَ هَذَا شَأْنُهُ وَهِمَّتُهُ فِي الشَّرِّ، فَكَيْفَ الْخَلَاصُ مِنْهُ إِلَّا بِمَعُونَةِ اللَّهِ وَتَأْيِيدِهِ وَإِعَاذَتِهِ! وَلَا يُمْكِنُ حَصْرُ أَجْنَاسِ شَرِّهِ فَضْلًا عَنْ آحَادِهَا، إِذْ كُلُّ شَرٍّ فِي الْعَالَمِ فَهُوَ السَّبَبُ فِيهِ، وَلَكِنْ يَنْحَصِرُ شَرُّهُ فِي سِتَّةِ أَجْنَاسٍ، لَا يَزَالُ بِابْنِ آدَمَ حَتَّى يَنَالَ مِنْهُ وَاحِدًا مِنْهَا أَوْ أَكْثَرَ:

If this is his reality and ambition in causing evil, then how can one be saved from him except through the assistance, support, and seeking refuge in Allah? It is impossible to enumerate all the types of his evil, let alone its individual manifestations as every evil in the world is caused by him. However, his evil can be classified into six categories, and he continues to target the children of Adam until he achieves one or more of these:

الشَّرُّ الْأَوَّلُ: شَرُّ الْكُفْرِ وَالشِّرْكِ وَمُعَادَاةِ اللَّهِ وَرَسُولِهِ، فَإِذَا ظَفِرَ بِذَلِكَ مِنَ ابْنِ آدَمَ بَرَدَ أَنِينُهُ، وَاسْتَرَاحَ مِنْ تَعَبِهِ مَعَهُ، وَهُوَ أَوَّلُ مَا يُرِيدُهُ مِنَ الْعَبْدِ، فَلَا يَزَالُ بِهِ حَتَّى يَنَالَهُ مِنْهُ، فَإِذَا نَالَ ذَلِكَ مِنْهُ صَيَّرَهُ مِنْ جُنُودِهِ وَعَسْكَرِهِ، وَاسْتَنَابَهُ عَلَى أَمْثَالِهِ وَأَشْكَالِهِ، فَصَارَ مِنْ دُعَاةِ إِبْلِيسَ وَنُوَّابِهِ.

1. The first type of evil is disbelief, polytheism, and enmity towards Allah and His Messenger. If he succeeds with a person, his moaning will be silenced, and he will find relief from further hardship. This is the primary thing he desires from a servant. He continues to pursue them until he achieves it, turning them into one of his soldiers and part of his legions, deputizing them to

[102] *Badā'i al Fawā'id, Tafsīr al Mu'awwidhatayn.*

recruit similar people. They become callers to the cause of *Shayṭān* and his deputies.

فَإِنْ يَئِسَ مِنْهُ مِنْ ذَلِكَ، وَكَانَ مِمَّنْ سَبَقَ لَهُ الْإِسْلَامُ فِي بَطْنِ أُمِّهِ، نَقَلَهُ إِلَى الْمَرْتَبَةِ الثَّانِيَةِ مِنَ الشَّرِّ، وَهِيَ الْبِدْعَةُ، وَهِيَ أَحَبُّ إِلَيْهِ مِنَ الْفُسُوقِ وَالْمَعَاصِي؛ لِأَنَّ ضَرَرَهَا فِي نَفْسِ الدِّينِ وَهُوَ ضَرَرٌ مُتَعَدٍّ، وَهِيَ ذَنْبٌ لَا يُتَابُ مِنْهُ، وَهِيَ مُخَالَفَةٌ لِدَعْوَةِ الرُّسُلِ، وَدَعْوَةٌ إِلَى خِلَافِ مَا جَاءُوا بِهِ، وَهِيَ بَابُ الْكُفْرِ وَالشِّرْكِ، فَإِذَا نَالَ مِنْهُ الْبِدْعَةَ وَجَعَلَهُ مِنْ أَهْلِهَا بَقِيَ أَيْضًا نَائِبَهُ وَدَاعِيًا مِنْ دُعَاتِهِ.

2. If he despairs achieving that with someone who was already predestined for Islam from their mother's womb, he moves them to the second level of evil, which is innovation (*bid'ah*). It is more believed to him than disobedience and sins because the harm of innovation extends to the very essence of the religion, and it is a sin not repented from. It contradicts the call of the messengers and calls for the opposite of what they came with. It is the gateway to disbelief and polytheism. If he succeeds in leading them into innovation, making them its adherents, they too become his deputies and callers.

فَإِنْ أَعْجَزَهُ مِنْ هَذِهِ الْمَرْتَبَةِ، وَكَانَ الْعَبْدُ مِمَّنْ سَبَقَتْ لَهُ مِنَ اللَّهِ مَوْهَبَةُ السُّنَّةِ وَمُعَادَاةُ أَهْلِ الْبِدَعِ وَالضَّلَالِ، نَقَلَهُ إِلَى الْمَرْتَبَةِ الثَّالِثَةِ مِنَ الشَّرِّ، وَهِيَ الْكَبَائِرُ عَلَى اخْتِلَافِ أَنْوَاعِهَا، فَهُوَ أَشَدُّ حِرْصًا عَلَى أَنْ يُوقِعَهُ فِيهَا، وَلَا سِيَّمَا إِنْ كَانَ عَالِمًا مَتْبُوعًا، فَهُوَ حَرِيصٌ عَلَى ذَلِكَ لِيُنَفِّرَ النَّاسَ عَنْهُ، ثُمَّ يُشِيعُ مِنْ ذُنُوبِهِ وَمَعَاصِيهِ فِي النَّاسِ وَيَسْتَنِيبُ مِنْهُمْ مَنْ يُشِيعُهَا وَيُذِيعُهَا تَدَيُّنًا وَتَقَرُّبًا بِزَعْمِهِ إِلَى اللَّهِ تَعَالَى، وَهُوَ نَائِبُ إِبْلِيسَ وَلَا يَشْعُرُ،

3. If he fails to achieve that level with someone predestined to possess the blessing of adhering to the Sunnah and opposing the people of innovation and misguidance, he takes them to the third level of evil, which includes major sins in their various forms. He is more eager to ensnare them in this category, especially if they are knowledgeable and followed. He is eager for this to turn

people away from them. Then he spreads their sins and transgressions among the people and deputizes those who spread and publicize them, claiming that they do so for the sake of the religion and to seek nearness to Allah. They become deputies of Satan without realizing.

فَإِنَّ الَّذِينَ يُحِبُّونَ أَنْ تَشِيعَ الْفَاحِشَةُ فِي الَّذِينَ آمَنُوا لَهُمْ عَذَابٌ أَلِيمٌ، هَذَا إِذَا أَحَبُّوا إِشَاعَتَهَا وَإِذَاعَتَهَا، فَكَيْفَ إِذَا تَوَلَّوْا هُمْ إِشَاعَتَهَا وَإِذَاعَتَهَا لَا نَصِيحَةً مِنْهُمْ، وَلَكِنْ طَاعَةً لِإِبْلِيسَ وَنِيَابَةً عَنْهُ؟! كُلَّ ذَلِكَ لِيَنْفِرَ النَّاسَ عَنْهُ، وَعَنِ الِانْتِفَاعِ بِهِ، وَذُنُوبُ هَذَا وَلَوْ بَلَغَتْ عَنَانَ السَّمَاءِ أَهْوَنُ عِنْدَ اللَّهِ مِنْ ذُنُوبِ هَؤُلَاءِ،

Those who love to spread obscenity among the believers will face a painful punishment. That is the case if they love to spread and propagate it. So, what if they spread and propagate it, not out of sincere advice but out of obedience to Satan and his deputies? All of this is done to distance people from benefiting from them. Even if the sins (of those defamed) were to reach the skies, they are insignificant before Allah compared to the sins of these individuals.

فَإِنَّهَا ظُلْمٌ مِنْهُ لِنَفْسِهِ، إِذَا اسْتَغْفَرَ اللَّهَ وَتَابَ إِلَيْهِ قَبِلَ اللَّهُ وَتَوْبَتَهُ، وَبَدَّلَ سَيِّئَاتِهِ حَسَنَاتٍ، وَأَمَّا ذُنُوبُ أُولَئِكَ فَظُلْمٌ لِلْمُؤْمِنِينَ وَتَتَبُّعٌ لِعَوْرَتِهِمْ وَقَصْدٌ لِفَضِيحَتِهِمْ، وَاللَّهُ -سُبْحَانَهُ- بِالْمِرْصَادِ لَا تَخْفَى عَلَيْهِ كَمَائِنُ الصُّدُورِ وَدَسَائِسُ النُّفُوسِ.

Their sins are an injustice to themselves. However, if they seek forgiveness from Allah, repent to Him, and replace their evil deeds with good ones, Allah accepts their repentance. As for the sins of those individuals, they are an injustice to the believers, a violation of their honor and are done out of an intention to disgrace them. Allah is ever watchful, and the secrets of hearts and the schemes of souls are not hidden from Him.

فَإِنْ أَعْجَزَ الشَّيْطَانَ عَنْ هَذِهِ الْمَرَاتِبِ، نَقَلَهُ إِلَى الْمَرْتَبَةِ الرَّابِعَةِ وَهِيَ: الصَّغَائِرُ الَّتِي إِذَا اجْتَمَعَتْ فَرُبَّمَا أَهْلَكَتْ صَاحِبَهَا، كَمَا قَالَ النَّبِيُّ صَلَّى اللَّهُ عَلَيْهِ وَسَلَّمَ:

**"إِيَّاكُمْ وَمُحَقَّرَاتِ الذُّنُوبِ، فَإِنَّ مَثَلَ ذَلِكَ مَثَلُ قَوْمٍ نَزَلُوا بِفَلَاةٍ مِنَ الْأَرْضِ ... "،** وَذَكَرَ حَدِيثًا مَعْنَاهُ: أَنَّ كُلَّ وَاحِدٍ مِنْهُمْ جَاءَ بِعُودِ حَطَبٍ حَتَّى أَوْقَدُوا نَارًا عَظِيمَةً فَطَبَخُوا وَاشْتَوَوْا، وَلَا يَزَالُ يُسَهِّلُ عَلَيْهِ أَمْرَ الصَّغَائِرِ حَتَّى يَسْتَهِينَ بِهَا، فَيَكُونُ صَاحِبُ الْكَبِيرَةِ الْخَائِفُ مِنْهَا أَحْسَنَ حَالًا مِنْهُ.

If he escapes *Shayṭān* in the previous level, he moves the person to the fourth level, which is the minor sins. When these minor sins accumulate, they may destroy the person. As the Prophet (ﷺ) said, "**Beware of the minor sins, for they gather on a person until they destroy him, like a group of people descending into a valley...**" Then he (ﷺ) mentioned a narration that means: Each of them gathers firewood, bringing one stick after another, until they kindle a great fire and cook their food. *Shayṭān* continues to make minor sins seem easy and insignificant to people, to such an extent that someone who commits a major sin while being afraid (of punishment) is in a better condition than them.

فَإِنْ أَعْجَزَهُ الْعَبْدُ مِنْ هَذِهِ الْمَرْتَبَةِ، نَقَلَهُ إِلَى الْمَرْتَبَةِ الْخَامِسَةِ، وَهِيَ إِشْغَالُهُ بِالْمُبَاحَاتِ الَّتِي لَا ثَوَابَ فِيهَا وَلَا عِقَابَ، بَلْ عِقَابُهَا فَوَاتُ الثَّوَابِ الَّذِي ضَاعَ عَلَيْهِ بِاشْتِغَالِهِ بِهَا.

If the servant escapes the influence of minor sins, *Shayṭān* takes them to the fifth level, which involves preoccupying them with permissible matters that neither brings reward nor punishment. However, the punishment in engaging in these permissible matters is missing out on the reward that could have been attained (if one had been preoccupied with more virtuous actions.)

فَإِنْ أَعْجَزَهُ الْعَبْدُ مِنْ هَذِهِ الْمَرْتَبَةِ وَكَانَ حَافِظًا لِوَقْتِهِ شَحِيحًا بِهِ، يَعْلَمُ مِقْدَارَ أَنْفَاسِهِ وَانْقِطَاعَهَا وَمَا يُقَابِلُهَا مِنَ النَّعِيمِ وَالْعَذَابِ، نَقَلَهُ إِلَى الْمَرْتَبَةِ السَّادِسَةِ، وَهُوَ: أَنْ يُشْغِلَهُ بِالْعَمَلِ الْمُفَضَّلِ عَمَّا هُوَ أَفْضَلُ مِنْهُ، لِيَزِحَّ عَنْهُ الْفَضِيلَةَ وَيُفَوِّتَهُ

ثَوَابَ الْعَمَلِ الْفَاضِلِ، فَيَأْمُرُهُ بِفِعْلِ الْخَيْرِ الْمُفَضَّلِ، وَيُحَضِّهِ عَلَيْهِ، وَيُحْسِنُهُ لَهُ، إِذَا تَضَمَّنَ تَرْكَ مَا هُوَ أَفْضَلُ وَأَعْلَى مِنْهُ،

If the servant escapes him in this level, and if they are mindful of their time and aware of the value of their passing moments and the consequences that follow of (eternal) bliss and punishment (in the Hereafter), *Shayṭān* moves them to the sixth level. In this level, *Shayṭān* distracts the person with lesser deeds while neglecting more virtuous and superior actions. *Shayṭān* commands them to perform the lesser good deeds, encourages them to do so, and beautifies them in their eyes. Thus, they neglect what is better and higher in favor of the lesser.

وَقَلَّ مِنْ يَتَنَبَّهُ لِهَذَا مِنَ النَّاسِ، فَإِنَّهُ إِذَا رَأَى فِيهِ دَاعِيًا قَوِيًّا وَمُحَرِّكًا إِلَى نَوْعٍ مِنَ الطَّاعَةِ لَا يَشُكُّ أَنَّهُ طَاعَةٌ وَقُرْبَةٌ، فَإِنَّهُ لَا يَكَادُ يَقُولُ: إِنَّ هَذَا الدَّاعِي مِنَ الشَّيْطَانِ، فَإِنَّ الشَّيْطَانَ لَا يَأْمُرُ بِخَيْرٍ، وَيَرَى أَنَّ هَذَا خَيْرٌ، فَيَقُولُ: هَذَا الدَّاعِي مِنَ اللَّهِ، وَهُوَ مَعْذُورٌ، وَلَمْ يَصِلْ عِلْمُهُ إِلَى أَنَّ الشَّيْطَانَ يَأْمُرُهُ بِسَبْعِينَ بَابًا مِنْ أَبْوَابِ الْخَيْرِ، إِمَا لِيَتَوَصَّلَ بِهَا إِلَى بَابٍ وَاحِدٍ مِنَ الشَّرِّ، وَإِمَا لِيُفَوِّتَ بِهَا خَيْرًا أَعْظَمَ مِنْ تِلْكَ السَّبْعِينَ بَابًا وَأَجَلَّ وَأَفْضَلَ.

Unfortunately, very few people are aware of this reality. When they encounter an inner summoning that is strong and motivates them towards a particular type of obedience, they do not doubt it to be an act of obedience and nearness to Allah. They do not consider that it may be an inner summoning from *Shayṭān*. They believe the caller is from Allah and are excused for doing so. They are unaware that Satan may command them with seventy gates of goodness, either to lead them to one gate of evil or to make them miss out on a more excellent and virtuous opportunity.

وَهَذَا لَا يُتَوَصَّلُ إِلَى مَعْرِفَتِهِ إِلَّا بِنُورٍ مِنَ اللَّهِ يَقْذِفُهُ فِي قَلْبِ الْعَبْدِ يَكُونُ سَبَبُهُ تَجْرِيدَ مُتَابَعَةِ الرَّسُولِ - صَلَّى اللَّهُ عَلَيْهِ وَسَلَّمَ - وَشِدَّةِ عِنَايَتِهِ بِمَرَاتِبِ الْأَعْمَالِ

عِنْدَ اللَّهِ وَأَحَبَّهَا إِلَيْهِ وَأَرْضَاهَا لَهُ، وَأَنْفَعَهَا لِلْعَبْدِ، وَأَعَمَّهَا نَصِيحَةً لِلَّهِ - تَعَالَى - وَلِرَسُولِهِ وَلِكِتَابِهِ وَلِعِبَادِهِ الْمُؤْمِنِينَ خَاصَّتِهِمْ وَعَامَّتِهِمْ، وَلَا يَعْرِفُ هَذَا إِلَّا مَنْ كَانَ مِنْ وَرَثَةِ الرَّسُولِ - صَلَّى اللَّهُ عَلَيْهِ وَسَلَّمَ - وَنَوَابِهِ فِي الْأُمَّةِ وَخُلَفَائِهِ فِي الْأَرْضِ، وَأَكْثَرُ الْخَلْقِ مَحْجُوبُونَ عَنْ ذَلِكَ فَلَا يَخْطُرُ بِقُلُوبِهِمْ، وَاللَّهُ تَعَالَى يَمُنُّ بِفَضْلِهِ عَلَى مَنْ يَشَاءُ مِنْ عِبَادِهِ.

This understanding can only be attained through divine guidance and illumination in the servant's heart. This illumination is achieved by closely following the Messenge This illumination is achieved by closely following the Messenger (ﷺ), understanding the ranks of deeds in the sight of Allah, and knowing which deeds are more beloved to Him, more pleasing to Him, more beneficial to the servant, and more sincere for Allah, His Messenger, His Book, and His believing servants from the laypeople and the leaders. Only the Prophet's (ﷺ) inheritors, his deputies in the ummah, and his successors on Earth possess this knowledge. Most people are veiled from this understanding, and Allah (سُبْحَانَهُ وَتَعَالَى) bestows His favor on whom He wills among His servants.

فَإِذَا أَعْجَزَهُ الْعَبْدُ مِنْ هَذِهِ الْمَرَاتِبِ السِّتِّ وَأَعْيَا عَلَيْهِ سَلَّطَ عَلَيْهِ حِزْبَهُ مِنَ الْإِنْسِ وَالْجِنِّ بِأَنْوَاعِ الْأَذَى وَالتَّكْفِيرِ لَهُ وَالتَّضْلِيلِ وَالتَّبْدِيعِ وَالتَّحْذِيرِ مِنْهُ، وَقَصْدِ إِخْمَالِهِ وَإِطْفَائِهِ لِيُشَوِّشَ عَلَيْهِ قَلْبَهُ وَيُشْغِلَ بِحَرْبِهِ فِكْرَهُ، وَلِيَمْنَعَ النَّاسَ مِنَ الِانْتِفَاعِ بِهِ، فَيَبْقَى سَعْيُهُ فِي تَسْلِيطِ الْمُبْطِلِينَ مِنْ شَيَاطِينِ الْإِنْسِ وَالْجِنِّ عَلَيْهِ، لَا يَفْتُرُ وَلَا يَنِي، فَحِينَئِذٍ يَلْبَسُ الْمُؤْمِنُ لَأْمَةَ الْحَرْبِ وَلَا يَضَعُهَا عَنْهُ إِلَى الْمَوْتِ، وَمَتَى وَضَعَهَا أُسِرَ أَوْ أُصِيبَ، فَلَا يَزَالُ فِي جِهَادٍ حَتَّى يَلْقَى اللَّهَ.

When the servant escapes him in these six levels and exhausts his efforts, he unleashes his troops of jinn and humans upon the person. They inflict harm upon them, accuse them of disbelief, label them as misguided, accuse them of innovation, warn others against them, and seek to diminish their status and extinguish their influence. They aim is to confuse the person's heart, occupy their thoughts with the battle, and prevent people from benefiting from them. He continues striving, unfaltering and unrelenting, to unleash the people of falsehood from the devils of the humans and jinn against him. At this point, the believer clothes himself in the mantle of war and does not remove it until death. Whenever he removes it, he is either taken captive or injured. So he does not relinquish the struggle until he meets Allah.

فَتَأَمَّلْ هَـذَا الْفَصْلَ وَتَدَبَّرْ مَوْقِعَهُ وَعَظِيمَ مَنْفَعَتِهِ، وَاجْعَلْهُ مِيزَانًا لَكَ تَزِنُ بِهِ النَّاسَ وَتَزِنُّ بِهِ الْأَعْمَالَ، فَإِنَّهُ يُطْلِعُكَ عَلَى حَقَائِقِ الْوُجُودِ وَمَرَاتِبِ الْخَلْقِ، وَاللَّهُ الْمُسْتَعَانُ، وَعَلَيْهِ التُّكْلَانُ، وَلَوْ لَمْ يَكُنْ فِي هَـذَا التَّعْلِيقِ إِلَّا هَـذَا الْفَصْلُ لَكَانَ نَافِعًا لِمَنْ تَدَبَّرَهُ وَوَعَاهُ.

Reflect upon this discussion, ponder its significance, and use it as a criterion to weigh people and actions. It will reveal to you the realities of existence and the ranks of creation. Allah is sought for assistance and trusted. If this section alone were the only in this commentary, it would benefit those who reflect upon it and take heed."

# Chapter 4

## Angels, Devils, & the War Within

*Humility is One of the Greatest Causes of Angelic Support*

*The Touch of an Angel & the Touch of a Devil*

*A Broad Outline of the War Within*

*A Fuller Description of the War Within*

# 4. ANGELS, DEVILS, & THE WAR WITHIN

The angels are the allies of the believers in this world and the next. Allah (سُبْحَانَهُ وَتَعَالَىٰ) said:

{نَحْنُ أَوْلِيَاؤُكُمْ فِي الْحَيَاةِ الدُّنْيَا وَفِي الْآخِرَةِ ۖ وَلَكُمْ فِيهَا مَا تَشْتَهِي أَنفُسُكُمْ وَلَكُمْ فِيهَا مَا تَدَّعُونَ}

**"We [angels] were your allies in worldly life and [are so] in the Hereafter. And you will have therein whatever your souls desire, and you will have therein whatever you request [or wish]."**

Ibn Kathīr (d. 774 AH رَحِمَهُ ٱللَّهُ) comments:[103]

"أَيْ: قُرَنَاءَكُمْ فِي الْحَيَاةِ الدُّنْيَا، نُسَدِّدُكُمْ وَنُوَفِّقُكُمْ، وَنَحْفَظُكُمْ بِأَمْرِ اللَّهِ، وَكَذَلِكَ نَكُونُ مَعَكُمْ فِي الْآخِرَةِ نُؤْنِسُ مِنكُمُ الْوَحْشَةَ فِي الْقُبُورِ، وَعِنْدَ النَّفْخَةِ فِي الصُّورِ، وَنُؤَمِّنُكُمْ يَوْمَ الْبَعْثِ وَالنُّشُورِ، وَنُجَاوِزُ بِكُمُ الصِّرَاطَ الْمُسْتَقِيمَ، وَنُوصِلُكُمْ إِلَى جَنَّاتِ النَّعِيمِ".

"That is, your companions in this worldly life, we support, guide, and protect you by the command of Allah. And likewise, we will be with you in the Hereafter, alleviating your loneliness in the graves, and during the blowing in the trumpet. We will provide you with security on the Day of Resurrection and gathering, guide you across the straight path, and lead you to the Gardens of Bliss."

---

[103] *Tafsīr al Qur'ān al 'Aẓīm.*

Burhān al-Dīn al Baqā'ī (d 885 AH رَحِمَهُ ٱللَّهُ) says:[104]

"{**نَحْنُ أَوْلِيَاؤُكُمْ**} أَيْ أَقْرَبُ الْأَقْرِبَاءِ إِلَيْكُمْ، فَنَحْنُ نَفْعَلُ مَعَكُمْ كُلَّ مَا يُمْكِنُ أَنْ يَفْعَلَهُ الْقَرِيبُ {**فِي الْحَيَاةِ الدُّنْيَا**} نَجْتَلِبُ لَكُمُ الْمَسَرَّاتِ وَنُبْعِدُ عَنْكُمُ الْمَضَرَّاتِ وَنَحْمِلُكُمْ عَلَى جَمِيعِ الْخَيْرَاتِ بِحَيْثُ يَكُونُ لَكُمْ فِيهَا مَا تُؤْثِرُهُ الْعُقُولُ بِالْامْتِنَاعِ مِمَّا تَهْوَاهُ النُّفُوسُ، وَإِنْ تَرَاءَى لِلرَّائِينَ فِي الدُّنْيَا أَنَّ الْأَمْرَ بِخِلَافِ ذَلِكَ، فَنُوقِظُكُمْ مِنَ الْمَنَامِ، وَنَحْمِلُكُمْ عَلَى الصَّلَاةِ وَالصِّيَامِ، وَنُبْعِدُكُمْ عَنِ الْآثَامِ، ضِدَّ مَا تَفْعَلُهُ الشَّيَاطِينُ مَعَ أَوْلِيَائِهِمْ".

"'**We were your allies**' that is, we are the closest of those near and dear to you, so we do everything with you that a close relative does; "**in worldly life**," [meaning] we bring you causes of joy, ward off harm from you, and drive you towards all that is good to the point that your intellect prefers it over what your souls desire. Even if it appears to the onlookers in this life that the situation is contrary to this. We awaken you from your sleep, guide you towards prayer and fasting, and keep you away from sins, contrary to what the devils do with their allies."

---

Al-Sa'dī (d. 1376 AH رَحِمَهُ ٱللَّهُ) commented on this verse:[105]

"يَحُثُّونَهُمْ فِي الدُّنْيَا عَلَى الْخَيْرِ، وَيُزَيِّنُونَهُ لَهُمْ، وَيُرَهِّبُونَهُمْ عَنِ الشَّرِّ، وَيُقَبِّحُونَهُ فِي قُلُوبِهِمْ، وَيَدْعُونَ اللَّهَ لَهُمْ، وَيُثَبِّتُونَهُمْ عِنْدَ الْمَصَائِبِ وَالْمَخَاوِفِ، وَخُصُوصًا عِنْدَ الْمَوْتِ وَشِدَّتِهِ، وَالْقَبْرِ وَظُلْمَتِهِ، وَفِي الْقِيَامَةِ وَأَهْوَالِهَا، وَعَلَى الصِّرَاطِ، وَفِي الْجَنَّةِ يُهَنِّئُونَهُمْ بِكَرَامَةِ رَبِّهِمْ، وَيَدْخُلُونَ عَلَيْهِمْ مِنْ كُلِّ بَابٍ {**سَلَامٌ عَلَيْكُمْ بِمَا صَبَرْتُمْ فَنِعْمَ عُقْبَى الدَّارِ**}".

"They encourage them towards goodness in this world, beautify it for them, deter them from evil and make it unattractive

---

[104] *Naẓm al-Durar fī Tanāsub al Ayāt wal-Suwar* (17/184).

[105] *Tafsīr al-Sa'dī.*

in their hearts. They pray to Allah for them, and offer them support during hardships and fears, especially during the severity of death, in the darkness of the grave, during the horrors of the Day of Resurrection, and on the Path of Righteousness. In Paradise, they congratulate them on the generosity of their Lord, and they enter upon them from every gate, saying '**Peace be upon you for your patience. So how excellent is the final home'**."

---

Ibn al Qayyim (رَحِمَهُ ٱللَّهُ) explains in greater detail this angelic support for the believers and contrasts it with the demonic support for the wicked. He says:[106]

"فَالنَّفْسُ السَّمَاوِيَّةُ بَيْنَهَا وَبَيْنَ الْمَلَائِكَةِ وَالرَّفِيقِ الْأَعْلَىٰ مُنَاسَبَةٌ طَبِيعِيَّةٌ بِهَا مَالَتْ إِلَىٰ أَوْصَافِهِمْ، وَأَخْلَاقِهِمْ، وَأَعْمَالِهِمْ.

"The heavenly soul has a naturally affinity for the angels and *al-rafīq al 'alā* (the deceased heavenly souls,) by way of which they incline towards their qualities, morals and actions.

فَالْمَلَائِكَةُ أَوْلِيَاءُ هَذَا النَّوْعِ فِي الدُّنْيَا وَالآخِرَةِ، قال تعالى: {**إِنَّ الَّذِينَ قَالُوا رَبُّنَا اللَّهُ ثُمَّ اسْتَقَامُوا تَتَنَزَّلُ عَلَيْهِمُ الْمَلَائِكَةُ أَلَّا تَخَافُوا وَلَا تَحْزَنُوا وَأَبْشِرُوا بِالْجَنَّةِ الَّتِي كُنْتُمْ تُوعَدُونَ (30) نَحْنُ أَوْلِيَاؤُكُمْ فِي الْحَيَاةِ الدُّنْيَا وَفِي الْآخِرَةِ وَلَكُمْ فِيهَا مَا تَشْتَهِي [98 أ] أَنْفُسُكُمْ وَلَكُمْ فِيهَا مَا تَدَّعُونَ (31) نُزُلًا مِنْ غَفُورٍ رَحِيمٍ**}.

The angels are the protectors of this type of soul in this world and the Hereafter. Allah (سُبْحَانَهُ وَتَعَالَىٰ) says: **"Verily, those who say: 'Our Lord is Allah (Alone),' and then they stand firm, on them the angels will descend (at the time of their death) (saying): 'Fear not, nor grieve! But receive the glad tidings of**

---

[106] Rawḍah al Muḥibbīn, chapter 20 (p. 367).

**Paradise which you have been promised! We have been your friends in the life of this world and are (so) in the Hereafter. Therein you shall have (all) that your inner selves desire, and therein you shall have (all) for which you ask for. An entertainment from (Allah), the Oft-Forgiving, Most Merciful."**[107]

فَالْمَلَكُ يَتَوَلَّىٰ مَنْ يُنَاسِبُهُ بِالنُّصْحِ لَهُ، وَالْإِرْشَادِ، وَالتَّثْبِيتِ، وَالتَّعْلِيمِ، وَإِلْقَاءِ الصَّوَابِ عَلَىٰ لِسَانِهِ، وَدَفْعِ عَدُوِّهِ عَنْهُ، وَالِاسْتِغْفَارِ لَهُ إِذَا زَلَّ، وَتَذَكُّرِهِ إِذَا نَسِيَ، وَتَسْلِيَتِهِ إِذَا حَزِنَ، وَإِلْقَاءِ السَّكِينَةِ فِي قَلْبِهِ إِذَا خَافَ، وَإِيقَاظِهِ لِلصَّلَاةِ إِذَا نَامَ عَنْهَا، وَإِيعَادِ صَاحِبِهِ بِالْخَيْرِ، وَحَضِّهِ عَلَىٰ التَّصْدِيقِ بِالْوَعْدِ، وَتَحْذِيرِهِ مِنَ الرُّكُونِ إِلَىٰ الدُّنْيَا، وَتَقْصِيرِ أَمَلِهِ، وَتَرْغِيبِهِ فِيمَا عِنْدَ اللَّهِ،

The angel takes care of those who are suitable for them by advising, guidance, reinforcement, education, conveying the truth on his tongue, repelling his enemy from him, seeking forgiveness for him if he errs, reminding him if he forgets, consoling him if he is sad, instilling tranquility in his heart if he is afraid, waking him up for prayer if he is asleep at its time, promising him goodness for righteousness, encouraging him to believe in (Allah's) promise, warning him against being attached to this world, limiting his worldly hopes, and urging him towards what Allah has.

فَهُوَ أَنِيسُهُ فِي الْوَحْدَةِ، وَوَلِيُّهُ، وَمُعَلِّمُهُ، وَمُثَبِّتُهُ، وَمُسَكِّنُ جَأْشِهِ، وَمُرَغِّبُهُ فِي الْخَيْرِ، وَمُحَذِّرُهُ مِنَ الشَّرِّ، يَسْتَغْفِرُ لَهُ إِنْ أَسَاءَ، وَيَدْعُو لَهُ بِالثَّبَاتِ إِنْ أَحْسَنَ، وَإِنْ بَاتَ طَاهِرًا يَذْكُرُ اللَّهَ؛ بَاتَ مَعَهُ فِي شِعَارِهِ، فَإِنْ قَصَدَهُ عَدُوٌّ لَهُ بِسُوءٍ وَهُوَ نَائِمٌ؛ دَفَعَهُ عَنْهُ.

He is his companion in solitude and his protector, teacher, reinforcement, soother of his temperament, encourager of good deeds, and warner against evil. If he errs, he seeks forgiveness for

---

[107] Fussilat, 30-32.

him, and if he does well, he prays for his steadfastness. If he goes to sleep in a state of ritual purity while in remembrance of Allah, he spends the night with him in his hair. If any enemy intends to harm him while he is asleep, he defends him from it.

وَالشَّيَاطِينُ أَوْلِيَاءُ النَّوْعِ الثَّانِي، يُخْرِجُونَهُمْ مِنَ النُّورِ إِلَى الظُّلُمَاتِ. قال الله تعالى: {**تَاللَّهِ لَقَدْ أَرْسَلْنَا إِلَى أُمَمٍ مِنْ قَبْلِكَ فَزَيَّنَ لَهُمُ الشَّيْطَانُ أَعْمَالَهُمْ فَهُوَ وَلِيُّهُمُ الْيَوْمَ**} وقال تعالى: {**كُتِبَ عَلَيْهِ أَنَّهُ مَنْ تَوَلَّاهُ فَأَنَّهُ يُضِلُّهُ وَيَهْدِيهِ إِلَى عَذَابِ السَّعِيرِ**} وقال تعالى: {**وَمَنْ يَتَّخِذِ الشَّيْطَانَ وَلِيًّا مِنْ دُونِ اللَّهِ فَقَدْ خَسِرَ خُسْرَانًا مُبِينًا (119) يَعِدُهُمْ وَيُمَنِّيهِمْ وَمَا يَعِدُهُمُ الشَّيْطَانُ إِلَّا غُرُورًا (120) أُولَئِكَ مَأْوَاهُمْ جَهَنَّمُ وَلَا يَجِدُونَ عَنْهَا مَحِيصًا**}، وقال تعالى: {**وَإِذْ قُلْنَا لِلْمَلَائِكَةِ اسْجُدُوا لِآدَمَ فَسَجَدُوا إِلَّا إِبْلِيسَ كَانَ مِنَ الْجِنِّ فَفَسَقَ عَنْ أَمْرِ رَبِّهِ أَفَتَتَّخِذُونَهُ وَذُرِّيَّتَهُ أَوْلِيَاءَ مِنْ دُونِي وَهُمْ لَكُمْ عَدُوٌّ بِئْسَ لِلظَّالِمِينَ بَدَلًا**}.

And the devils are the allies of the second type [of people], leading them from light to darkness. Allah (سُبْحَانَهُ وَتَعَالَىٰ) says: "**By Allah, We indeed sent (Messengers) to the nations before you (O Muhammad ﷺ), but Shayṭān made their deeds fair-seeming to them. So he is their Wali (helper) today (i.e. in this world).**"[108] And He (سُبْحَانَهُ وَتَعَالَىٰ) also says: "**For him (the devil) it is decreed that whosoever follows him, he will mislead him, and will drive him to the torment of the Fire.**"[109] And He (سُبْحَانَهُ وَتَعَالَىٰ) says: "**And whoever takes Shayṭān as a Wali (protector or helper) instead of Allah, has surely suffered a manifest loss. He makes promises to them, and arouses in them false desires; and Shayṭān's (Satan) promises are nothing but deceptions.**"[110] And He (سُبْحَانَهُ وَتَعَالَىٰ) says: "**And (remember) when We said to the angels; 'Prostrate to Adam.'**

---

[108] An-Nahl: 63.

[109] Al-Hajj: 4.

[110] An-Nisa: 119-121.

**So they prostrated except Iblis. He was one of the jinn; he disobeyed the Command of his Lord. Will you then take him (Iblis) and his offspring as protectors and helpers rather than Me while they are enemies to you? What an evil is the exchange for the wrong-doers."**[111]

فَهَذَا النَّوْعُ بَيْنَ نُفُوسِهِمْ وَبَيْنَ الشَّيَاطِينِ مُنَاسَبَةٌ طَبِيعِيَّةٌ، بِهَا مَالَتْ إِلَى أَوْصَافِهِمْ، وَأَخْلَاقِهِمْ، وَأَعْمَالِهِمْ، فَالشَّيَاطِينُ تَتَوَلَّاهُمْ بِضَدِّ مَا تَتَوَلَّى بِهِ الْمَلَائِكَةُ مَنْ نَاسَبَهُمْ، فَتَؤُزُّهُمْ إِلَى الْمَعَاصِي أَزًّا، وَتُزْعِجُهُمْ إِلَيْهَا إِزْعَاجًا، وَيُزَيِّنُونَ لَهُمُ الْقَبَائِحَ، وَيُخَفِّفُونَهَا عَلَى قُلُوبِهِمْ، وَيُحِلُّونَهَا فِي نُفُوسِهِمْ،

This type [of people] have a natural affinity with the devils by which they incline towards their qualities, morals and actions. The devils support and influence those inclined towards wrongdoing, while the angels protect and watch over those deserving of their guidance. The devils tempt them towards sinful actions and lead them toward distress. They do not feel settled with them, and they beautify ugliness for them, easing it into their hearts and legitimizing it in their souls.

ويُثَقِّلُونَ عَلَيْهِم الطَّاعَاتِ، ويُثَبِّطونهم عنها، ويقبِّحُونها في أعينهم، ويُلْقُونَ عَلَى ألسنَتِهِمْ أَنْوَاعَ الْقَبِيحِ مِنَ الْكَلَامِ، وما لا يُفِيدُ، وَيُزَيِّنُونَهُ في أَسْمَاعَ مَنْ يَسْمَعُهُ مِنْهُمْ

They make obedience heavy for them, discourage them from it, and make it appear ugly. They fill their tongues with all kinds of ugly speech and useless talk, beautifying it for those who hear it from them.

يُبَيِّتُونَ مَعَهُمْ حَيْثُ بَاتُوا وَيُقَيِّلُونَ مَعَهُمْ حَيْثُ قَالُوا، وَيُشَارِكُونَهُمْ فِي أَمْوَالِهِمْ وَأَوْلَادِهِمْ وَنِسَائِهِمْ، يَأْكُلُونَ مَعَهُمْ، وَيَشْرَبُونَ مَعَهُمْ، وَيُجَامِعُونَ مَعَهُمْ، وَيَنَامُونَ مَعَهُمْ. لَا يَسْتَقِرُّونَ مَعَهُ،

---

[111] Al-Kahf: 50.

They spend the night where they stay and speak with them where they speak. They share in their wealth, children, and wives, eating, drinking, having sexual relations, and sleeping with them.

قال الله تعالى: {**وَمَنْ يَكُنِ الشَّيْطَانُ لَهُ قَرِينًا فَسَاءَ قَرِينًا**}، وقال تعالى: {**وَمَنْ يَعْشُ عَنْ ذِكْرِ الرَّحْمَنِ نُقَيِّضْ لَهُ شَيْطَانًا فَهُوَ لَهُ قَرِينٌ (36) وَإِنَّهُمْ لَيَصُدُّونَهُمْ عَنِ السَّبِيلِ وَيَحْسَبُونَ أَنَّهُمْ مُهْتَدُونَ (37) حَتَّى إِذَا جَاءَنَا قَالَ يَالَيْتَ بَيْنِي وَبَيْنَكَ بُعْدَ الْمَشْرِقَيْنِ فَبِئْسَ الْقَرِينُ**}.

Allah (سُبْحَانَهُ وَتَعَالَىٰ) said: "**And whoever is an ally of Shayṭān - then indeed, he is to him a [dangerous] enemy.**"[112] And He (سُبْحَانَهُ وَتَعَالَىٰ) also said: "**And whoever turns away from the remembrance of the Most Merciful - We appoint for him a devil, and he is to him a companion [who misleads].**"[113]

---

[112] Al-Nisā': 38.

[113] Al-Zukhruf: 43:36-37

## HUMILITY IS ONE OF THE GREATEST CAUSES OF ANGELIC SUPPORT

One of the greatest means of angelic support for the believer is humility towards the truth and dealings with people. Allah's Messenger (ﷺ) is reported to have said:[114]

"مَا مِنْ آدَمِيٍ إِلَّا فِي رَأْسِهِ حَكَمَةٌ بِيَدِ مَلَكٍ فَإِذَا تَوَاضَعَ قِيلَ لِلْمَلَكِ ارْفَعْ حَكَمَتَه وَإِذَا تَكَبَّرَ قِيلَ لِلْمَلَكِ ضَعْ حَكَمَتَه"

**"There is no human but there is a jaw-latch in his head, in the hand of an angel. When he is humble, it is said to the angel, 'lift up his jaw-latch.' And when he is arrogant, it is said to the angel, 'put down his jaw-latch (i.e., let go of the reins).'"**

Ibn al Anbārī (d. 328 AH رَحِمَهُ ٱللَّهُ) said:[115]

"قَالَ إِبْرَاهِيمُ: فَمَعْنَى قَوْلِهِ: فِي رَأْسِهِ حَكَمَةٌ مَثَلٌ، قَالَ: وَالْحَكَمَةُ: حَدِيدَةٌ فِي اللِّجَامِ، مُسْتَدِيْرَةٌ عَلَى الْحَنَكِ، تَمْنَعُ الْفَرَسَ مِنَ الْفَسَادِ وَالْجَرِيِّ ... فَلَمَّا كَانَتْ الْحِكْمَةُ تَأْخُذُ بِفَمِ الدَّابَّةِ، وَكَانَ الْحَنَكُ مُتَّصِلًا بِالرَّأْسِ، جَعَلَهَا رَسُولُ اللَّهِ تَمْنَعُ مَنْ هُوَ فِي رَأْسِهِ مِنَ الْكِبْرِ، كَمَا تَمْنَعُ الْحَكَمَةُ الدَّابَّةَ مِنَ الْفَسَادِ وَالْجَرِيِّ."

"Ibrahim said: The meaning of his statement 'in his head is a '*ḥakamah*' (a harness jaw-latch) is a similitude. A '*ḥakamah*' is an iron piece in the harness, revolving on the jaw preventing the horse from misbehaving and running off… So as the jaw-latch bit takes hold of the mouth of the riding animal, and the jaw is

[114] Collected by al-Ṭabarāni in *al Kabīr* from Ibn 'Abbās and al Bazzār in *al Musnad* from Abū Hurayrah. Graded *ḥasan li ghayrihi* by al Albānī in *al-Ṣaḥīḥah* (538) and *Ṣaḥīḥ al-Targhīb wal-Tarhīb* (2895).

[115] *Al-Zāhir fī Ma'ānī Kalimāt al-Nās* (1/397).

connected to the head, the Prophet (ﷺ) made (this similitude) as preventing one who has such a jaw-latch in his head from being arrogant, just as the harness jaw-latch prevents the riding animal from misbehaving and running off."

---

Al Fayūmī (d. 870 AH رَحِمَهُ ٱللَّهُ) said:[116]

"لِأَنَّ الْفَرَسَ إِذَا جَذَبَ حَكَمَتَهُ إِلَى فَوْقَ رَفَعَ رَأْسَهُ، فَكَنَّى بِرَفْعِ الرَّأْسِ عَنْ رَفْعِ الْمَنْزِلَةِ وَالْقَدْرِ. قَالَ الْجَبَّانُ: وَقَدْ يُقَالُ لِلْفَرَسِ كَمَا هُوَ حَكَمَةٌ وَلَهُ عِنْدَنَا حَكَمَةٌ أَيْ قَدْرٌ وَمَنْزِلَةٌ وَهُوَ عَالِي الْحَكَمَةِ. وَقِيلَ الْحَكَمَةُ مِنَ الْإِنْسَانِ أَسْفَلُ وَجْهِهِ مُسْتَعَارٌ مِنْ مَوْضِعِ حَكَمَةِ اللِّجَامِ وَرَفْعِهَا كِنَايَةً عَنِ الْإِعْزَازِ لِأَنَّ مِنْ صِفَةِ الذَّلِيلِ تَنْكِيسُ رَأْسِهِ"

"For the horse, when its reins are pulled upward, it raises its head, hence the metaphor for raising one's status and value by raising the head. Al-Jabān said: The horse can also be referred to as '*ḥakamah*' and be considered by us as having '*ḥakamah*' meaning value and status, hence 'high in *ḥakamah*'. And it's said that person's '*ḥakamah'* is the lower part of his face, metaphorically taken from the position of the reins of the harness and raising it signifies honor because one of the characteristics of the humble is to bow their heads."

---

Al Munāwī (d. 1031 AH رَحِمَهُ ٱللَّهُ) said:[117]

"(حَكَمَةٌ) مَا يُجْعَلُ تَحْتَ حَنَكِ الْدَّابَّة يَمْنَعُهَا الْمُخَالَفَة كَالْلِّجَام (بِيَدِ مَلَكٍ) مُوَكَّلٍ بِهِ (فَإِذَا تَوَاضَعَ) لِلْحَقِّ وَالْخَلْقِ (قِيلَ لِلْمَلَكِ) مِنْ قِبَلِ اللَّهِ (ارْفَعْ حَكَمَتَهُ) أَي قَدْرَهُ وَمَنْزِلَتَهُ (واذا تَكَبَّرَ قِيل لِلْمَلَكِ ضَعْ حَكَمَتَهُ) كِنَايَةٌ عَنْ اِذْلَالِهِ فَإِنَّ مِنْ

---

[116] *Fatḥ al Qarīb al Mujīb 'alāl-Targhīb wal-Tarhīb* (11/587).

[117] *Al-Taysīr* (2/356).

صِفَةِ الذَّلِيلِ تَنْكِيسَ رَأْسِهِ، فَثَمَرَةُ الْتَّكَبُّرِ فِي الدُّنْيَا الْذِّلَّةُ بَيْنَ الْخَلْقِ وَفِي الْآخِرَةِ النَّارُ".

"'**A ḥakamah** (harness throat-jaw-latch)' is placed placed under the animal's jaw to prevent it from disobeying, like a harness, '**in the hand of an angel**' assigned to it. So, '**when one humbles oneself**' for the truth and people, '**Allah says to the angel,**' '**Raise his bit**,' meaning his value and status. And '**when one is arrogant, it is said to the angel, lower his bit**,' which is a metaphor for his humiliation because one of the characteristics of the degraded person is bowing their head. Thus, the fruit of arrogance in this world is humiliation among people and in the hereafter, it is hellfire."

# THE TOUCH OF AN ANGEL & THE TOUCH OF A DEVIL

'Abdullah b. Mas'ūd (رَضِيَ ٱللَّهُ عَنْهُ) said:[118]

"إِنَّ لِلشَّيْطَانِ لَمَّةً مِنْ ابْنِ آدَمٍ، وَلِلْمَلَكِ لَمَّةً. فَأَمَّا لَمَّةُ الشَّيْطَانِ، فَإِيعَادٌ بِالشَّرِّ، وَتَكْذِيبٌ بِالْحَقِّ. وَأَمَّا لَمَّةُ الْمَلَكِ، فَإِيعَادٌ بِالْخَيْرِ، وَتَصْدِيقٌ بِالْحَقِّ".

"Indeed, Shayṭān has a touch on the son of Adam, and the angel also has a touch. As for Satan's touch, it is a prompt to do evil and a denial of the truth. As for the angel's touch, it is a prompt to do good and an affirmation of the truth.

Ibn al Athīr (d. 606 AH رَحِمَهُ ٱللَّهُ) explained Ibn Mas'ūd's (رَضِيَ ٱللَّهُ عَنْهُ) statement, saying:[119]

"اللَّمَّة: الْهِمَّة والخَطْرَة تَقَع فِي الْقَلْبِ، أَرَادَ إِلْمَام المَلَكِ أَوِ الشَّيْطَانِ بِهِ والقُرْب مِنْهُ، فما كَانَ مِنْ خَطَرَات الخَيْر، فَهُوَ مِنَ المَلَك، وَمَا كَانَ مِن خَطَرَات الشَّرِّ، فَهُوَ مِنَ الشَّيطان".

"The '*lammah*': is a thought or an idea that occurs in the heart, meaning the angel's or the devil's direct interaction with it and closeness to it. Whatever comes from good thoughts, it is from the angel, and whatever comes from evil thoughts, it is from the *shayṭān*."

---

[118] This narration is reported in *Mawqūf* form as a statement of Ibn Mas'ūd (رَضِيَ ٱللَّهُ عَنْهُ). The *mawqūf* report is repored by al-Ṭabarī in his Tafsīr [*Jāmi' al Bayān*] (6176), and graded *Ṣaḥīḥ li Ghayrihi* by Maḥmūd Shākir (رَحِمَهُ ٱللَّهُ) in his checking. Abu Zur'ah al-Rāzī and Abu Ḥātim al-Rāzī both said that it is authentic as a statement of Ibn Mas'ūd. It is not authentic as a statement of the Prophet (صَلَّى ٱللَّهُ عَلَيْهِ وَسَلَّمَ) according to many scholars of *ḥadīth*. And Allah knows best.

[119] *Al-Nihāyah fī Gharīb al Ḥadīth* (4/273).

Al Imām Ibn al Qayyim (d. 751 AH رَحِمَهُ ٱللَّهُ) elaborates further, saying:[120]

وَإِذَا تَأَمَّلْتَ حَالَ "الْقَلْبِ" مَعَ الْمَلَكِ وَالشَّيْطَانِ رَأَيْتَ أَعْجَبَ الْعَجَائِبِ، فَهَذَا يُلِمُّ بِهِ مَرَّةً، وَهَذَا يُلِمُّ بِهِ مَرَّةً، فَإِذَا أَلَمَّ بِهِ الْمَلَكُ حَدَثَ مِنْ لَمَّتِهِ الانْفِسَاحُ، وَالْانْشِرَاحُ، وَالنُّورُ، وَالرَّحْمَةُ، وَالْإِخْلَاصُ، وَالْإِنَابَةُ، وَمَحَبَّةُ اللَّهِ، وَإِيثَارُهُ عَلَى مَا سِوَاهُ، وَقِصَرُ الْأَمَلِ، وَالتَّجَافِي عَنْ دَارِ الْبَلَاءِ وَالِامْتِحَانِ وَالْغُرُورِ، فَلَوْ دَامَتْ لَهُ تِلْكَ الْحَالَةُ لَكَانَ فِي أَهْنَأِ عَيْشٍ وَأَلَذِّهِ وَأَطْيَبِهِ.

"When you contemplate the state of the *heart* with the angel and the devil, you witness the most extraordinary of wonders. This one comes near and touches it at times, and that one touches it at other times. When the angel touches it, its touch results in its openness, expansion, light, mercy, sincerity, return to Allah, love of Allah, preference of Allah over anything else, limitation of (worldly) hope, and an aversion from the world of misfortune, trial and delusion. If this condition continues, it is the most comfortable, pleasurable, and delightful life.

وَلَكِنْ تَأْتِيهِ لَمَّةُ الشَّيْطَانِ، فَتُحْدِثُ لَهُ مِنَ الضِّيقِ، وَالظُّلْمَةِ، وَالْهَمِّ، وَالْغَمِّ، وَالْخَوْفِ، وَالسَّخَطِ عَلَى الْمُقَدَّرِ، وَالشَّكِّ فِي الْحَقِّ، وَالْحِرْصِ عَلَى الدُّنْيَا وَعَاجِلِهَا، وَالْغَفْلَةِ عَنِ اللَّهِ — مَا هُوَ مِنْ أَعْظَمِ عَذَابِ "الْقَلْبِ".

However, the touch of the devil comes and it brings it distress, darkness, worry, sorrow, fear, displeasure with what is predestined, doubt about the truth, greed for the world and its immediacy, and negligence of Allah - all of which are among the greatest torments of the 'heart'.

ثُمَّ لِلنَّاسِ فِي هَذِهِ الْمِحْنَةِ مَرَاتِبُ لَا يُحْصِيهَا إِلَّا اللَّهُ عَزَّ وَجَلَ:

[120] *Al-Tibyān fī Aymān al Qur'ān* (p. 631).

Then, people have ranks in this ordeal that none but Allah (سُبْحَانَهُ وَتَعَالَىٰ) can fully enumerate:

فَمِنْهُمْ مَنْ تَكُونُ لَمَّةُ الْمَلَكِ أَغْلَبَ عَلَيْهِ مِنْ لَمَّةِ الشَّيْطَانِ وَأَقْوَى، فَإِذَا أَلَمَّ بِهِ الشَّيْطَانُ وَجَدَ مِنَ الْأَلَمِ، وَالضِّيقِ، وَالْحَصْرِ، وَسُوءِ الْحَالِ بِحَسَبِ مَا عِنْدَهُ مِنْ حَيَاةِ "الْقَلْبِ"، يُبَادِرُ إِلَى مَحْوِ تِلْكَ اللَّمَّةِ، وَلَا يَدَعُهَا تَسْتَحْكِمُ فَيَصْعُبُ تَدَارُكُهَا. فَهُوَ دَائِمٌ بَيْنَ اللَّمَّتَيْنِ، يُدَالُ لَهُ مَرَّةً، وَيُدَالُ عَلَيْهِ مَرَّةً أُخْرَى، وَالْعَاقِبَةُ لِلتَّقْوَى.

Among them are those whose angel's touch is more dominant and robust than the devil's. When the devil pains them, they feel pain, distress, constraint, and adversity proportional to the life in their 'heart.' They rush to erase that touch and do not let it take hold, lest it becomes challenging to control. They constantly alternate between the two touches: once it is in their favor, another time it is against them. And the finality of affairs favors the righteous.

وَمِنْهُمْ مَنْ تَكُونُ لَمَّةُ الشَّيْطَانِ أَغْلَبَ عَلَيْهِ مِنْ لَمَّةِ الْمَلَكِ وَأَقْوَى، فَلَا تَزَالُ تَغْلِبُ لَمَّةَ الْمَلَكِ حَتَّى تَسْتَحْكِمَ وَتَصِيرَ الْحُكْمُ لَهَا، فَيَمُوتُ "الْقَلْبُ"، فَلَا يُحِسُّ بِمَا نَالَهُ الشَّيْطَانُ، مَعَ أَنَّهُ فِي غَايَةِ الْعَذَابِ، وَالْأَلَمِ، وَالضِّيقِ، وَالْحَصْرِ، وَلَكِنَّ سُكْرَ الشَّهْوَةِ وَالْغَفْلَةِ حَجَبَ عَنْهُ الْإِحْسَاسَ بِذَلِكَ الْمُؤْلِمِ.

Among them are those whose devil's touch is more dominant and robust than the angel's. The devil's touch continues to dominate the angel's touch until it takes control and the ruling is for it, and the 'heart' dies. They don't feel what the devil has afflicted them, even though they are in extreme torment, pain, distress, and constraint. However, the drunkenness of desire and negligence has obscured their senses from that pain.

فَإِذَا كُشِفَ عَنْهُ بَعْضُ غِطَائِهِ أَدْرَكَ سُوءَ حَالِهِ، وَعَلِمَ مَا هُوَ فِيهِ، فَإِنِ اسْتَمَرَّ لَهُ كَشْفُ الْغِطَاءِ أَمْكَنَهُ تَدَارُكُ هَذَا الدَّاءِ وَحَسْمُهُ، وَإِنْ عَادَ الْغِطَاءُ عَادَ الْأَمْرُ كَمَا كَانَ، حَتَّى يُكْشَفَ عَنْهُ وَقْتَ الْمُفَارَقَةِ، فَتَظْهَرُ حِينَئِذٍ تِلْكَ الْآلَامُ، وَالْهُمُومُ،

وَالْغُمُومُ، وَالْأَحْزَانُ، وَهِيَ لَمْ تَتَجَدَّدْ لَهُ، وَإِنَّمَا كَانَتْ كَامِنَةً فِيهِ، تُوَارِيهَا الشَّوَاغِلُ، فَلَمَّا زَالَتِ الشَّوَاغِلُ ظَهَرَ مَا كَانَ كَامِنًا، وَتَجَدَّدَ لَهُ أَضْعَافُهُ.

If some of their covering is removed, they realize their poor state and understand what they are going through. If the lifting of the covering continues, they can control this disease and nip it in the bud. But if the cover returns, everything returns to how it was until it is ultimately exposed at the time of departure (from this world.) At that time, pains, worries, gloom, and sorrows appear. They did not arise anew to them; instead, they were hidden within them. Distractions had hidden them, and when the distractions are gone, what was hidden appears, and new degrees of it multiply many times over.

وَالشَّيْطَانُ يُلِمُّ بِـ "الْقَلْبِ" لِمَا لَهُ هُنَاكَ مِنْ جَوَاذِبِ تَجْذِبُهُ، وَهِيَ نَوْعَانِ: صِفَاتٌ، وَإِرَادَاتٌ.

"And the *shayṭān* approaches the heart for what he has thereof attractors that appeal to him, and they are of two types: characteristics and desires.

فَإِذَا كَانَتِ الْجَوَاذِبُ صِفَاتٍ قَوِيَ سُلْطَانُهُ هُنَاكَ، وَاسْتَفْحَلَ أَمْرُهُ، وَوَجَدَ مَوْطِنًا وَمَقَرًّا، فَتَبْقَى الْأَذْكَارُ وَالدَّعَوَاتُ وَالتَّعَوُّذَاتُ الَّتِي يَأْتِي بِهَا الْإِنْسَانُ حَدِيثَ نَفْسٍ، لَا تَدْفَعُ سُلْطَانَ الشَّيْطَانِ؛ لِأَنَّ مَرْكَبَهُ صِفَةٌ لَازِمَةٌ.

When a person possesses traits that attract the devil, his influence and authority over that individual become potent, exacerbating the situation. Therefore, remembrances, supplications, and invocations for divine refuge that a human comes with are (merely) personal thoughts that do not repel the authority of the devil, as his hold is deeply rooted in persistent characteristics.

فَإِذَا قَلَعَ الْعَبْدُ تِلْكَ الصِّفَاتِ مِنْ قَلْبِهِ ، وَعَمِلَ عَلَى التَّطَهُّرِ مِنْهَا وَالِاغْتِسَالِ، بَقِيَ لِلشَّيْطَانِ بِـ "الْقَلْبِ" خَطَرَاتٌ، وَوَسَاوِسُ، وَلَمَّاتٌ مِنْ غَيْرِ اسْتِقْرَارٍ، وَذَلِكَ يُضْعِفُهُ، وَيُقَوِّي لَمَّةَ الْمَلَكِ، فَتَأْتِي الْأَذْكَارُ، وَالدَّعَوَاتُ، وَالتَّعَوُّذَاتُ؛ فَتَدْفَعُهُ بِأَسْهَلِ شَيْءٍ.

When the servant uproots these characteristics from his heart and works on purifying and washing himself from them, what remains for the devil in the 'heart' are mere fleeting thoughts, whispers, and fleeting touches that do not settle. This weakens him and strengthens the angel's touch. Therefore, remembrances, supplications, and invocations come and repel him quite easily.

وَإِذَا أَرَدْتَ لِذَلِكَ مِثَالًا مُطَابِقًا: فَمَثَلُهُ مَثَلُ كَلْبٍ جَائِعٍ، شَدِيدِ الْجُوعِ، وَبَيْنَكَ وَبَيْنَهُ لَحْمٌ أَوْ خُبْزٌ، وَهُوَ يَتَأَمَّلُكَ، فَيَرَاكَ لَا تُقَاوِمُهُ وَهُوَ قَدْ اقْتَرَبَ مِنْكَ، فَأَنْتَ تَزْجُرُهُ، وَتَصِيحُ عَلَيْهِ، وَهُوَ يَأْبَى إِلَّا الْهُجُومَ عَلَيْكَ، وَالْغَارَةَ عَلَى مَا بَيْنَ يَدَيْكَ.

And if you want a similar example, it is like a hungry dog, severely starving, and between you and it is meat or bread, and it is watching you. It sees that you do not resist it while it is close to you, so you growl and shout in an attempt to deter it. However, the dog persists in attacking and seizing what is in front of you.

فَالْأَذْكَارُ بِمَنْزِلَةِ الصِّيَاحِ عَلَيْهِ، وَالزَّجْرِ لَهُ، وَلَكِنَّ مَعْلُومَهُ وَمُرَادَهُ عِنْدَكَ، وَقَدْ قَوَّيْتَهُ عَلَيْكَ، فَإِذَا لَمْ يَكُنْ بَيْنَ يَدَيْكَ شَيْءٌ يَصْلُحُ لَهُ - وَقَدْ تَأَمَّلَكَ فَرَآكَ أَقْوَى مِنْهُ - فَإِنَّكَ تَزْجُرُهُ فَيَنْزَجِرُ، وَتَصِيحُ عَلَيْهِ فَيَذْهَبُ. وَكَذَلِكَ "الْقَلْبُ" الْخَالِي عَنْ قُوتِ الشَّيْطَانِ يَنْزَجِرُ بِمُجَرَّدِ الذِّكْرِ.

The remembrances are like shouting at it and growling at it, but it knows that you have what it wants, and you have empowered it against yourself. If nothing in front of you is suitable for it - and it watches you and sees you stronger than it - then you growl at it, and it backs down, and you shout at it, and it goes away. And thus, the heart devoid of the devil's food backs down merely by the remembrance.

وَأَمَّا الْقَلْبُ الَّذِي فِيهِ تِلْكَ الصِّفَاتُ الَّتِي هِيَ مَرْكَبُهُ وَمَوْطِنُهُ، يَقَعُ الذِّكْرُ فِي حَوَاشِيهَا وَجَوَانِبِهَا، وَلَا يَقْوَى عَلَى إِخْرَاجِ الْعَدُوِّ.

As for the 'heart' that holds qualities that are his (i.e., *Shayṭān's*) vehicle and habitat, the remembrance happens at its outskirts and edges and cannot drive out the enemy.

وَمِصْدَاقُ ذَلِكَ تَجِدُهُ فِي الصَّلَاةِ، فَتَأَمَّلِ الْحَالَ، وَانْظُرْ: هَلْ تُخْرِجُ الصَّلَاةُ وَأَذْكَارُهَا وَقِرَاءَتُهَا الشَّيْطَانَ مِنْ قَلْبِكَ، وَتُفَرِّغُهُ كُلَّهُ لِلَّهِ تَعَالَى، وَتُقِيمُهُ بَيْنَ يَدَيْهِ مُقْبِلًا بِكُلِّيَّتِهِ عَلَيْهِ، يُصَلِّي لِلَّهِ - تَعَالَى - كَأَنَّهُ يَرَاهُ، قَدْ اجْتَمَعَ هَمُّهُ كُلُّهُ عَلَى اللَّهِ، وَصَارَ ذِكْرُهُ، وَمُرَاقَبَتُهُ، وَمُحَبَّتُهُ، وَالْأُنْسُ بِهِ؛ فِي مَحَلِّ الْخَوَاطِرِ وَالْوَسَاوِسِ؛ أَمْ لَا؟ فَاللَّهُ الْمُسْتَعَانُ.

And the affirmation of this can be found during the prayer, so contemplate the condition (of the heart) and let him look: Does the prayer, its remembrances, and its recitation expel the devil from your heart, free it completely for Allah, and place it in front of Him, focusing it entirely on Him, so that he prays for Allah (سُبْحَانَهُ وَتَعَالَىٰ) as if he sees Him, having gathered all his concern on Allah? And is one's constant remembrance of Allah, self-supervision, love, and seeking comfort in His presence enough to replace fleeting thoughts and whispers? Allah is the One sought for assistance.

وَهَاهُنَا نُكْتَةٌ يَنْبَغِي التَّفَطُّنُ لَهَا، وَهِيَ أَنَّ الْقُلُوبَ مُمْتَلِئَةٌ بِالْأَخْلَاطِ الرَّدِيئَةِ. وَالْعِبَادَاتُ وَالْأَذْكَارُ وَالتَّعَوُّذَاتُ أَدْوِيَةٌ لِتِلْكَ الْأَخْلَاطِ، كَمَا يُثِيرُ الدَّوَاءُ أَخْلَاطَ الْبَدَنِ، فَإِنْ كَانَ قَبْلَ الدَّوَاءِ وَبَعْدَهُ حِمْيَةٌ نَفَعَ ذَلِكَ الدَّوَاءُ، وَقَلَعَ الدَّاءَ أَوْ أَكْثَرَهُ، وَإِنْ لَمْ يَكُنْ قَبْلَهُ وَلَا بَعْدَهُ حِمْيَةٌ لَمْ يَزِدِ الدَّوَاءُ عَلَى إِثَارَتِهِ، وَإِنْ أَزَالَ مِنْهُ شَيْئًا مَا. فَمَدَارُ الْأَمْرِ عَلَى شَيْئَيْنِ: الْحِمْيَةِ، وَاسْتِعْمَالِ الْأَدْوِيَةِ»

And here is a point that should be noted: hearts are filled with harmful mixtures. And acts of worship, remembrances, and invocations for seeking divine refuge are medicines for these mixtures, just as medicine aggravates physical imbalances. If there is a dietary regiment (limiting food intake) before and after the medicine, then that medicine benefits and uproots the disease entirely or mostly. If there is no dietary regimen before or after, the medicine does nothing more than aggravate (the sickness) even if it partially removes it. So, the matter revolves around a strict dietary regimen and medicines."

## A BROAD OUTLINE OF THE WAR WITHIN

Ibn al Qayyim (رَحِمَهُ ٱللَّهُ) said:[121]

"أَلْقَى اللَّهُ سُبْحَانَهُ الْعَدَاوَةَ بَيْنَ الشَّيْطَانِ وَبَيْنَ الْمَلَكِ، وَالْعَدَاوَةَ بَيْنَ الْعَقْلِ وَبَيْنَ الْهَوَى، وَالْعَدَاوَةَ بَيْنَ النَّفْسِ الْأَمَّارَةِ وَبَيْنَ الْقَلْبِ، وَابْتَلَى الْعَبْدَ بِذَلِكَ، وَجَمَعَ لَهُ بَيْنَ هَؤُلَاءِ، وَأَمَدَّ كُلَّ حِزْبٍ بِجُنُودٍ وَأَعْوَانٍ؛

Allah has placed enmity between the *Shayṭān* and the angel, between reason and desires, and between the insistent self and the heart. He has tested His servant with this and gathered them together, providing each party with soldiers and supporters.

فَلَا تَزَالُ الْحَرْبُ سِجَالًا وَدُوَلًا بَيْنَ الْفَرِيقَيْنِ إِلَى أَنْ يَسْتَوْلِيَ أَحَدُهُمَا عَلَى الْآخَرِ وَيَكُونَ الْآخَرُ مَقْهُورًا مَعَهُ.

The war continues, alternating between the two sides until one dominates the other and the other becomes subjugated.

فَإِذَا كَانَتِ النَّوْبَةُ لِلْقَلْبِ وَالْعَقْلِ وَالْمَلَكِ؛ فَهُنَالِكَ السُّرُورُ، وَالنَّعِيمُ، وَاللَّذَّةُ، وَالْبَهْجَةُ، وَالْفَرَحُ، وَقُرَّةُ الْعَيْنِ، وَطِيبُ الْحَيَاةِ، وَانْشِرَاحُ الصَّدْرِ، وَالْفَوْزُ بِالْغَنَائِمِ.

When victory belongs to the heart, the intellect, and the angel, there is happiness, bliss, pleasure, delight, joy, the coolness of the eyes, the sweetness of life, the expansion of the chest, and the gain of spoils.

وَإِذَا كَانَتِ النَّوْبَةُ لِلنَّفْسِ وَالْهَوَى وَالشَّيْطَانِ؛ فَهُنَالِكَ الْغُمُومُ، وَالْهُمُومُ، وَالْأَحْزَانُ، وَأَنْوَاعُ الْمَكَارِهِ، وَضِيقُ الصَّدْرِ، وَحَبْسُ الْمَلِكِ.

But when victory belongs to the self, the desires, and *Shayṭān*, there is sorrow, worry, grief, a variety of hated outcomes, constriction of the chest, and imprisonment of the king.

---

[121] Al Fawā'id, p. 83.

فَمَا ظَنُّكَ بِمَلِكٍ اسْتَوْلَى عَلَيْهِ عَدُوُّهُ، فَأَنْزَلَهُ عَنْ سِرِّيرِ مُلْكِهِ، وَأَسَرَهُ، وَحَبَسَهُ، وَحَالَ بَيْنَهُ وَبَيْنَ خَزَائِنِهِ وَذَخَائِرِهِ وَخَدَمِهِ، وَصَيَّرَهَا لَهُ، وَمَعَ هَذَا فَلَا يَتَحَرَّكُ الْمَلِكُ لِطَلَبِ ثَأْرِهِ، وَلَا يَسْتَغِيثُ بِمَنْ يُغِيثُهُ، وَلَا يَسْتَنْجِدُ بِمَنْ يُنْجِدُهُ؟!

So, what do you think of a king whose enemy has taken control, demoted him from his royal seat, captured him, imprisoned him, and prevented him from accessing his treasures, wealth, and servants, and then allocated all of this for himself? Despite all of this, the king does not move to seek his vengeance, nor does he call for help from those who can assist him, nor does he ask for rescue from those who can save him?!

وَفَوْقَ هَذَا الْمَلِكِ مَلِكٌ قَاهِرٌ لَا يُقْهَرُ، وَغَالِبٌ لَا يُغْلَبُ، وَعَزِيزٌ لَا يُذَلُّ، فَأَرْسَلَ إِلَيْهِ: إِنِ اسْتَنْصَرْتَنِي نَصَرْتُكَ، وَإِنِ اسْتَغَثْتَ بِي أَغَثْتُكَ، وَإِنِ التَّجَأْتَ إِلَيَّ أَخَذْتُ بِثَأْرِكَ، وَإِنْ هَرَبْتَ إِلَيَّ وَأَوَيْتَ إِلَيَّ سَلَّطْتُكَ عَلَى عَدُوِّكَ، وَجَعَلْتُهُ تَحْتَ أَسْرِكَ

Above this king is a supreme King who cannot be vanquished, an invincible Victor who cannot be defeated, a Mighty One who cannot be humiliated. He sends a message to the imprisoned king: "*If you seek my help, I will help you. If you call upon me, I will come to your aid. If you take refuge in me, I will avenge you. If you flee to me and seek shelter with me, I will grant you authority over your enemy and make him your captive.*"

فَإِنْ قَالَ هَذَا الْمَلِكُ الْمَأْسُورُ: قَدْ شَدَّ عَدُوِّي وَثَاقِي، وَأَحْكَمَ رِبَاطِي، وَاسْتَوْثَقَ مِنِّي بِالْقُيُودِ، وَمَنَعَنِي مِنَ النُّهُوضِ إِلَيْكَ وَالْفِرَارِ إِلَيْكَ وَالْمَسِيرِ إِلَى بَابِكَ؛ فَإِنْ أَرْسَلْتَ جُنْدًا مِنْ عِنْدَكَ يَحُلُّ وَثَاقِي وَيَفُكُّ قُيُودِي وَيُخْرِجُنِي مِنْ حَبْسِهِ؛ أَمْكَنَنِي أَنْ أُوَافِيَ بَابَكَ، وَإِلَّا لَمْ يُمْكِنِّي مُفَارَقَةُ مَحْبُوسِي وَلَا كَسْرُ قُيُودِي.

If the imprisoned king says, "*My enemy has tightened my bonds, secured my restraints, and shackled me with chains, preventing me from rising to you, fleeing to you, or approaching your door. I can reach your door if you send an army from your side to break my chains, release my shackles, and set me free from his prison. Otherwise, I cannot escape my confinement or break my chains."*

فَإِنْ قَالَ ذَلِكَ احْتِجَاجًا عَلَى ذَلِكَ السُّلْطَانِ، وَدَفْعًا لِرِسَالَتِهِ، وَرِضًا بِمَا هُوَ فِيهِ عِنْدَ عَدُوِّهِ؛ خَلَّاهُ السُّلْطَانُ الْأَعْظَمُ وَحَالَهُ وَوَلَّاهُ مَا تَوَلَّى.

If the king says this as an objection against the supreme King, rejection of His message and accepting his condition under his enemy, the supreme King will leave him alone and let him deal with the situation as he wishes.

وَإِنْ قَالَ ذَلِكَ افْتِقَارًا إِلَيْهِ، وَإِظْهَارًا لِعَجْزِهِ وَذُلِّهِ، وَأَنَّهُ أَضْعَفُ وَأَعْجَزُ مِنْ أَنْ يَسِيرَ إِلَيْهِ بِنَفْسِهِ، وَيَخْرُجَ مِنْ حَبْسِ عَدُوِّهِ، وَيَتَخَلَّصَ مِنْهُ بِحَوْلِهِ وَقُوَّتِهِ، وَأَنَّ مِنْ تَمَامِ نِعْمَةِ ذَلِكَ الْمَلِكِ عَلَيْهِ -كَمَا أَرْسَلَ إِلَيْهِ هَذِهِ الرِّسَالَةَ- أَنْ يَمُدَّهُ مِنْ جُنُودِهِ وَمَمَالِيكِهِ بِمَنْ يُعِينُهُ عَلَى الْخَلَاصِ وَيَكْسِرَ بَابَ مَحْبِسِهِ وَيَفُكَّ قُيُودَهُ؛ فَإِنْ فَعَلَ بِهِ ذَلِكَ فَقَدْ أَتَمَّ إِنْعَامَهُ عَلَيْهِ، وَإِنْ تَخَلَّى عَنْهُ فَلَمْ يَظْلِمْهُ وَلَا مَنَعَهُ حَقًّا هُوَ لَهُ.

However, if the king says this out of need for the supreme King, acknowledging his weakness and humiliation, admitting that he is too weak and incapable of journeying to the supreme King by himself, or escaping from the prison of his enemy and freeing himself through his own power and strength, and if he understands that the supreme King's favor towards him — as shown by sending this message — is to provide him with His soldiers and servants to help him attain salvation, to break the door of his prison, and to release his shackles, then, if the supreme King does so, He has completed His favor upon him. And if He abandons him, He has not wronged him nor withheld any right of his.

وَأَنَّ حَمْدَهُ وَحِكْمَتَهُ اقْتَضَى مَنْعَهُ وَتَخْلِيَتَهُ فِي مَحْبَسِهِ، وَلَا سِيَّمَا إِذَا عَلِمَ أَنَّ الْحَبْسَ حَبْسُهُ، وَأَنَّ هَذَا الْعَدُوَّ الَّذِي حَبَسَهُ مَمْلُوكٌ مِنْ مَمَالِيكِهِ، وَعَبْدٌ مِنْ عَبِيدِهِ، نَاصِيَتُهُ بِيَدِهِ، لَا يَتَصَرَّفُ إِلَّا بِإِذْنِهِ وَمَشِيئَتِهِ؛ فَهُوَ غَيْرُ مُلْتَفِتٍ إِلَيْهِ، وَلَا خَائِفٍ مِنْهُ، وَلَا مُعْتَقِدٍ أَنَّ لَهُ شَيْئًا مِنَ الْأَمْرِ وَلَا بِيَدِهِ نَفْعٌ وَلَا ضَرٌّ، بَلْ هُوَ نَاظِرٌ

إِلَى مَالِكِهِ وَمُتَوَلِّي أَمْرِهِ وَمَنْ نَاصِيَتُهُ بِيَدِهِ، قَدْ أَفْرَدَهُ بِالْخَوْفِ وَالرَّجَاءِ وَالتَّضَرُّعِ إِلَيْهِ وَالِالْتِجَاءِ وَالرَّغْبَةِ وَالرَّهْبَةِ؛ فَهُنَاكَ تَأْتِيهِ جُيُوشُ النَّصْرِ وَالظَّفَرِ.

The king acknowledges the greatness and wisdom of the supreme King, realizing that it is fitting for the supreme King to withhold help and allow him to remain in confinement. He understands that his imprisonment is part of the supreme King's will and that his enemy, who has confined him, is merely a servant of the supreme King, obeying His commands. Consequently, the king does not pay attention to his enemy or fear or believe in the enemy's power to do him good or harm. Instead, he focuses entirely on the supreme King, who controls his fate and has complete authority over him. He directs all his emotions of fear, hope, supplication, seeking refuge, longing, and awe solely toward the supreme King. In this state, the armies of victory and triumph would come to his aid.

## A Fuller Description of the War Within

Ibn al Qayyim (رَحِمَهُ ٱللَّهُ) said:[122]

"وَمِنْ عُقُوبَاتِهَا: أَنَّهَا مَدَدٌ مِنَ الْإِنْسَانِ يَمُدُّ بِهِ عَدُوَّهُ عَلَيْهِ، وَجَيْشٌ يُقَوِّيهِ بِهِ عَلَى حَرْبِهِ، وَذَلِكَ أَنَّ اللَّهَ سُبْحَانَهُ ابْتَلَى هَذَا الْإِنْسَانَ بِعَدُوٍّ لَا يُفَارِقُهُ طَرْفَةَ عَيْنٍ، وَلَا يَنَامُ مِنْهُ وَلَا يَغْفُلُ عَنْهُ، يَرَاهُ هُوَ وَقَبِيلُهُ مِنْ حَيْثُ لَا يَرَاهُ، يَبْذُلُ جَهْدَهُ فِي مُعَادَاتِهِ فِي كُلِّ حَالٍ، وَلَا يَدَعُ أَمْرًا يَكِيدُهُ بِهِ يَقْدِرُ عَلَى إِيصَالِهِ إِلَيْهِ إِلَّا أَوْصَلَهُ إِلَيْهِ، وَيَسْتَعِينُ عَلَيْهِ بِبَنِي جِنْسِهِ مِنْ شَيَاطِينِ الْجِنِّ، وَغَيْرِهِمْ مِنْ شَيَاطِينِ الْإِنْسِ،

"And among the punishments [of sins]: It is a means by which the person provides reinforcements that his enemy uses against him and an armed force which strengthens him in his war. This is because Allah has tested the human being with an enemy who does not leave him for a blink of an eye, does not sleep from (attacking) him and is not heedless of him. He and his tribe see him from where he does not see them. He exerts his efforts in hostility against him in every situation and does not abandon any matter he can scheme to make befall him except that he causes it to reach him. And he seeks out his own kind, from the devils of the *jinn*, to aid against him, and others from the devils of humans.

فَقَدْ نَصَبَ لَهُ الْحَبَائِلَ، وَبَغَى لَهُ الْغَوَائِلَ، وَمَدَّ حَوْلَهُ الْأَشْرَاكَ، وَنَصَبَ لَهُ الْفِخَاخَ وَالشِّبَاكَ، وَقَالَ لِأَعْوَانِهِ: دُونَكُمْ عَدُوَّكُمْ وَعَدُوَّ أَبِيكُمْ لَا يَفُوتُكُمْ وَلَا يَكُونُ حَظُّهُ الْجَنَّةَ وَحَظُّكُمُ النَّارَ، وَنَصِيبُهُ الرَّحْمَةَ وَنَصِيبُكُمُ اللَّعْنَةَ، وَقَدْ عَلِمْتُمْ أَنَّ مَا جَرَى عَلَيَّ وَعَلَيْكُمْ مِنَ الْخِزْيِ وَالْإِبْعَادِ مِنْ رَحْمَةِ اللَّهِ بِسَبَبِهِ وَمِنْ أَجْلِهِ،

So he has laid traps for him, seeks to cause him peril, spread out snares, laid nets for him and said to his helpers: "*Your enemy and the enemy of your fathers is before you. Do not let him escape, lest*

[122] *Al-Dā' wal-Dawā* (*al Jawāb al Kāfī*).

*his portion is Paradise and yours Hellfire, His share be mercy, and yours should be accursedness. You know that what happened to me and you, of humiliation and being distanced from Allah's mercy, was caused by him and was done for his sake.*

فَابْذُلُوا جَهْدَكُمْ أَنْ يَكُونُوا شُرَكَاءَنَا فِي هَذِهِ الْبَلِيَّةِ، إِذْ قَدْ فَاتَنَا شَرِكَةُ صَالِحِيهِمْ فِي الْجَنَّةِ.

*So work to your utmost to make them our partners in this calamity since we missed out on being partners with the righteous of them in Paradise."*

وَقَدْ أَعْلَمَنَا اللَّهُ سُبْحَانَهُ بِذَلِكَ كُلِّهِ مِنْ عَدُوِّنَا وَأَمَرَنَا أَنْ نَأْخُذَ لَهُ أُهْبَتَهُ وَنُعِدَّ لَهُ عُدَّتَهُ.

Allah has informed all of us about all of this pertaining to our enemy and has commanded us to take precautions against him and to prepare for him.

وَلَمَّا عَلِمَ سُبْحَانَهُ أَنَّ آدَمَ وَبَنِيهِ قَدْ بُلُوا بِهَذَا الْعَدُوِّ وَأَنَّهُ قَدْ سُلِّطَ عَلَيْهِمْ أَمَدَّهُمْ بِعَسَاكِرَ وَجُنْدٍ يَلْقَوْنَهُمْ بِهَا، وَأَمَدَّ عَدُوَّهُمْ أَيْضًا بِجُنْدٍ وَعَسَاكِرَ يَلْقَاهُمْ بِهَا،

Since Allah (سُبْحَانَهُ وَتَعَالَى) knew that this enemy tested Adam and his children and that he was unleashed against them, He reinforced them with armies and forces to confront them with while also providing their enemy with armies and forces to confront them with.

وَأَقَامَ سُوقَ الْجِهَادِ فِي هَذِهِ الدَّارِ فِي مُدَّةِ الْعُمُرِ الَّتِي هِيَ بِالْإِضَافَةِ إِلَى الْآخِرَةِ كَنَفَسٍ وَاحِدٍ مِنْ أَنْفَاسِهَا،

He (جَلَّ وَعَلَا) established the market of *jihād* in this world for the duration of one's lifespan, which, when compared to the afterlife, is like a single momentary breath…

وَاشْتَرَى مِنَ الْمُؤْمِنِينَ أَنْفُسَهُمْ وَأَمْوَالَهُمْ بِأَنَّ لَهُمُ الْجَنَّةَ، يُقَاتِلُونَ فِي سَبِيلِ اللَّهِ فَيَقْتُلُونَ وَيُقْتَلُونَ، وَأَخْبَرَ أَنَّ ذَلِكَ وَعْدٌ مُؤَكَّدٌ عَلَيْهِ فِي أَشْرَفِ كُتُبِهِ، وَهِيَ التَّوْرَاةُ وَالْإِنْجِيلُ وَالْقُرْآنُ، وَأَخْبَرَ أَنَّهُ لَا أَوْفَى بِعَهْدِهِ مِنْهُ سُبْحَانَهُ، ثُمَّ أَمَرَهُمْ أَنْ يَسْتَبْشِرُوا بِهَذِهِ الصَّفْقَةِ الَّتِي مَنْ أَرَادَ أَنْ يَعْرِفَ قَدْرَهَا فَلْيَنْظُرْ إِلَى الْمُشْتَرِي مَنْ هُوَ؟ وَإِلَى الثَّمَنِ الْمَبْذُولِ فِي هَذِهِ السِّلْعَةِ، وَإِلَى مَنْ جَرَى عَلَى يَدَيْهِ هَذَا الْعَقْدُ، فَأَيُّ فَوْزٍ أَعْظَمُ مِنْ هَذَا؟ وَأَيُّ تِجَارَةٍ أَرْبَحُ مِنْهُ؟

He bought from the believers their souls and their wealth in exchange for Paradise. They fight in the way of Allah, slaying and being slayed, and He has informed us that this promise is confirmed in His noblest books, the Torah, the Gospel, and the Quran, and He has informed us that no one is more faithful to his promise than He (سُبْحَانَهُ وَتَعَالَى). Furthermore, He commanded them to rejoice at this deal, which, whoever wants to understand its value, let him look at the Purchaser, the price paid for this commodity, and the One who contracted this agreement. What victory is more excellent than this? And what trade is more profitable than it?

ثُمَّ أَكَّدَ سُبْحَانَهُ مَعَهُمْ هَذَا الْأَمْرَ بِقَوْلِهِ: **{يَاأَيُّهَا الَّذِينَ آمَنُوا هَلْ أَدُلُّكُمْ عَلَى تِجَارَةٍ تُنْجِيكُمْ مِنْ عَذَابٍ أَلِيمٍ - تُؤْمِنُونَ بِاللَّهِ وَرَسُولِهِ وَتُجَاهِدُونَ فِي سَبِيلِ اللَّهِ بِأَمْوَالِكُمْ وَأَنْفُسِكُمْ ذَلِكُمْ خَيْرٌ لَكُمْ إِنْ كُنْتُمْ تَعْلَمُونَ - يَغْفِرْ لَكُمْ ذُنُوبَكُمْ وَيُدْخِلْكُمْ جَنَّاتٍ تَجْرِي مِنْ تَحْتِهَا الْأَنْهَارُ وَمَسَاكِنَ طَيِّبَةً فِي جَنَّاتِ عَدْنٍ ذَلِكَ الْفَوْزُ الْعَظِيمُ - وَأُخْرَى تُحِبُّونَهَا نَصْرٌ مِنَ اللَّهِ وَفَتْحٌ قَرِيبٌ وَبَشِّرِ الْمُؤْمِنِينَ}** .

Then He (Allah) affirmed this matter with them by saying: '**O you who have believed, shall I guide you to a transaction that will save you from a painful punishment? [It is that] you believe in Allah and His Messenger and strive in the cause of Allah with your wealth and your lives. That is best for you, if you should know. He will forgive for you your sins and admit you into gardens beneath which rivers flow and pleasant dwellings in gardens of perpetual residence. That is**

**the great attainment. And [you will obtain] another [favor] that you love - victory from Allah and an imminent conquest; and give good tidings to the believers.'**[123]

وَلَمْ يُسَلِّطْ سُبْحَانَهُ هَذَا الْعَدُوَّ عَلَى عَبْدِهِ الْمُؤْمِنِ الَّذِي هُوَ أَحَبُّ الْمَخْلُوقَاتِ إِلَيْهِ، إِلَّا لِأَنَّ الْجِهَادَ أَحَبُّ شَيْءٍ إِلَيْهِ، وَأَهْلَهُ أَرْفَعُ الْخَلْقِ عِنْدَهُ دَرَجَاتٍ، وَأَقْرَبُهُمْ إِلَيْهِ وَسِيلَةً، فَعَقَدَ سُبْحَانَهُ لِوَاءَ هَذِهِ الْحَرْبِ لِخُلَاصَةِ مَخْلُوقَاتِهِ، وَهُوَ الْقَلْبُ الَّذِي مَحَلُّ مَعْرِفَتِهِ وَمَحَبَّتِهِ، وَعُبُودِيَّتِهِ وَالْإِخْلَاصِ لَهُ، وَالتَّوَكُّلِ عَلَيْهِ وَالْإِنَابَةِ إِلَيْهِ، فَوَلَّاهُ أَمْرَ هَذِهِ الْحَرْبِ، وَأَيَّدَهُ بِجُنْدٍ مِنَ الْمَلَائِكَةِ لَا يُفَارِقُونَهُ {**لَهُ مُعَقِّبَاتٌ مِنْ بَيْنِ يَدَيْهِ وَمِنْ خَلْفِهِ يَحْفَظُونَهُ مِنْ أَمْرِ اللَّهِ**} .

And He (سُبْحَانَهُ وَتَعَالَىٰ) did not unleash this enemy upon His believing servant, who is the dearest of creation to Him, except because that striving (*jihad*) is the most beloved thing to Him. Its people are the highest of creation in rank with Him, and the nearest of them to Him in the means taken. So, He (سُبْحَانَهُ وَتَعَالَىٰ) has fastened the banner of this war to the choicest thing He created, which is the heart, in which there resides knowledge of Him, love of Him, servitude for Him, sincerity to Him, reliance on Him, and turning to Him. He entrusted it with the task of this war, and supported it with an army of angels who never leave it, '**For each (person,) there are angels in succession, before and behind him. They guard him by the command of Allah.**''[124]

يَعْقُبُ بَعْضُهُمْ بَعْضًا، كُلَّمَا ذَهَبَ بَدَلٌ جَاءَ بَدَلٌ آخَرُ يُثَبِّتُونَهُ وَيَأْمُرُونَهُ بِالْخَيْرِ وَيَحُضُّونَهُ عَلَيْهِ، وَيَعِدُونَهُ بِكَرَامَةِ اللَّهِ وَيُصَبِّرُونَهُ، وَيَقُولُونَ: إِنَّمَا هُوَ صَبْرُ سَاعَةٍ وَقَدِ اسْتَرَحْتَ رَاحَةَ الْأَبَدِ.

---

[123] Al-Saff: 10-13.

[124] Ar-Rad: 11.

They follow each other in succession, every time one shift departs, another comes,[125] reinforcing his resolve and ordering and urging him to do good. They promise him the honorable reward of Allah and encourage him. They say: *It's only an hour of patience, and then you will have eternal rest.*

ثُمَّ أَمَدَّهُ سُبْحَانَهُ بِجُنْدٍ آخَرَ مِنْ وَحْيِهِ وَكَلَامِهِ، فَأَرْسَلَ إِلَيْهِ رَسُولَهُ صلى الله عليه وسلم وَأَنْزَلَ إِلَيْهِ كِتَابَهُ، فَازْدَادَ قُوَّةً إِلَى قُوتِهِ، وَمَدَدًا إِلَى مَدَدِهِ، وَعُدَّةً إِلَى عُدَّتِهِ، وَأَمَدَّهُ مَعَ ذَلِكَ بِالْعَقْلِ وَزِيرًا لَهُ وَمُدَبِّرًا، وَبِالْمَعْرِفَةِ مُشِيرَةً عَلَيْهِ نَاصِحَةً لَهُ، وَبِالْإِيمَانِ مُثَبِّتًا لَهُ وَمُؤَيِّدًا وَنَاصِرًا، وَبِالْيَقِينِ كَاشِفًا لَهُ عَنْ حَقِيقَةِ الْأَمْرِ، حَتَّى كَأَنَّهُ يُعَايِنُ مَا وَعَدَ اللَّهُ تَعَالَى أَوْلِيَاءَهُ وَحِزْبَهُ عَلَى جِهَادِ أَعْدَائِهِ،

Then He (سُبْحَانَهُ وَتَعَالَىٰ) supported him with another army from His revelation and speech. So, He sent His Messenger (صَلَّى ٱللَّٰهُ عَلَيْهِ وَسَلَّمَ) to him and sent down His book to him, increasing his strength, support, and preparation. And He (سُبْحَانَهُ وَتَعَالَىٰ) supported him with intellect as an advisor and manager, and with knowledge as a counselor and adviser, and with *emān* as a resolve strengthener, helper and champion, and with certainty to clarify the reality of matters, until it is as if he sees what Allah promised His allies and His party in striving against His enemies.

فَالْعَقْلُ يُدَبِّرُ أَمْرَ جَيْشِهِ، وَالْمَعْرِفَةُ تَصْنَعُ لَهُ أُمُورَ الْحَرْبِ وَأَسْبَابَهَا وَمَوَاضِعَهَا اللَّائِقَةَ بِهَا، وَالْإِيمَانُ يُثَبِّتُهُ وَيُقَوِّيهِ وَيُصَبِّرُهُ، وَالْيَقِينُ يُقْدِمُ بِهِ وَيَحْمِلُ بِهِ الْحَمَلَاتِ الصَّادِقَةَ.

Reason plans the army's strategies, knowledge guides the aspects of war, including causes and suitable situations. Faith strengthens and empowers, while certainty motivates and propels one to undertake sincere campaigns.

---

125 meaning that they alternate at time of *Fajr* prayer and *'Aṣr* prayer as comes authentically in the *ḥadīth.*

ثُمَّ أَمَدَّ سُبْحَانَهُ الْقَائِمَ بِهَذِهِ الْحَرْبِ بِالْقُوَى الظَّاهِرَةِ وَالْبَاطِنَةِ، فَجَعَلَ الْعَيْنَ طَلِيعَتَهُ، وَالْأُذُنَ صَاحِبَ خَبَرِهِ، وَاللِّسَانَ تُرْجُمَانَهُ، وَالْيَدَيْنِ وَالرِّجْلَيْنِ أَعْوَانَهُ، وَأَقَامَ مَلَائِكَتَهُ وَحَمَلَةَ عَرْشِهِ يَسْتَغْفِرُونَ لَهُ وَيَسْأَلُونَ لَهُ أَنْ يَقِيَهُ السَّيِّئَاتِ وَيُدْخِلَهُ الْجَنَّاتِ،

"Then He (سُبْحَانَهُوَتَعَالَى) provided the one who stands in this war with outward and inward strengths. He made the eye his vanguard, the ear his carrier of news, the tongue his interpreter, and the hands and feet his aides. And He stationed His angels and the carriers of His throne to seek forgiveness, ask Him to protect him from sins, and admit him into Paradise.

وَتَوَلَّى سُبْحَانَهُ الدَّفْعَ وَالدِّفَاعَ عَنْهُ بِنَفْسِهِ وَقَالَ: هَؤُلَاءِ حِزْبِي، وَحِزْبُ اللَّهِ هُمُ الْمُفْلِحُونَ، قَالَ اللَّهُ تَعَالَى: {أُولَئِكَ حِزْبُ اللَّهِ أَلَا إِنَّ حِزْبَ اللَّهِ هُمُ الْمُفْلِحُونَ} .

And He (سُبْحَانَهُوَتَعَالَى) personally undertook his defense and protection, saying: '*These are my party, and the party of Allah are the successful ones.*' Allah, the Exalted, said: '**Those are the party of Allah. Unquestionably, the party of Allah - they are the successful.**'[126]

وَهَؤُلَاءِ جُنْدِي {**وَإِنَّ جُنْدَنَا لَهُمُ الْغَالِبُونَ**}.

And these are my soldiers, '**And indeed, Our soldiers will be those who overcome.**'[127]

وَعَلَّمَ عِبَادَهُ كَيْفِيَّةَ هَذِهِ الْحَرْبِ وَالْجِهَادِ، فَجَمَعَهَا لَهُمْ فِي أَرْبَعِ كَلِمَاتٍ فَقَالَ:

And He taught His servants how to wage this war and struggle, and He summarized it for them in four words and said:

126 Al-Mujadila: 22.

127 Surat As-Saffat: 173.

{يَاأَيُّهَا الَّذِينَ آمَنُوا اصْبِرُوا وَصَابِرُوا وَرَابِطُوا وَاتَّقُوا اللَّهَ لَعَلَّكُمْ تُفْلِحُونَ}

**'O you who believe! Endure and be more patient [than your enemy], and guard your territory [by stationing army units permanently at the places from where the enemy can attack you], and fear Allah, so that you may be successful.'**[128]

وَلَا يَتِمُّ أَمْرُ هَذَا الْجِهَادِ إِلَّا بِهَذِهِ الْأُمُورِ الْأَرْبَعَةِ، فَلَا يَتِمُّ الصَّبْرُ إِلَّا بِمُصَابَرَةِ الْعَدُوِّ، وَهُوَ مُقَاوَمَتُهُ وَمُنَازَلَتُهُ،

And this *Jihad* cannot be completed except with these four matters, so patience is not complete except perseverance against the enemy, which is to resist and face him.

فَإِذَا صَابَرَ عَدُوَّهُ احْتَاجَ إِلَى أَمْرٍ آخَرَ وَهِيَ الْمُرَابَطَةُ، وَهِيَ لُزُومُ ثَغْرِ الْقَلْبِ وَحِرَاسَتُهُ لِئَلَّا يَدْخُلَ مِنْهُ الْعَدُوُّ، وَلُزُومُ ثَغْرِ الْعَيْنِ وَالْأُذُنِ وَاللِّسَانِ وَالْبَطْنِ وَالْيَدِ وَالرِّجْلِ، فَهَذِهِ الثُّغُورُ يَدْخُلُ مِنْهَا الْعَدُوُّ فَيَجُوسُ خِلَالَ الدِّيَارِ وَيُفْسِدُ مَا قَدَرَ عَلَيْهِ،

So when he perseveres against the enemy, he needs another matter: *Ribāṭ* (guard duty). It is sticking to the guard post of the heart and guarding it so that the enemy does not enter from it, and sticking to the guard-post of the eye, ear, tongue, stomach, hand and foot, for these guard-posts are penetrated by the enemy who probes the innermost part of the dwellings and ruins whatever he can.

فَالْمُرَابَطَةُ لُزُومُ هَذِهِ الثُّغُورِ، وَلَا يُخَلِّي مَكَانَهَا فَيُصَادِفَ الْعَدُوُّ الثَّغْرَ خَالِيًا فَيَدْخُلَ مِنْهُ.

[128] Surah Al-Imran: 200.

*Al Murābaṭa* (guarding the frontier) is staying at these guard-posts and not leaving their location, lest the enemy finds the guard-post empty and infiltrates therefrom.[129]

فَهَؤُلَاءِ أَصْحَابُ رَسُولِ اللَّهِ صلى الله عليه وسلم خَيْرُ الْخَلْقِ بَعْدَ النَّبِيِّينَ وَالْمُرْسَلِينَ، وَأَعْظَمُهُمْ حِمَايَةً وَحِرَاسَةً مِنَ الشَّيْطَانِ، وَقَدْ أَخْلَوُا الْمَكَانَ الَّذِي أُمِرُوا بِلُزُومِهِ يَوْمَ أُحُدٍ، فَدَخَلَ مِنْهُ الْعَدُوُّ، فَكَانَ مَا كَانَ.

So here you have the Companions of the Allah's Messenger (رَضِيَ ٱللَّهُ عَنْهُمْ), the best of creation after the prophets and the messengers (عَلَيْهِمُ ٱلسَّلَامُ), and the greatest of them in protection and guarding against *Shayṭān.* They left the place they were ordered to stick to on the day of *Uḥud*, so the enemy entered from it, and the consequences of their actions unfolded.

وَجِمَاعُ هَذِهِ الثَّلَاثَةِ وَعُمُودُهَا الَّذِي تَقُومُ بِهِ هُوَ تَقْوَى اللَّهِ تَعَالَى، فَلَا يَنْفَعُ الصَّبْرُ وَلَا الْمُصَابَرَةُ وَلَا الْمُرَابَطَةُ إِلَّا بِالتَّقْوَى، وَلَا تَقُومُ التَّقْوَى إِلَّا عَلَى سَاقِ الصَّبْرِ.

And the combination of these three and the pillar upon which they stand is the fear of Allah (جَلَّ وَعَلَا), for patience, endurance, and *Ribāṭ* (standing guard) do not benefit except with fear of Allah, and fearing Allah does not stand except on the leg of patience."

## THE CONFRONTATION OF THE TWO ARMIES

فَانْظُرِ الْآنَ فِيكَ إِلَى الْتِقَاءِ الْجَيْشَيْنِ، وَاصْطِدَامِ الْعَسْكَرَيْنِ وَكَيْفَ تُدَالُ مَرَّةً، وَيُدَالُ عَلَيْكَ أُخْرَى؟ أَقْبَلَ مَلِكُ الْكَفَرَةِ بِجُنُودِهِ وَعَسَاكِرِهِ، فَوَجَدَ الْقَلْبَ فِي حِصْنِهِ جَالِسًا عَلَى كُرْسِيِّ مَمْلَكَتِهِ، أَمْرُهُ نَافِذٌ فِي أَعْوَانِهِ، وَجُنْدُهُ قَدْ حَفُّوا بِهِ،

[129] Ibn al Qayyim says in 'Idah al-Ṣābirīn (p. 34), ch. 4: "Guard duty, just as it is the stationing at the frontier from which an enemy attack is feared in the physical world, it is also the protection of the heart's frontier, lest desires and Satan enter and remove it from its kingdom."

يُقَاتِلُونَ عَنْهُ وَيُدَافِعُونَ عَنْ حَوْزَتِهِ، فَلَمْ يُمْكِنْهُمُ الْهُجُومُ عَلَيْهِ إِلَّا بِمُخَامَرَةِ بَعْضِ أُمَرَائِهِ وَجُنْدِهِ عَلَيْهِ،

Now, look within you to the encounter of the two armies, the collision of the two forces. How are you, at times, the aggressor, and at others, the one aggressed upon? The king of disbelief approaches with his soldiers and armies and finds the heart in its fortress, seated upon the throne of its kingdom. His command is executed among his aides, he is surrounded by his troops, fighting and defending his territory. They could not attack him except by enticing some of his chiefs and soldiers against him.

فَسَأَلَ عَنْ أَخَصِّ الْجُنْدِ بِهِ وَأَقْرَبِهِمْ مِنْهُ مَنْزِلَةً، فَقِيلَ لَهُ: **هِيَ النَّفْسُ،**

They inquired about the closest and most beloved of his troops, and they were told: it was the self.

[What follows from this point is a illustrative discussion of *Iblīs* with the devils of the *jinn*.]

فَقَالَ لِأَعْوَانِهِ: ادْخُلُوا عَلَيْهَا مِنْ مُرَادِهَا، وَانْظُرُوا مَوَاقِعَ مَحَبَّتِهَا وَمَا هُوَ مَحْبُوبُهَا فَعِدُوهَا بِهِ وَمَنُّوهَا إِيَّاهُ وَانْقُشُوا صُورَةَ الْمَحْبُوبِ فِيهَا فِي يَقَظَتِهَا وَمَنَامِهَا،

So (*Iblīs*) said to his helpers: Approach it with its desires, look at the points of its love and what it holds as beloved, promise it and arouse false desires within it. Imprint within it the image of the beloved during its wakefulness and sleep.

فَإِذَا اطْمَأَنَّتْ إِلَيْهِ وَسَكَنَتْ عِنْدَهُ فَاطْرَحُوا عَلَيْهَا كَلَالِيبَ الشَّهْوَةِ وَخَطَاطِيفَهَا، ثُمَّ جُرُّوهَا بِهَا إِلَيْكُمْ، فَإِذَا خَامَرَتْ عَلَى الْقَلْبِ وَصَارَتْ مَعَكُمْ عَلَيْهِ مَلَكْتُمْ ثَغْرَ الْعَيْنِ وَالْأُذُنِ وَاللِّسَانِ وَالْفَمِ وَالْيَدِ وَالرِّجْلِ،

First, make it feel comfortable and at peace with you, then ensnare it with the temptations and allurements of lust. Draw it closer to you using these enticements. Once it conspires against the heart and allies with you, you will gain control over the watchposts of the eye, ear, tongue, mouth, hand, and leg.

فَرَابِطُوا عَلَى هَذِهِ الثُّغُورِ كُلَّ الْمُرَابَطَةِ، فَمَتَى دَخَلْتُمْ مِنْهَا إِلَى الْقَلْبِ فَهُوَ قَتِيلٌ أَوْ أَسِيرٌ، أَوْ جَرِيحٌ مُثْخَنٌ بِالْجُرَاحَاتِ،

Guard these guard posts with all vigilance. Once you enter the heart through them, it becomes dead, captive, or wounded and loaded with injuries.

وَلَا تُخْلُوا هَذِهِ الثُّغُورَ، وَلَا تُمَكِّنُوا سَرِيَّةً تَدْخُلُ فِيهَا إِلَى الْقَلْبِ فَتُخْرِجَكُمْ مِنْهَا،

Don't abandon these frontiers; don't let a raiding party enter through them to reach the heart and drive you out.

وَإِنْ غُلِبْتُمْ فَاجْتَهِدُوا فِي إِضْعَافِ السَّرِيَّةِ وَوَهَنِهَا، حَتَّى لَا تَصِلَ إِلَى الْقَلْبِ، فَإِنْ وَصَلَتْ إِلَيْهِ وَصَلَتْ ضَعِيفَةً لَا تُغْنِي عَنْهُ شَيْئًا.

If defeated, strive to weaken the raiding party and debilitate it until it doesn't reach the heart. If it reaches the heart, it does so while weakened and unable to help it.

## THE GUARD-POST OF VISION

فَإِذَا اسْتَوْلَيْتُمْ عَلَى هَذِهِ الثُّغُورِ فَامْنَعُوا ثَغْرَ الْعَيْنِ أَنْ يَكُونَ نَظَرُهُ اعْتِبَارًا، بَلِ اجْعَلُوا نَظَرَهُ تَفَرُّجًا وَاسْتِحْسَانًا وَتَلَهِّيًا، فَإِنِ اسْتَرَقَ نَظْرَةُ عِبْرَةٍ فَأَفْسِدُوهَا عَلَيْهِ بِنَظَرِ الْغَفْلَةِ وَالِاسْتِحْسَانِ وَالشَّهْوَةِ،

(*Iblīs* advises the devils of the *jinn*) Once you have taken control of these strongholds, prevent the gaze of the eye from being contemplative. Instead, make its gaze one of indulgence, admiration, and distraction. If its gaze happens to steal a moment of reflection, spoil it with a glance of negligence, admiration, and lust.

فَإِنَّهُ أَقْرَبُ إِلَيْهِ وَأَعْلَقُ بِنَفْسِهِ وَأَخَفُّ عَلَيْهِ، وَدُونَكُمْ ثَغْرَ الْعَيْنِ، فَإِنَّ مِنْهُ تَنَالُونَ بُغْيَتَكُمْ، فَإِنِّي مَا أَفْسَدْتُ بَنِي آدَمَ بِشَيْءٍ مِثْلَ النَّظَرِ، فَإِنِّي أَبْذُرُ بِهِ فِي الْقَلْبِ بَذْرَ الشَّهْوَةِ، ثُمَّ أَسْقِيهِ بِمَاءِ الْأُمْنِيَّةِ، ثُمَّ لَا أَزَالُ أَعِدُهُ وَأُمَنِّيهِ حَتَّى أُقَوِّيَ عَزِيمَتَهُ وَأَقُودَهُ بِزِمَامِ الشَّهْوَةِ إِلَى الِانْخِلَاعِ مِنَ الْعِصْمَةِ،

It is the shortest route, has more of a connection with itself, and is the lightest thing. So go after the guard post of the eye. From it, you can attain your agenda. Indeed, I have corrupted the children of Adam with nothing like a glance. For I sow in the heart the seed of lust with it, then I water it with the water of enticement. Then I continue to tempt and entice it until I strengthen its resolution and lead it by the reins of lust to break away from protection.

فَلَا تُهْمِلُوا أَمْرَ هَذَا الثَّغْرِ وَأَفْسِدُوهُ بِحَسَبِ اسْتِطَاعَتِكُمْ، وَهَوِّنُوا عَلَيْهِ أَمْرَهُ، وَقُولُوا لَهُ: مِقْدَارُ نَظْرَةٍ تَدْعُوكَ إِلَى تَسْبِيحِ الْخَالِقِ وَالتَّأَمُّلِ لِبَدِيعِ صَنِيعِهِ، وَحُسْنِ هَذِهِ الصُّورَةِ الَّتِي إِنَّمَا خُلِقَتْ لِيَسْتَدِلَّ بِهَا النَّاظِرُ عَلَيْهِ، وَمَا خَلَقَ اللَّهُ لَكَ الْعَيْنَيْنِ سُدًى، وَمَا خَلَقَ اللَّهُ هَذِهِ الصُّورَةَ لِيَحْجُبَهَا عَنِ النَّظَرِ،

So do not neglect the importance of this guard-post and ruin it as much as you can, make its task easier for it, and say to it: Looking invites you to praise the Creator and contemplate the beauty of His creation and the beauty of this picture, which was created so that the viewer may infer proof of Him from it. Allah did not create your two eyes in vain, and Allah did not create this picture to hide it from view.

وَإِنْ ظَفِرْتُمْ بِهِ قَلِيلَ الْعِلْمِ فَاسِدَ الْعَقْلِ، فَقُولُوا لَهُ: هَذِهِ الصُّورَةُ مَظْهَرٌ مِنْ مَظَاهِرِ الْحَقِّ وَمَجْلًى مِنْ مَجَالِيهِ، فَادْعُوهُ إِلَى الْقَوْلِ بِالِاتِّحَادِ،

If you catch one of little knowledge with a corrupt intellect, say to him: This image is a manifestation of the True God and a display of His majesty, so invite him to the doctrine of pantheism (i.e., saying that the Creator and creation are one and the same).

فَإِنْ لَمْ يَقْبَلْ فَالْقَوْلُ بِالْحُلُولِ الْعَامِّ أَوِ الْخَاصِّ، وَلَا تَقْنَعُوا مِنْهُ بِدُونِ ذَلِكَ، فَإِنَّهُ يَصِيرُ بِهِ مِنْ إِخْوَانِ النَّصَارَى، فَمُرُوهُ حِينَئِذٍ بِالْعِفَّةِ وَالصِّيَانَةِ وَالْعِبَادَةِ وَالزُّهْدِ فِي الدُّنْيَا، وَاصْطَادُوا عَلَيْهِ وَبِهِ الْجُهَّالَ، فَهَذَا مِنْ أَقْرَبِ خُلَفَائِي وَأَكْبَرِ جُنْدِي، بَلْ أَنَا مِنْ جُنْدِهِ وَأَعْوَانِهِ.

If he does not accept that, invite him to the doctrine of the divine incarnation in a broad or a detailed way, and do not be satisfied with less than that from him, for, by doing so, he becomes one of the brothers of Christians. Then at that point, command him with chastity, abstinence, worship, and asceticism in worldly matters, and use the ignorant ones to prey on him to prey on them. This one is from the closest of my successors and the largest of my army, instead, I am from his army and his aides.

## THE GUARD-POST OF HEARING

ثُمَّ امْنَعُوا ثَغْرَ الْأُذُنِ أَنْ يَدْخُلَ عَلَيْهِ مَا يُفْسِدُ عَلَيْكُمُ الْأَمْرَ، فَاجْتَهِدُوا أَنْ لَا تُدْخِلُوا مِنْهُ إِلَّا الْبَاطِلَ، فَإِنَّهُ خَفِيفٌ عَلَى النَّفْسِ تَسْتَحْلِيهِ وَتَسْتَحْسِنُهُ،

(*Shayṭān* instructs the devils): Next, prevent anything from entering the guard-post of the ear that could spoil your affair. Strive to admit nothing to pass through it but falsehood. This is easy for the self, which enjoys it and approves of it.

تَخَيَّرُوا لَهُ أَعْذَبَ الْأَلْفَاظِ وَأَسْحَرَهَا لِلْأَلْبَابِ، وَامْزِجُوهُ بِمَا تَهْوَى النَّفْسُ مَزْجًا. وَأَلْقُوا الْكَلِمَةَ فَإِنْ رَأَيْتُمْ مِنْهُ إِصْغَاءً إِلَيْهَا فَزُجُّوهُ بِأَخَوَاتِهَا، وَكُلَّمَا صَادَفْتُمْ مِنْهُ اسْتِحْسَانَ شَيْءٍ فَالْهَجُوا لَهُ بِذِكْرِهِ،

Choose the sweetest and most enchanting words for the intellect, and mix them with what the self desires. Release the statement, and if you see from it an inclination towards it, lure it with others like it. Whenever you encounter its liking for something, constantly entice it with the mention of that thing.

وَإِيَّاكُمْ أَنْ يَدْخُلَ مِنْ هَذَا الثَّغْرِ شَيْءٌ مِنْ كَلَامِ اللَّهِ أَوْ كَلَامِ رَسُولِهِ صلى الله عليه وسلم أَوْ كَلَامِ النُّصَحَاءِ، فَإِنْ غُلِبْتُمْ عَلَى ذَلِكَ وَدَخَلَ مِنْ ذَلِكَ شَيْءٌ، فَحُولُوا بَيْنَهُ وَبَيْنَ فَهْمِهِ وَتَدَبُّرِهِ وَالتَّفَكُّرِ فِيهِ وَالْعِظَةِ بِهِ،

Beware not to let anything from the words of Allah, His Messenger (ﷺ) or the words of wise advisors enter through this stronghold. If you're overpowered and something of the sort enters, interfere with his understanding, his contemplation, and his reflection on it, as well as any lessons he may draw from it.

إِمَّا بِإِدْخَالِ ضِدِّهِ عَلَيْهِ، وَإِمَّا بِتَهْوِيلِ ذَلِكَ وَتَعْظِيمِهِ وَأَنَّ هَذَا أَمْرٌ قَدْ حِيلَ بَيْنَ النُّفُوسِ وَبَيْنَهُ فَلَا سَبِيلَ لَهَا إِلَيْهِ، وَهُوَ حِمْلٌ يَثْقُلُ عَلَيْهَا لَا تَسْتَقِلُّ بِهِ، وَنَحْوِ ذَلِكَ، وَإِمَّا بِإِرْخَاصِهِ عَلَى النُّفُوسِ، وَأَنَّ الِاشْتِغَالَ يَنْبَغِي أَنْ يَكُونَ بِمَا هُوَ أَعْلَى عِنْدَ النَّاسِ، وَأَعَزُّ عَلَيْهِمْ، وَأَغْرَبُ عِنْدَهُمْ، وَزَبُونُهُ الْقَابِلُونَ لَهُ أَكْثَرُ،

Do this by presenting the opposite of the truth or exaggerating and making it seem unattainable, suggesting that it is beyond one's capabilities. Convince the self that it is a burden too significant to bear alone. Or by cheapening it to the self, stating that people should be engaged in what is loftier, more valuable, and uncommon, that would garner more customers.

وَأَمَّا الْحَقُّ فَهُوَ مَهْجُورٌ، وَقَائِلُهُ مُعَرِّضٌ نَفْسَهُ لِلْعَدَاوَةِ، وَالرَّابِحُ بَيْنَ النَّاسِ أَوْلَى بِالْإِيثَارِ وَنَحْوِ ذَلِكَ،

As for the truth, it's abandoned, and the one who speaks it exposes himself to animosity. (Persuade them) that what people perceive as profitable deserves priority, and so on.

فَتُدْخِلُونَ الْبَاطِلَ عَلَيْهِ فِي كُلِّ قَالَبٍ يَقْبَلُهُ وَيَخِفُّ عَلَيْهِ، وَتُخْرِجُونَ لَهُ الْحَقَّ فِي كُلِّ قَالَبٍ يَكْرَهُهُ وَيَثْقُلُ عَلَيْهِ.

Therefore, you introduce falsehood to him in every form that he can accept, which is easy for him, while you present the truth to him in every form that he despises and finds burdensome.

وَإِذَا شِئْتَ أَنْ تَعْرِفَ ذَلِكَ فَانْظُرْ إِلَى إِخْوَانِهِمْ مِنْ شَيَاطِينِ الْإِنْسِ، كَيْفَ يُخْرِجُونَ الْأَمْرَ بِالْمَعْرُوفِ وَالنَّهْيَ عَنِ الْمُنْكَرِ فِي قَالَبِ كَثْرَةِ الْفُضُولِ، وَتَتَبُّعِ عَثَرَاتِ النَّاسِ، وَالتَّعَرُّضِ مِنَ الْبَلَاءِ لِمَا لَا يُطِيقُ، وَإِلْقَاءِ الْفِتَنِ بَيْنَ النَّاسِ، وَنَحْوِ ذَلِكَ،

And if you wish to know this, look at their brothers from the human devils, see how they project the matter of enjoining good and forbidding evil in the mold of excessive curiosity, searching for people's missteps, exposing themselves to affliction that they cannot bear, inciting strife among people and the like.

وَيُخْرِجُونَ اتِّبَاعَ السُّنَّةِ وَوَصْفَ الرَّبِّ تَعَالَى بِمَا وَصَفَ بِهِ نَفْسَهُ وَوَصَفَهُ بِهِ رَسُولُهُ صلى الله عليه وسلم فِي قَالَبِ التَّجْسِيمِ وَالتَّشْبِيهِ وَالتَّكْيِيفِ،

And they project the adherence to the Sunnah and the description of the Lord (عَزَّوَجَلَّ) as He has described Himself and as His messenger (صَلَّىٱللَّهُعَلَيْهِوَسَلَّمَ) has described Him in the mold of *tajsīm* (making Allah similar to a created body), *tashbīh* (likening Allah to the creation), and *takyīf* (asking how Allah's descriptions are beyond what is apparent).

وَيُسَمُّونَ عُلُوَّ اللَّهِ عَلَى خَلْقِهِ وَاسْتِوَاءَهُ عَلَى عَرْشِهِ وَمُبَايَنَتَهُ لِمَخْلُوقَاتِهِ، تَحَيُّزًا،

They call the highness of Allah over His creation, His ascension above His throne, and His clearness from His creatures as localization.

وَيُسَمُّونَ نُزُولَهُ إِلَى سَمَاءِ الدُّنْيَا، وَقَوْلَهُ: مَنْ يَسْأَلُنِي فَأُعْطِيَهُ، تَحَرُّكًا وَانْتِقَالًا،

They call His descent to the lowest heaven and His saying: 'Who asks Me that I may give him,' as moving and transitioning.

وَيُسَمُّونَ مَا وَصَفَ بِهِ نَفْسَهُ مِنَ الْيَدِ وَالْوَجْهِ أَعْضَاءَ وَجَوَارِحَ،

They call what He described Himself with — such as the hand and face — organs and limbs.

وَيُسَمُّونَ مَا يَقُومُ بِهِ مِنْ أَفْعَالِهِ حَوَادِثَ، وَمَا يَقُومُ مِنْ صِفَاتِهِ أَعْرَاضًا،

They call what is affirmed from His actions as occurrences and what is affirmed from His attributes as accidents.

ثُمَّ يَتَوَصَّلُونَ إِلَى نَفْيِ مَا وَصَفَ بِهِ نَفْسَهُ بِهَذِهِ الْأُمُورِ، وَيُوهِمُونَ الْأَغْمَارَ وَضُعَفَاءَ الْبَصَائِرِ، أَنَّ إِثْبَاتَ الصِّفَاتِ الَّتِي نَطَقَ بِهَا كِتَابُ اللَّهِ وَسُنَّةُ رَسُولِهِ صلى الله عليه وسلم تَسْتَلْزِمُ هَذِهِ الْأُمُورَ، وَيُخْرِجُونَ هَذَا التَّعْطِيلَ فِي قَالَبِ التَّنْزِيهِ وَالتَّعْظِيمِ،

Then they deny what He described Himself with of these things, and they delude the ignorant and those with weak insight that affirm the attributes mentioned in the Book of Allah and the Sunnah of His messenger (ﷺ) necessitates these matters. They project this denial in the mold of transcendence and exaltation.

وَأَكْثَرُ النَّاسِ ضُعَفَاءُ الْعُقُولِ يَقْبَلُونَ الشَّيْءَ بِلَفْظٍ وَيَرُدُّونَهُ بِعَيْنِهِ بِلَفْظٍ آخَرَ، قَالَ اللَّهُ تَعَالَى: {**وَكَذَلِكَ جَعَلْنَا لِكُلِّ نَبِيٍّ عَدُوًّا شَيَاطِينَ الْإِنْسِ وَالْجِنِّ يُوحِي بَعْضُهُمْ إِلَى بَعْضٍ زُخْرُفَ الْقَوْلِ غُرُورًا**} فَسَمَّاهُ زُخْرُفًا، وَهُوَ بَاطِلٌ، لِأَنَّ صَاحِبَهُ يُزَخْرِفُهُ وَيُزَيِّنُهُ مَا اسْتَطَاعَ، وَيُلْقِيهِ إِلَى سَمْعِ الْمَغْرُورِ فَيَغْتَرُّ بِهِ.

Most people with weak intellect accept a thing in one wording and reject the same thing in another. Allah (عَزَّوَجَلَّ) said, **'And thus We have made for every prophet an enemy - devils from mankind and jinn, inspiring to one another decorative speech in delusion.'**[130] He called it decorative speech, which is falsehood, because its owner decorates it, adorns it as much as he

[130] Surah Al-An'am: 112

can, and throws it to the hearing of the deluded, who is then deceived by it.

وَالْمَقْصُودُ: أَنَّ الشَّيْطَانَ قَدْ لَزِمَ ثَغرَ الأُذُنِ، أَنْ يُدْخِلَ فِيهَا مَا يَضُرُّ الْعَبْدَ وَلَا يَنْفَعُهُ، وَيَمْنَعَ أَنْ يَدْخُلَ إِلَيْهَا مَا يَنْفَعُهُ، وَإِنْ دَخَلَ بِغَيْرِ اخْتِيَارِهِ أَفْسَدَهُ عَلَيْهِ.

The point is that the devil has insisted on the gateway of the ear, to insert into it what harms the servant and does not benefit him, and prevents what benefits him from entering it, and if it enters without his choice, he corrupts it for him."

## THE GUARD-POST OF THE TONGUE

ثُمَّ يَقُولُ: قُومُوا عَلَى ثَغْرِ اللِّسَانِ، فَإِنَّهُ الثَّغْرُ الْأَعْظَمُ، وَهُوَ قَبَالَةُ الْمَلِكِ، فَأَجْرُوا عَلَيْهِ مِنَ الْكَلَامِ مَا يَضُرُّهُ وَلَا يَنْفَعُهُ، وَامْنَعُوهُ أَنْ يَجْرِيَ عَلَيْهِ شَيْءٌ مِمَّا يَنْفَعُهُ: مِنْ ذِكْرِ اللَّهِ تَعَالَى وَاسْتِغْفَارِهِ، وَتِلَاوَةِ كِتَابِهِ، وَنَصِيحَةِ عِبَادِهِ، وَالتَّكَلُّمِ بِالْعِلْمِ النَّافِعِ،

Then (*Shayṭān*) says (to the devils of the *jinn*): Take control of the guard-post of the tongue, for it is the greatest passage and the King's representative. Place upon it speech that harms it and does not benefit it, and prevent it from uttering anything that benefits it, such as remembrance of Allah (سُبْحَانَهُ وَتَعَالَىٰ), seeking His forgiveness, reciting His book, sincerely advising His servants, and speaking about beneficial knowledge.

وَيَكُونُ لَكُمْ فِي هَذَا الثَّغْرِ أَمْرَانِ عَظِيمَانِ، لَا تُبَالُونَ بِأَيِّهِمَا ظَفِرْتُمْ:

You have two great matters at this stronghold, and you shouldn't be concerned about which you achieve.

**أَحَدُهُمَا:** التَّكَلُّمُ بِالْبَاطِلِ، فَإِنَّمَا الْمُتَكَلِّمُ بِالْبَاطِلِ أَخٌ مِنْ إِخْوَانِكُمْ، وَمِنْ أَكْبَرِ جُنْدِكُمْ وَأَعْوَانِكُمْ.

The first matter is speaking falsehood, for the one who speaks falsehood is a brother among your brothers and one of your greatest soldiers and supporters.

**الثَّانِي:** السُّكُوتُ عَنِ الْحَقِّ، فَإِنَّ السَّاكِتَ عَنِ الْحَقِّ أَخٌ لَكُمْ أَخْرَسُ، كَمَا أَنَّ الْأَوَّلَ أَخٌ نَاطِقٌ، وَرُبَّمَا كَانَ الْأَخُ الثَّانِي أَنْفَعَ أَخَوَيْكُمْ لَكُمْ، أَمَا سَمِعْتُمْ قَوْلَ النَّاصِحِ: الْمُتَكَلِّمُ بِالْبَاطِلِ شَيْطَانٌ نَاطِقٌ، وَالسَّاكِتُ عَنِ الْحَقِّ شَيْطَانٌ أَخْرَسُ؟

The second matter is silence in the face of the truth, for the one who remains silent about the truth is a mute brother of yours. It may be that the second brother is more beneficial to you than the first. Have you not heard the saying of the advisor: The one who speaks falsehood is a speaking devil, and the one who remains silent about the truth is a mute devil?[131]

فَالرِّبَاطَ الرِّبَاطَ عَلَى هَذَا الثَّغْرِ أَنْ يَتَكَلَّمَ بِحَقٍّ أَوْ يُمْسِكَ عَنْ بَاطِلٍ، وَزَيِّنُوا لَهُ التَّكَلُّمَ بِالْبَاطِلِ بِكُلِّ طَرِيقٍ، وَخَوِّفُوهُ مِنَ التَّكَلُّمِ بِالْحَقِّ بِكُلِّ طَرِيقٍ.

So, avidly guard this guard-post so that he neither speaks the truth nor refrains from falsehood, and adorn for him the act of speaking falsehood in every way, and instill fear in him of speaking the truth in every way.

وَاعْلَمُوا يَا بَنِيَّ أَنَّ ثَغْرَ اللِّسَانِ هُوَ الَّذِي أُهْلِكُ مِنْهُ بَنِي آدَمَ، وَأَكُبُّهُمْ مِنْهُ عَلَى مَنَاخِرِهِمْ فِي النَّارِ، فَكَمْ لِي مِنْ قَتِيلٍ وَأَسِيرٍ وَجَرِيحٍ أَخَذْتُهُ مِنْ هَذَا الثَّغْرِ؟

And know, O my children, that the guard-post of the tongue is the one from which the children of Adam are destroyed, and it is what will lead most of them to their destruction in the Fire. How many killed, captured, and wounded, have I taken from this stronghold?

[131] This is reported from Abū ʿAlī al-Daqqāq al-Naysābūrī (d. 406 AH رَحِمَهُ ٱللَّهُ).

وَأُوصِيكُمْ بِوَصِيَّةٍ فَاحْفَظُوهَا: لِيَنْطِقْ أَحَدُكُمْ عَلَى لِسَانِ أَخِيهِ مِنَ الْإِنْسِ بِالْكَلِمَةِ، وَيَكُونُ الْآخَرُ عَلَى لِسَانِ السَّامِعِ فَيَنْطِقُ بِاسْتِحْسَانِهَا وَتَعْظِيمِهَا وَالتَّعَجُّبِ مِنْهَا وَيَطْلُبُ مِنْ أَخِيهِ إِعَادَتَهَا،

And I advise you (i.e., *Shayṭān* advises the devils) with a piece of advice, so memorize it: let one of you speak a word on the tongue of his human associate, and let another (devil) speak on the listener's tongue. Make the latter express his admiration, his reverence, and his astonishment at it and ask his friend to repeat it.

وَكُونُوا أَعْوَانًا عَلَى الْإِنْسِ بِكُلِّ طَرِيقٍ، وَادْخُلُوا عَلَيْهِمْ مِنْ كُلِّ بَابٍ، وَاقْعُدُوا لَهُمْ كُلَّ مَرْصَدٍ، أَمَا سَمِعْتُمْ قَسَمِي الَّذِي أَقْسَمْتُ بِهِ لِرَبِّهِمْ حَيْثُ قُلْتُ: {**فَبِمَا أَغْوَيْتَنِي لَأَقْعُدَنَّ لَهُمْ صِرَاطَكَ الْمُسْتَقِيمَ - ثُمَّ لَآتِيَنَّهُمْ مِنْ بَيْنِ أَيْدِيهِمْ وَمِنْ خَلْفِهِمْ وَعَنْ أَيْمَانِهِمْ وَعَنْ شَمَائِلِهِمْ وَلَا تَجِدُ أَكْثَرَهُمْ شَاكِرِينَ**} .

Be helpers against humans in every way, enter upon them from every door, and occupy every observation point for them. Have you not heard my oath that I swore to their Lord, when I said, '**Then I will come to them from before them and from behind them and on their right and on their left, and You will not find most of them grateful.**'[132]

أَوَمَا تَرَوْنِي قَدْ قَعَدْتُ لِابْنِ آدَمَ بِطُرُقِهِ كُلِّهَا، فَلَا يَفُوتُنِي مِنْ طَرِيقٍ إِلَّا قَعَدْتُ لَهُ بِطَرِيقٍ غَيْرِهِ، حَتَّى أُصِيبَ مِنْهُ حَاجَتِي أَوْ بَعْضَهَا؟ وَقَدْ حَذَّرَهُمْ ذَلِكَ رَسُولُهُمْ صلى الله عليه وسلم وَقَالَ لَهُمْ: «إِنَّ الشَّيْطَانَ قَدْ قَعَدَ لِابْنِ آدَمَ بِطُرُقِهِ كُلِّهَا، وَقَعَدَ لَهُ بِطَرِيقِ الْإِسْلَامِ، فَقَالَ لَهُ: أَتُسْلِمُ وَتَذَرُ دِينَكَ وَدِينَ آبَائِكَ؟ فَخَالَفَهُ وَأَسْلَمَ، فَقَعَدَ لَهُ بِطَرِيقِ الْهِجْرَةِ، فَقَالَ: أَتُهَاجِرُ وَتَذَرُ أَرْضَكَ وَسَمَاءَكَ؟ فَخَالَفَهُ وَهَاجَرَ، فَقَعَدَ لَهُ بِطَرِيقِ الْجِهَادِ، فَقَالَ: أَتُجَاهِدُ فَتُقْتَلَ فَيُقَسَّمَ الْمَالُ وَتُنْكَحَ الزَّوْجَةُ؟»

132 See Surah Al-A'raf, 7:16-17.

(*Shayṭān* advises the devils): "Do you not see how I have positioned myself for the son of Adam in all his paths? He never escapes me in a single path except that I have positioned myself for him on another until I attain my need, if only partially. Their Messenger (ﷺ) warned them of this and said, 'Indeed, Shayṭān has positioned himself for the son of Adam in all his ways, and he has positioned himself for him in the path of Islam.' He asked, 'Will you submit and abandon your religion and those of your forefathers?' So he opposed him and embraced Islam. Then he positioned himself for him in the path of migration and said, 'Will you migrate and abandon your earth and sky?' So he opposed him and migrated. Then he positioned himself for him in the path of jihad and said, 'Will you strive and be killed, and your wealth be divided, and your wife be married to someone else?'"

فَكَهَذَا فَاقْعُدُوا لَهُمْ بِكُلِّ طُرُقِ الْخَيْرِ، فَإِذَا أَرَادَ أَحَدُهُمْ أَنْ يَتَصَدَّقَ فَاقْعُدُوا لَهُ عَلَى طَرِيقِ الصَّدَقَةِ، وَقُولُوا لَهُ فِي نَفْسِهِ: أَتُخْرِجُ الْمَالَ فَتَبْقَى مِثْلَ هَذَا السَّائِلِ وَتَصِيرَ بِمَنْزِلَتِهِ أَنْتَ وَهُوَ سَوَاءٌ؟ أَوَمَا سَمِعْتُمْ مَا أَلْقَيْتُ عَلَى لِسَانِ رَجُلٍ سَأَلَهُ آخَرُ أَنْ يَتَصَدَّقَ عَلَيْهِ، قَالَ: هِيَ أَمْوَالُنَا إِذَا أَعْطَيْنَاكُمُوهَا صِرْنَا مِثْلَكُمْ.

So, in this fashion, position yourselves for them in every path of goodness. When one of them intends to give charity, position yourselves for him in the path of charity and say to him inwardly, 'Will you give away your wealth, making you and the beggar equal?' Have you not heard what a man said when another asked him to give charity? He said, 'This is our wealth. If we give it to you, we would become like you.'

وَاقْعُدُوا لَهُ بِطَرِيقِ الْحَجِّ، فَقُولُوا: طَرِيقُهُ مَخُوفَةٌ مُشِقَّةٌ، يَتَعَرَّضُ سَالِكُهَا لِتَلَفِ النَّفْسِ وَالْمَالِ، وَهَكَذَا فَاقْعُدُوا لَهُ عَلَى سَائِرِ طُرُقِ الْخَيْرِ بِالتَّنْفِيرِ عَنْهَا وَذِكْرِ صُعُوبَتِهَا وَآفَاتِهَا، ثُمَّ اقْعُدُوا لَهُمْ عَلَى طُرُقِ الْمَعَاصِي فَحَسِّنُوهَا فِي أَعْيُنِ بَنِي

آدَمَ، وَزَيِّنُوهَا فِي قُلُوبِهِمْ، وَاجْعَلُوا أَكْثَرَ أَعْوَانِكُمْ عَلَى ذَلِكَ النِّسَاءَ، فَمِنْ أَبْوَابِهِنَّ فَادْخُلُوا عَلَيْهِمْ، فَنِعْمَ الْعَوْنُ هُنَّ لَكُمْ.

(*Shayṭān* advises the devils): Position yourselves for them in the path of Hajj and say, 'Its path is fearful and arduous, and those who traverse it are exposed to the loss of life and wealth.' Likewise, position yourselves for them on all paths of goodness by discouraging them from it and mentioning its difficulties and harms. Then position yourselves for them in the paths of sins and beautify them in the eyes of the children of Adam, and adorn them in their hearts. Let women be your most effective helpers in this. Enter upon them through their doors, for they greatly help you.

ثُمَّ الْزَمُوا ثَغْرَ الْيَدَيْنِ وَالرِّجْلَيْنِ، فَامْنَعُوهَا أَنْ تَبْطِشَ بِمَا يَضُرُّكُمْ وَتَمْشِي فِيهِ.

Then hold your position at the guard posts of the hands and the feet, preventing them from striking or walking in any way they harm you (i.e., your cause)."

## THE INSISTENT SELF IS SHAYṬĀN'S GREATEST ALLY

وَاعْلَمُوا أَنَّ أَكْبَرَ أَعْوَانِكُمْ عَلَى لُزُومِ هَذِهِ الثُّغُورِ مُصَالَحَةُ النَّفْسِ الْأَمَّارَةِ، فَأَعِينُوهَا وَاسْتَعِينُوا بِهَا، وَأَمِدُّوهَا وَاسْتَمِدُّوا مِنْهَا،

(*Shayṭān* advises the devils): And know that your greatest allies in holding your positions at these guard-posts are attained by contracting peace with the *insistent self*. So support it, seek assistance from it, strengthen it, and derive strength from it.

وَكُونُوا مَعَهَا عَلَى حَرْبِ النَّفْسِ الْمُطْمَئِنَّةِ، فَاجْتَهِدُوا فِي كَسْرِهَا وَإِبْطَالِ قُوَاهَا، وَلَا سَبِيلَ إِلَى ذَلِكَ إِلَّا بِقَطْعِ مَوَادِّهَا عَنْهَا،

Stand with it in the relentless war against the *assured, tranquil self*. Strive to break it and neutralize its power. There is no way to achieve this except by cutting off its resources.

فَإِذَا انْقَطَعَتْ مَوَادُّهَا وَقَوِيَتْ مَوَادُّ النَّفْسِ الْأَمَّارَةِ، وَانْطَاعَتْ لَكُمْ أَعْوَانُهَا، فَاسْتَنْزِلُوا الْقَلْبَ مِنْ حِصْنِهِ، وَاعْزِلُوهُ عَنْ مَمْلَكَتِهِ، وَوَلُّوا مَكَانَهُ النَّفْسَ الْأَمَّارَةَ،

So when its supplies are cut off and the supplies of the insistent self are strengthened, and its allies are obedient to you, then bring down the heart from its fortress, isolate it from its kingdom and appoint in its place the insistent self.

فَإِنَّهَا لَا تَأْمُرُ إِلَّا بِمَا تَهْوَوْنَهُ وَتُحِبُّونَهُ، وَلَا تَجِيئُكُمْ بِمَا تَكْرَهُونَهُ أَلْبَتَّةَ، مَعَ أَنَّهَا لَا تُخَالِفُكُمْ فِي شَيْءٍ تُشِيرُونَ بِهِ عَلَيْهَا، بَلْ إِذَا أَشَرْتُمْ عَلَيْهَا بِشَيْءٍ بَادَرَتْ إِلَى فِعْلِهِ،

For it only commands what it desires and what you love, and it does not bring to you anything that you detest. Alongside that, it does not oppose you in anything you advice it to do, but rather when you advice it to do something, it hastens to act.

فَإِنْ أَحْسَسْتُمْ مِنَ الْقَلْبِ مُنَازَعَةً إِلَى مَمْلَكَتِهِ، وَأَرَدْتُمُ الْأَمْنَ مِنْ ذَلِكَ، فَاعْقِدُوا بَيْنَهُ وَبَيْنَ النَّفْسِ عَقْدَ النِّكَاحِ، فَزَيِّنُوهَا وَجَمِّلُوهَا، وَأَرُوهَا إِيَّاهُ فِي أَحْسَنِ صُورَةِ عَرُوسٍ تُوجَدُ،

(*Shayṭān* advises the devils): If you sense from the heart any yearning to return to its dominion and want to be safe from that, establish a marriage contract between it and the insistent self. Adorn it and beautify it, and present her to it in the best possible appearance of a bride.

وَقُولُوا لَهُ ذُقْ طَعْمَ هَذَا الْوِصَالِ وَالتَّمَتُّعِ بِهَذِهِ الْعَرُوسِ كَمَا ذُقْتَ طَعْمَ الْحَرْبِ، وَبَاشَرْتَ مَرَارَةَ الطَّعْنِ وَالضَّرْبِ، ثُمَّ وَازِنْ بَيْنَ لَذَّةِ هَذِهِ الْمَسْأَلَةِ، وَمَرَارَةِ تِلْكَ الْمُحَارَبَةِ، فَدَعِ الْحَرْبَ تَضَعُ أَوْزَارَهَا، فَلَيْسَتْ بِيَوْمٍ وَتَنْقَضِي، وَإِنَّمَا هُوَ حَرْبٌ مُتَّصِلٌ بِالْمَوْتِ، وَقُوَاكَ تَضْعُفُ عَنْ حَرْبٍ دَائِمٍ.

Say to it, 'Taste the sweetness of this union and the enjoyment of this bride, just as you have tasted war and the bitterness of wounds and blows. Then contrast between the pleasure of this matter and the bitterness of that, and let the war lay down its burdens. It is not just a day, after which it ends, but rather an ongoing war lasting to death, and you are not strong enough to engage in perpetual war.'

وَاسْتَعِينُوا يَا بَنِيَّ بِجُنْدَيْنِ عَظِيمَيْنِ لَنْ تُغْلَبُوا مَعَهُمَا:

(*Shayṭān* advises the devils): Seek assistance, O my children, from two mighty armies alongside whom you will never be defeated:

أَحَدُهُمَا: جُنْدُ الْغَفْلَةِ، فَأَغْفِلُوا قُلُوبَ بَنِي آدَمَ عَنِ اللَّهِ تَعَالَى وَالدَّارِ الْآخِرَةِ بِكُلِّ طَرِيقٍ، فَلَيْسَ لَكُمْ شَيْءٌ أَبْلَغَ فِي تَحْصِيلِ غَرَضِكُمْ مِنْ ذَلِكَ، فَإِنَّ الْقَلْبَ إِذَا غَفَلَ عَنِ اللَّهِ تَعَالَى تَمَكَّنْتُمْ مِنْهُ وَمِنْ إِغْوَائِهِ.

The first is the army of heedlessness, so make the hearts of the children of Adam oblivious to Allah the Exalted and the Hereafter in every way. There is nothing more effective for you in attaining your objective than this. When the heart becomes heedless of Allah, you will gain control over it and its seduction.

الثَّانِي: جُنْدُ الشَّهَوَاتِ، فَزَيِّنُوهَا فِي قُلُوبِهِمْ، وَحَسِّنُوهَا فِي أَعْيُنِهِمْ، وَصُولُوا عَلَيْهِمْ بِهَذَيْنِ الْعَسْكَرَيْنِ، فَلَيْسَ لَكُمْ فِي بَنِي آدَمَ أَبْلَغُ مِنْهُمَا،

The second is the army of desires, so beautify them in their hearts and make them appealing in their eyes. Engage them with these two armies, for there is nothing more effective for you among the children of Adam.

وَاسْتَعِينُوا عَلَى الْغَفْلَةِ بِالشَّهَوَاتِ، وَعَلَى الشَّهَوَاتِ بِالْغَفْلَةِ، وَاقْرِنُوا بَيْنَ الْغَافِلِينَ، ثُمَّ اسْتَعِينُوا بِهِمَا عَلَى الذَّاكِرِ، وَلَا يَغْلِبُ وَاحِدٌ خَمْسَةً، فَإِنَّ مَعَ الْغَافِلَيْنِ شَيْطَانَيْنِ صَارُوا أَرْبَعَةً، وَشَيْطَانُ الذَّاكِرِ مَعَهُمْ،

Seek the support of desires for heedlessness and heedlessness for desires. Companion yourself with those who are heedless, then seek assistance from them against the one who remembers. One alone cannot overpower five, for with two heedless people, two devils become four, and the devil of the one who remembers is also with them.

وَإِذَا رَأَيْتُمْ جَمَاعَةً مُجْتَمِعِينَ عَلَى مَا يَضُرُّكُمْ - مِنْ ذِكْرِ اللَّهِ وَمُذَاكَرَةِ أَمْرِهِ وَنَهْيِهِ وَدِينِهِ، وَلَمْ تَقْدِرُوا عَلَى تَفْرِيقِهِمْ - فَاسْتَعِينُوا عَلَيْهِمْ بِبَنِي جِنْسِهِمْ مِنَ الْإِنْسِ الْبَطَّالِينَ، فَقَرِّبُوهُمْ مِنْهُمْ، وَشَوِّشُوا عَلَيْهِمْ بِهِمْ.

When you see a group gathered upon something that harms you – such as mentioning Allah, discussing His commandments, prohibitions, and religion – and you cannot disperse them, seek assistance against them with individuals of their kind among idle humans. Bring them close to them and create confusion among them."

وَبِالْجُمْلَةِ فَأَعِدُّوا لِلْأُمُورِ أَقْرَانَهَا، وَادْخُلُوا عَلَى كُلِّ وَاحِدٍ مِنْ بَنِي آدَمَ مِنْ بَابِ إِرَادَتِهِ وَشَهْوَتِهِ، فَسَاعِدُوهُ عَلَيْهَا، وَكُونُوا لَهُ أَعْوَانًا عَلَى تَحْصِيلِهَا،

(*Shayṭān* advises the devils): And in general, prepare counterparts for matters, and enter every one of the children of Adam through the door of their will and desire. Assist them in fulfilling their desires, and be their allies in achieving them.

وَإِذَا كَانَ اللَّهُ قَدْ أَمَرَهُمْ أَنْ يَصْبِرُوا لَكُمْ وَيُصَابِرُوكُمْ وَيُرَابِطُوا عَلَيْكُمُ الثُّغُورَ، فَاصْبِرُوا أَنْتُمْ وَصَابِرُوا وَرَابِطُوا عَلَيْهِمْ بِالثُّغُورِ، وَانْتَهِزُوا فُرَصَكُمْ فِيهِمْ عِنْدَ الشَّهْوَةِ وَالْغَضَبِ، فَلَا تَصْطَادُوا بَنِي آدَمَ فِي أَعْظَمَ مِنْ هَذَيْنِ الْمَوْطِنَيْنِ.

And when Allah has commanded them to have patience for you, to endure for you, and to guard the fortifications for you, then you too should have patience and endure, and guard the fortifications against them. Seize your opportunities with them during moments of desire and anger, and do not ensnare the children of Adam in anything greater than these two realms.

وَاعْلَمُوا أَنَّ مِنْهُمْ مَنْ يَكُونُ سُلْطَانُ الشَّهْوَةِ عَلَيْهِ أَغْلَبَ وَسُلْطَانُ غَضَبِهِ ضَعِيفٌ مَقْهُورٌ، فَخُذُوا عَلَيْهِ طَرِيقَ الشَّهْوَةِ، وَدَعُوا طَرِيقَ الْغَضَبِ،

Know that among them are those whose desire has greater control over them, while the authority of their anger is weak and suppressed. So take them on the path of desire and leave the path of anger.

وَمِنْهُمْ مَنْ يَكُونُ سُلْطَانُ الْغَضَبِ عَلَيْهِ أَغْلَبَ، فَلَا تُخْلُوا طَرِيقَ الشَّهْوَةِ قَلْبَهُ، وَلَا تُعَطِّلُوا ثَغْرَهَا، فَإِنْ لَمْ يَمْلِكْ نَفْسَهُ عِنْدَ الْغَضَبِ، فَإِنَّهُ الْحَرِيُّ أَنْ لَا يَمْلِكَ نَفْسَهُ عِنْدَ الشَّهْوَةِ،

And among them are those whose anger has greater control over them. Do not leave their hearts void of desire nor obstruct its passageway. If they cannot control themselves in moments of anger, then it is more likely that they will not control themselves in moments of desire.

فَزَوِّجُوا بَيْنَ غَضَبِهِ وَشَهْوَتِهِ، وَامْزِجُوا أَحَدَهُمَا بِالْآخَرِ، وَادْعُوهُ إِلَى الشَّهْوَةِ مِنْ بَابِ الْغَضَبِ، وَإِلَى الْغَضَبِ مِنْ طَرِيقِ الشَّهْوَةِ.

Therefore, marry desire to anger and mix one with the other, and invite desire through the avenue of anger, and invite anger through the path of desire.

وَاعْلَمُوا أَنَّهُ لَيْسَ لَكُمْ فِي بَنِي آدَمَ سِلَاحٌ أَبْلَغُ مِنْ هَذَيْنِ السِّلَاحَيْنِ، وَإِنَّمَا أَخْرَجْتُ أَبَوَيْهِمْ مِنَ الْجَنَّةِ بِالشَّهْوَةِ، وَإِنَّمَا أَلْقَيْتُ الْعَدَاوَةَ بَيْنَ أَوْلَادِهِمْ بِالْغَضَبِ، فَبِهِ قَطَّعْتُ أَرْحَامَهُمْ، وَسَفَكْتُ دِمَاءَهُمْ، وَبِهِ قَتَلَ أَحَدُ ابْنَيْ آدَمَ أَخَاهُ.

And know that there is no weapon more effective for you among the children of Adam than these two weapons. Indeed, I expelled their parents from Paradise through desire and caused enmity among their children through anger. Through them, I severed their ties and shed their blood, and by means of them, one of the sons of Adam killed his brother.

وَاعْلَمُوا أَنَّ الْغَضَبَ جَمْرَةٌ فِي قَلْبِ ابْنِ آدَمَ، وَالشَّهْوَةَ تَثُورُ مِنْ قَلْبِهِ، وَإِنَّمَا تُطْفَأُ النَّارُ بِالْمَاءِ وَالصَّلَاةِ وَالذِّكْرِ وَالتَّكْبِيرِ، فَإِيَّاكُمْ أَنْ تُمَكِّنُوا ابْنَ آدَمَ عِنْدَ غَضَبِهِ وَشَهْوَتِهِ مِنْ قُرْبَانِ الْوُضُوءِ وَالصَّلَاةِ، فَإِنَّ ذَلِكَ يُطْفِئُ عَنْهُمْ نَارَ الْغَضَبِ وَالشَّهْوَةِ، وَقَدْ أَمَرَهُمْ نَبِيُّهُمْ بِذَلِكَ فَقَالَ: «إِنَّ الْغَضَبَ جَمْرَةٌ فِي قَلْبِ ابْنِ آدَمَ، أَمَا رَأَيْتُمْ مِنِ احْمِرَارِ عَيْنَيْهِ وَانْتِفَاخِ أَوْدَاجِهِ، فَمَنْ أَحَسَّ بِذَلِكَ فَلْيَتَوَضَّأْ» .

Know that anger is a fire that burns in the heart of the children of Adam, and desire erupts from their hearts. Indeed, the fire is extinguished with water, prayer, remembrance, and the utterance of "Allahu Akbar" (Allah is the Greatest.) So beware of enabling the son of Adam in moments of anger and desire through performing ablution and offering prayers, for that will extinguish the fire of anger and desire within them. Allah has commanded them, saying, "Indeed, anger is a burning coal in the heart of the son of Adam. Have you not seen his eyes' redness and veins' swelling? So whoever experiences that, let him perform ablution."

وَقَالَ لَهُمْ: «إِنَّمَا تُطْفَأُ النَّارُ بِالْمَاءِ» ، وَقَدْ أَوْصَاهُمُ اللَّهُ أَنْ يَسْتَعِينُوا عَلَيْكُمْ بِالصَّبْرِ وَالصَّلَاةِ، فَحُولُوا بَيْنَهُمْ وَبَيْنَ ذَلِكَ، وَأَنْسُوهُمْ إِيَّاهُ،

(*Shayṭān* advises the devils): And he (i.e., the Prophet ﷺ) told them, **"Indeed, fire is extinguished by water."** Allah has advised them to seek assistance against you through patience and prayer. So create a barrier between them and that, and make them forget it.

وَاسْتَعِينُوا عَلَيْهِمْ بِالشَّهْوَةِ وَالْغَضَبِ، وَأَبْلَغُ أَسْلِحَتِكُمْ فِيهِمْ وَأَنْكَاهَا: الْغَفْلَةُ وَاتِّبَاعُ الْهَوَى. وَأَعْظَمُ أَسْلِحَتِهِمْ فِيكُمْ وَأَمْنَعُ حُصُونِهِمْ ذِكْرُ اللَّهِ وَمُخَالَفَةُ الْهَوَى، فَإِذَا رَأَيْتُمُ الرَّجُلَ مُخَالِفًا لِهَوَاهُ فَاهْرَبُوا مِنْ ظِلِّهِ وَلَا تَدْنُوا مِنْهُ.

Seek assistance against them with desire and anger; your most potent weapons against them are heedlessness and following one's whims. And their greatest weapons against you — and the most fortified citadels — are the remembrance of Allah and going against one's whims. So when you see a person going against their whims, flee from their shade and do not approach them."

وَالْمَقْصُودُ أَنَّ الذُّنُوبَ وَالْمَعَاصِيَ سِلَاحٌ وَمَدَدٌ يَمُدُّ بِهَا الْعَبْدُ أَعْدَاءَهُ وَيُعِينُهُمْ بِهَا عَلَى نَفْسِهِ، فَيُقَاتِلُونَ بِسِلَاحِهِ، وَيَكُونُ مَعَهُمْ عَلَى نَفْسِهِ، وَهَذَا غَايَةُ الْجَهْلِ.

The intended meaning is that sins and transgressions are weapons and supports with which a servant arms his enemies and assists them against himself. They fight with these weapons, and the servant allows them to prevail over himself. This is the height of ignorance.

مَا يَبْلُغُ الْأَعْدَاءُ مِنْ جَاهِلٍ ... مَا يَبْلُغُ الْجَاهِلُ مِنْ نَفْسِهِ

Enemies cannot achieve against an ignorant person... What an ignorant person can achieve against himself.

وَمِنَ الْعَجَائِبِ أَنَّ الْعَبْدَ يَسْعَى بِجُهْدِهِ فِي هَوَانِ نَفْسِهِ، وَهُوَ يَزْعُمُ أَنَّهُ لَهَا مُكْرِمٌ وَيَجْتَهِدُ فِي حِرْمَانِهَا أَعْلَى حُظُوظِهَا وَأَشْرَفَهَا وَهُوَ يَزْعُمُ أَنَّهُ يَسْعَى فِي حَظِّهَا، وَيَبْذُلُ جُهْدَهُ فِي تَحْقِيرِهَا وَتَصْغِيرِهَا وَتَدْنِيسِهَا، وَهُوَ يَزْعُمُ أَنَّهُ يُعْلِيهَا وَيَرْفَعُهَا وَيُكْبِرُهَا.

Among the wonders is that a servant strives to degrade his soul while believing that he honors it. He deprives it of its highest and noblest aspirations, thinking he strives for its benefit. He exerts effort to belittle it, degrade it, and defile it while claiming to elevate, honor and magnify it.

وَكَانَ بَعْضُ السَّلَفِ يَقُولُ فِي خُطْبَتِهِ: أَلَا رُبَّ مُهِينٍ لِنَفْسِهِ وَهُوَ يَزْعُمُ أَنَّهُ لَهَا مُكْرِمٌ، وَمُذِلٌّ لِنَفْسِهِ وَهُوَ يَزْعُمُ أَنَّهُ لَهَا مُعِزٌّ، وَمُصَغِّرٌ لِنَفْسِهِ وَهُوَ يَزْعُمُ أَنَّهُ لَهَا

مُكَبِّرٌ، وَمُضِيعٌ لِنَفْسِهِ وَهُوَ يَزْعُمُ أَنَّهُ مُرَاعٍ لِحِفْظِهَا، وَكَفَى بِالْمَرْءِ جَهْلًا أَنْ يَكُونَ مَعَ عَدُوِّهِ عَلَى نَفْسِهِ، يَبْلُغُ مِنْهَا بِفِعْلِهِ مَا لَا يَبْلُغُهُ عَدُوُّهُ، وَاللَّهُ الْمُسْتَعَانُ

Some of the pious predecessors used to say in their sermons: "How astonishing is the one who humiliates his self while claiming to honor it, who debases his self while claiming to exalt it, who belittles his self while claiming to magnify it, who wastes his self while claiming to protect it. It is sufficient ignorance for a person to be with his enemy against himself, allowing his enemy to achieve what his enemy himself cannot achieve through his actions. And Allah is the one sought for help."

# Conclusion

## The Never-ending Conflict Between The Inner-States of the Self & Its Traits

# Conclusion: The Never-ending Conflict Between The Inner-States of the Self & Its Traits

Ibn al Qayyim (رَحِمَهُ ٱللَّهُ) eloquently describes the lifelong state of conflict and dissonance within the human self. He says:[133]

"وَقَدْ امْتَحَنَ اللَّهُ سُبْحَانَهُ الْإِنْسَانَ بِهَاتَيْنِ النَّفْسَيْنِ: الْأَمَّارَةِ، وَاللَّوَّامَةِ؛ كَمَا أَكْرَمَهُ بِالْمُطْمَئِنَّةِ. فَهِيَ نَفْسٌ وَاحِدَةٌ تَكُونُ أَمَّارَةً، ثُمَّ لَوَّامَةً، ثُمَّ مُطْمَئِنَّةً. وَهِيَ غَايَةُ كَمَالِهَا وَصَلاحِهَا.

Allah tested the human with these two states of the self: the one insistently commanding with evil (*al ammārah*) and the self-reproaching soul (*al-lawwāmah*), just as He honored them with the tranquil self (*al muṭma'innah*). It is a single self that becomes first prone to evil, then is self-reproaching, and finally is tranquil, the latter being the self's ultimate perfection and rectitude.

وَأَيَّدَ الْمُطْمَئِنَّةَ بِجُنُودٍ عَدِيدَةٍ. فَجَعَلَ الْمَلَكَ قَرِينَهَا وَصَاحِبَهَا الَّذِي يَلِيهَا وَيُسَدِّدُهَا، وَيَقْذِفُ فِيهَا الْحَقَّ، وَيُرَغِّبُهَا فِيهِ، وَيُرِيهَا حُسْنَ صُورَتِهِ، وَيَزْجُرُهَا عَنِ الْبَاطِلِ، وَيُزَهِّدُهَا فِيهِ، وَيُرِيهَا قُبْحَ صُورَتِهِ. وَأَمَدَّهَا بِمَا عَلَّمَهَا مِنَ الْقُرْآنِ وَالْأَذْكَارِ وَأَعْمَالِ الْبِرِّ، وَجَعَلَ وُفُودَ الْخَيْرَاتِ وَأَمْدَادَ التَّوْفِيقِ تَنْتَابُهَا وَتَصِلُ إِلَيْهَا مِنْ كُلِّ نَاحِيَةٍ. وَكُلَّمَا تَلَقَّتْهَا بِالْقَبُولِ، وَالشُّكْرِ، وَالْحَمْدِ لِلَّهِ، وَرُؤْيَةِ أَوَّلِيَّتِهِ فِي ذَلِكَ كُلِّهِ، ازْدَادَ مَدَدُهَا، فَتَقْوَى عَلَى مُحَارَبَةِ الْأَمَّارَةِ.

Numerous troops support the tranquil self. Allah (عَزَّوَجَلَّ) made the angel its companion and the one who is close to it, guiding and directing it, casting the truth into it, encouraging it towards the truth, showing it the beauty of the truth, deterring it,

---

133 Al-Rūḥ.

disinteresting in and showing it the ugliness of falsehood. Allah supplied it with what it learned from the *Qur'an*, supplications, and good deeds. He (عَزَّوَجَلَّ) made the delegations of goodness and supplies of success reach it from all sides. Every time the soul receives (these spiritual blessings) with acceptance, thanks, praises Allah and sees His support, its supplies increase, and it becomes stronger in fighting the insistently commanding self.

فَمِنْ جُنُودِهَا — وَهُوَ سُلْطَانُ عَسَاكِرِهَا وَمَلِكُهَا — الْإِيمَانُ وَالْيَقِينُ. فَالْجُيُوشُ
الْإِسْلَامِيَّةُ كُلُّهَا تَحْتَ لِوَائِهِ نَاظِرَةٌ إِلَيْهِ. إِنْ ثَبَتَ ثَبَتَتْ، وَإِنِ انْهَزَمَ وَلَّتْ عَلَى
أَدْبَارِهَا.

Faith and certainty are among its troops — the commanders of its armies and its king. All the Islamic armies are under its banner, looking up to it. If it stands firm, they stand firm; if it is defeated, they turn their backs and flee.

ثُمَّ أُمَرَاءُ هَذَا الْجَيْشِ وَمُقَدَّمُو عَسَاكِرِهِ: شُعَبُ الْإِيمَانِ الْمُتَعَلِّقَةُ بِالْجَوَارِحِ عَلَى
اخْتِلَافِ أَنْوَاعِهَا، كَالصَّلَاةِ وَالزَّكَاةِ وَالصِّيَامِ وَالْحَجِّ وَالْجِهَادِ، وَالْأَمْرِ بِالْمَعْرُوفِ
وَالنَّهْيِ عَنِ الْمُنْكَرِ، وَنَصِيحَةِ الْخَلْقِ، وَالْإِحْسَانِ إِلَيْهِمْ بِأَنْوَاعِ الْإِحْسَانِ؛

Then the leaders of this army and the forefront of its troops are the branches of faith that are related to the limbs in their various forms, such as prayer, alms-giving, fasting, pilgrimage, *jihad*, commanding good, forbidding evil, sincerely advising the people, and various acts of kindness.

وَشُعَبُهُ الْبَاطِنَةُ الْمُتَعَلِّقَةُ بِالْقَلْبِ، كَالْإِخْلَاصِ وَالتَّوَكُّلِ وَالْإِنَابَةِ وَالتَّوْبَةِ وَالْمُرَاقَبَةِ
وَالصَّبْرِ وَالْحِلْمِ وَالتَّوَاضُعِ وَالْمَسْكَنَةِ، وَامْتِلَاءِ الْقَلْبِ مِنْ مَحَبَّةِ اللَّهِ وَرَسُولِهِ،
وَتَعْظِيمِ أَوَامِرِ اللَّهِ وَحُقُوقِهِ، وَالْغَيْرَةِ لِلَّهِ وَفِي اللَّهِ، وَالشَّجَاعَةِ وَالْعِفَّةِ وَالصِّدْقِ
وَالشَّفَقَةِ وَالرَّحْمَةِ.

There are also the internal branches related to the heart, such as sincerity, reliance on Allah, turning to Him, repentance, mindfulness, patience, forbearance, humility, contentment, filling the heart with the love of Allah and His Messenger, venerating Allah's commands and rights, having jealous protectiveness (*al ghayrah*) for Allah's sake and as relates to Allah, courage, chastity, truthfulness, compassion, and mercy.

**وَمِلاكُ ذَلِكَ كُلِّهِ الْإِخْلَاصُ وَالصِّدْقُ.** فَلَا يَتَعَنَّى الصَّادِقُ الْمُخْلِصُ، فَقَدْ أُقِيمَ عَلَى الصِّرَاطِ الْمُسْتَقِيمِ، فَيُسَارُ بِهِ وَهُوَ رَاقِدٌ. وَلَا يَتَهَنَّى مَنْ حُرِمَ الصِّدْقُ وَالْإِخْلَاصُ، فَقَدْ قُطِعَتْ عَلَيْهِ الطَّرِيقُ، وَاسْتَهْوَتْهُ الشَّيَاطِينُ فِي الْأَرْضِ حَيْرَانَ، فَإِنْ شَاءَ فَلْيَعْمَلْ، وَإِنْ شَاءَ فَلْيَتْرُكْ، فَلَا يَزِيدُهُ عَمَلُهُ مِنَ اللَّهِ إِلَّا بُعْدًا.

**The essential factor of all this is sincerity and truthfulness.** The sincere and truthful person does not fatigue; they are established on the straight path and are mobile even at rest. The one deprived of truthfulness and sincerity does not enjoy himself; their path is blocked, and they are confused by the devils on the earth. Whether they choose to do good deeds or to abandon them, their deeds will not bring them closer to Allah but distance them farther away.

وَبِالْجُمْلَةِ فَمَا كَانَ لِلَّهِ وَبِاللَّهِ، فَهُوَ مِنْ جُنْدِ النَّفْسِ الْمُطْمَئِنَّةِ.

In summary, whatever is for and by Allah (i.e., done seeking His assistance) belongs to the troops of the contented soul.

## THE COLLUSION BETWEEN THE INSISTENT SELF & SHAYTĀN

وَأَمَّا النَّفْسُ الْأَمَّارَةُ فَجُعِلَ الشَّيْطَانُ قَرِينَهَا وَصَاحِبَهَا الَّذِي يَلِيهَا، فَهُوَ يَعِدُهَا وَيُمَنِّيهَا، وَيَقْذِفُ فِيهَا الْبَاطِلَ، وَيَأْمُرُهَا بِالسُّوءِ وَيُزَيِّنُهُ لَهَا، وَيُطَالِبُهَا بِالْأَمَلِ، وَيُرِيهَا الْبَاطِلَ فِي صُورَةٍ تَقْبَلُهَا وَتَسْتَحْسِنُهَا، وَيُمِدُّهَا بِأَنْوَاعِ الْإِمْدَادِ الْبَاطِلِ مِنَ

الْأَمَانِي الْكَاذِبَةِ وَالشَّهَوَاتِ الْمُهْلِكَةِ. وَيَسْتَعِينُ عَلَيْهَا بِهَوَاهَا وَإِرَادَتِهَا، فَمِنْهُ يَدْخُلُ عَلَيْهَا، وَيُدْخِلُ عَلَيْهَا كُلَّ مَكْرُوهٍ.

As for the insistent self, *Shayṭān* has been made its companion and associate. He tempts and entices it, casts falsehood into it, commands it to do evil and beautifies it for the soul. He prolongs its hopes, shows it falsehood in a form that it accepts and approves of and provides it with various types of false support from false hopes and destructive desires. He uses its own desires and will to aid him against it; through these, he infiltrates it and introduces all that is detestable.

فَمَا اسْتَعَانَ عَلَى النُّفُوسِ بِشَيْءٍ هُوَ أَبْلَغُ مِنْ هَوَاهَا وَإِرَادَتِهَا الْبَتَّةَ. وَقَدْ عَلَّمَ ذَلِكَ إِخْوَانَهُ مِنْ شَيَاطِينِ الْإِنْسِ، فَلَا يَسْتَعِينُونَ عَلَى الصُّوَرِ الْمَمْنُوعَةِ مِنْهُمْ بِشَيْءٍ أَبْلَغَ مِنْ هَوَاهُمْ وَإِرَادَتِهِمْ، فَإِذَا أَعْيَتْهُمْ صُورَةٌ طَلَبُوا بِجَهْدِهِمْ مَا تُحِبُّهُ وَتَهْوَاهُ، ثُمَّ طَلَبُوا بِجَهْدِهِمْ تَحْصِيلَهُ، فَاصْطَادُوا بِهِ تِلْكَ الصُّوَرَ. فَإِذَا فَتَحَتْ لَهُمُ النَّفْسُ بَابَ الْهَوَى دَخَلُوا مِنْهُ، فَجَاسُوا خِلَالَ الدِّيَارِ، فَعَاثُوا وَأَفْسَدُوا، وَفَتَّكُوا وَسَبَوَا، وَفَعَلُوا مَا يَفْعَلُهُ الْعَدُوُّ بِبِلَادِ عَدُوِّهِ إِذَا تَحَكَّمَ فِيهَا.

He employs desires and intentions as the most effective means to control inner selves. He imparted this knowledge to his human devil brethren, who rely on their desires and will to pursue someone they cannot possess. When they fail to attain their desired object, they seek out what they love and desire, and then strive to obtain it, thus ensnaring their targets. Once desires open the door to them, they invade, cause havoc, corruption, destruction, and plunder, acting like an enemy would in overtaking their adversary's land.

فَهَدَّمُوا مَعَالِمَ الْإِيمَانِ وَالْقُرْآنِ وَالذِّكْرِ وَالصَّلَاةِ، وَخَرَّبُوا الْمَسَاجِدَ، وَعَمَّرُوا الْبِيَعَ وَالْكَنَائِسَ وَالْحَانَاتِ وَالْمَوَاخِيرَ. وَقَصَدُوا إِلَى الْمَلِكِ، فَأَسَرُوهُ، وَسَلَبُوهُ مُلْكَهُ، وَنَقَلُوهُ مِنْ عِبَادَةِ الرَّحْمَنِ إِلَى عِبَادَةِ الْبَغَايَا وَالْأَوْثَانِ، وَمِنْ عِزِّ الطَّاعَةِ إِلَى ذُلِّ الْمَعْصِيَةِ، وَمِنَ السَّمَاعِ الرَّحْمَانِيِّ إِلَى السَّمَاعِ الشَّيْطَانِيِّ، وَمِنَ الِاسْتِعْدَادِ لِلِقَاءِ

رَبِّ الْعَالَمِينَ إِلَى الِاسْتِعْدَادِ لِلِقَاءِ إِخْوَانِ الشَّيَاطِينِ. فَبَيْنَا هُوَ يُرَاعِي حُقُوقَ اللَّهِ وَمَا أَمَرَهُ بِهِ، إِذْ صَارَ يَرْعَى الْخَنَازِيرَ! وَبَيْنَا هُوَ مُنْتَصِبٌ لِخِدْمَةِ الْعَزِيزِ الرَّحِيمِ، إِذْ صَارَ مُنْتَصِبًا لِخِدْمَةِ كُلِّ شَيْطَانٍ رَجِيمٍ!

They demolish the landmarks of faith, the Quran, remembrance, and prayer, destroy mosques, and build markets, churches, bars, and brothels. They head to the king, capture him, rob him of his kingdom, and transfer him from the worship of the Most Merciful to the worship of prostitutes and idols, from the dignity of obedience to the humiliation of disobedience, from listening to what is recited from al-Raḥmān to listening to what is recited from *Shayṭān*, and from preparing to meet the Lord of the Worlds to preparing to meet the brethren of the devils. While he used to tend to Allah's rights and commands, he now tends to pigs! While he was devoted to serving the Almighty, the Merciful, he is now devoted to serving every accursed devil!

**وَالْمَقْصُودُ أَنَّ الْمَلَكَ قَرِينُ النَّفْسِ الْمُطْمَئِنَّةِ، وَالشَّيْطَانُ قَرِينُ الْأَمَّارَةِ.**

**The point is that the angel is the companion of the contented soul, and Shayṭān is the companion of the insistently commanding self.**

وَقَدْ رَوَى أَبُو الْأَحْوَصِ، عَنْ عَطَاءِ بْنِ السَّائِبِ، عَنْ مُرَّةَ، عَنْ عَبْدِ اللَّهِ قَالَ: قَالَ رَسُولُ اللَّهِ - صَلَّى اللَّهُ عَلَيْهِ وَسَلَّمَ -: «إِنَّ لِلشَّيْطَانِ لَمَّةً مِنَ ابْنِ آدَمَ، وَلِلْمَلَكِ لَمَّةً. فَأَمَّا لَمَّةُ الشَّيْطَانِ، فَإِيعَادٌ بِالشَّرِّ، وَتَكْذِيبٌ بِالْحَقِّ. وَأَمَّا لَمَّةُ الْمَلَكِ، فَإِيعَادٌ بِالْخَيْرِ، وَتَصْدِيقٌ بِالْحَقِّ. فَمَنْ وَجَدَ ذَلِكَ فَلْيَعْلَمْ أَنَّهُ مِنَ اللَّهِ، وَلْيَحْمَدِ اللَّهَ. وَمَنْ وَجَدَ الْآخَرَ فَلْيَتَعَوَّذْ بِاللَّهِ مِنَ الشَّيْطَانِ الرَّجِيمِ». ثُمَّ قَرَأَ: ﴿الشَّيْطَانُ يَعِدُكُمُ الْفَقْرَ وَيَأْمُرُكُمْ بِالْفَحْشَاءِ﴾

Abu Al-Ahwass narrated from Ata Ibn Al-Saib, from Murra, from Abdullah [Ibn Mas'ūd (رَضِيَ اللَّهُ عَنْهُ)], who said that the Messenger of Allah (ﷺ) said,[134] "Indeed, Shayṭān has a touch on the son of Adam, and the angel also has a touch. As for *Shayṭān's* touch, it is a prompt to do evil and a denial of the truth. As for the angel's touch, it is a prompt to do good and an affirmation of the truth. Whoever experiences the latter should know that it is from Allah and should praise Allah. Whoever experiences the former should seek refuge in Allah from the accursed *Shayṭān*." Then he recited, "**Shayṭān threatens you with poverty and orders you to immorality.**"[135]

وَقَدْ رَوَاهُ عَمْرٌو عَنْ عَطَاءِ بْنِ السَّائِبِ، وَزَادَ فِيهِ عَمْرٌو، قَالَ: سَمِعْنَا فِي هَذَا الْحَدِيثِ أَنَّهُ كَانَ يُقَالُ: «إِذَا أَحَسَّ أَحَدُكُمْ مِنْ لَمَّةِ الْمَلَكِ شَيْئًا فَلْيَحْمَدِ اللَّهَ، وَلْيَسْأَلْهُ مِنْ فَضْلِهِ. وَإِذَا أَحَسَّ مِنْ لَمَّةِ الشَّيْطَانِ شَيْئًا فَلْيَسْتَغْفِرِ اللَّهَ، وَلْيَتَعَوَّذْ مِنَ الشَّيْطَانِ».

'Amr narrated from Ata Ibn Al-Sā'ib and added in his narration, saying, "We heard about this *hadith* that it was said: 'If one of you feels something from the angel's touch, let him praise Allah and ask Him for His bounty. If one feels something from *Shayṭān's* touch, let him seek forgiveness from Allah and seek refuge in Him from *Shayṭān*.'"

فَالْمَلَكُ وَجُنْدُهُ مِنَ الْإِيمَانِ يَقْتَضِيَانِ مِنَ النَّفْسِ الْمُطْمَئِنَّةِ التَّوْحِيدَ، وَالْإِحْسَانَ وَالْبِرَّ، وَالتَّقْوَى وَالصَّبْرَ وَالتَّوَكُّلَ، وَالتَّوْبَةَ وَالْإِنَابَةَ وَالْإِقْبَالَ عَلَى اللَّهِ، وَقِصَرَ الْأَمَلِ وَالِاسْتِعْدَادَ لِلْمَوْتِ وَمَا بَعْدَهُ. وَالشَّيْطَانُ وَجُنْدُهُ مِنَ الْكُفْرِ يَقْتَضِيَانِ مِنَ النَّفْسِ الْأَمَّارَةِ ضِدَّ ذَلِكَ.

---

[134] This narration is reported in *Mawqūf* form as a statement of Ibn Mas'ūd (رضي الله عنه). It is not authentic as a statement of the Prophet (ﷺ) according to many scholars of ḥadīth. The *mawqūf* report is Repored by al-Ṭabarī (6176), and graded Ṣaḥīḥ li Ghayrihi by Maḥmūd Shākir (رحمه الله) in his checking. Abu Zur'ah and Abu Ḥātim both said that it is authentic as a statement of Ibn Mas'ūd.

[135] Al-Baqarah: 268.

The angel and his troops of faith demand from the contented soul monotheism, excellence, righteousness, piety, patience, reliance on Allah, repentance, turning back to Allah, focusing on Allah, shortening one's hopes, and preparing for death and what comes after. Shayṭān and his troops of disbelief demand the opposite from the insistent self..

وَقَدْ سَلَّطَ اللَّهُ سُبْحَانَهُ الشَّيْطَانَ عَلَى كُلِّ مَا لَيْسَ لَهُ، وَلَمْ يُرَدْ بِهِ وَجْهُهُ، وَلَا هُوَ طَاعَةٌ لَهُ. وَجَعَلَ ذَلِكَ إِقْطَاعَهُ، فَهُوَ يَسْتَنِيبُ النَّفْسَ الْأَمَّارَةَ عَلَى هَذَا الْعَمَلِ وَالْإِقْطَاعِ، وَيَتَقَاضَاهَا أَنْ تَأْخُذَ الْأَعْمَالَ مِنَ النَّفْسِ الْمُطْمَئِنَّةِ، فَتَجْعَلَهَا قُوَّةً لَهَا. فَهِيَ أَحْرَصُ شَيْءٍ عَلَى تَخْلِيصِ الْأَعْمَالِ كُلِّهَا لَهَا، وَأَنْ تَصِيرَ مِنْ حَظُوظِهَا،

Allah has granted Shayṭān authority over everything that does not belong to Him, is not intended for Him, and is not obedient to Him. Allah has made this Satan's domain, and he incites the insistent self to engage in this work and domain. He persuades the soul to take actions from the contented soul and make them a source of strength for itself. The insistent self is keen to claim all deeds for itself and make them part of its share.

فَأَصْعَبُ شَيْءٍ عَلَى النَّفْسِ الْمُطْمَئِنَّةِ تَخْلِيصُ الْأَعْمَالِ مِنَ الشَّيْطَانِ وَمِنَ الْأَمَّارَةِ لِلَّهِ. فَلَوْ وَصَلَ مِنْهَا عَمَلٌ وَاحِدٌ كَمَا يَنْبَغِي لَنَجَا بِهِ الْعَبْدُ، وَلَكِنْ أَبَتْ الْأَمَّارَةُ وَالشَّيْطَانُ أَنْ يَدَعَا لَهَا عَمَلًا وَاحِدًا يَصِلُ إِلَى اللَّهِ. كَمَا قَالَ بَعْضُ الْعَارِفِينَ بِاللَّهِ وَبِنَفْسِهِ: وَاللَّهُ لَوْ أَعْلَمُ أَنَّ لِيَ عَمَلًا وَاحِدًا وَصَلَ إِلَى اللَّهِ لَكُنْتُ أَفْرَحَ بِالْمَوْتِ مِنْ الْغَائِبِ يَقْدَمُ عَلَى أَهْلِهِ.

The most difficult thing for the contented soul is to free its deeds from Shayṭān and the insistent self for Allah. If a single deed from the contented soul reaches Allah as it should, the servant would be saved by it. However, the insistent self and Shayṭān refuse to let a single deed reach Allah. As one of those who know Allah and themselves said, "By Allah, if I knew that I had a single deed that reached Allah, I would be happier with death than the one who is absent coming back to his family."

وقال عبد الله بن عمر: لو أعلم أن الله تقبَّل مني سجدة واحدة لم يكن غائبٌ أحبَّ إليَّ من الموت، {إِنَّمَا يَتَقَبَّلُ اللَّهُ مِنَ الْمُتَّقِينَ} [المائدة: 27].

Abdullah ibn Umar said, "If I knew that Allah had accepted a single prostration from me, nothing that is absent would be dearer to me than death, 'Indeed, Allah only accepts from the righteous'."[136]

وَقَدْ انْتَصَبَتِ الْأَمَّارَةُ فِي مُقَابَلَةِ الْمُطْمَئِنَّةِ، فَكُلُّ مَا جَاءَتْ بِهِ تِلْكَ مِنْ خَيْرٍ ضَاهَتْهَا هَذِهِ وَجَاءَتْ مِنَ الشَّرِّ بِمَا يُقَابِلُهُ حَتَّى تُفْسِدَهُ عَلَيْهَا.

The insistent self has positioned itself to counteract the contented soul; for every good that the contented soul brings, the insistent self opposes and brings forth evil to corrupt it.

فَإِذَا جَاءَتْ بِالْإِيمَانِ وَالتَّوْحِيدِ جَاءَتْ هَذِهِ بِمَا يَقْدَحُ فِي الْإِيمَانِ مِنَ الشَّكِّ وَالنِّفَاقِ، وَمَا يَقْدَحُ فِي التَّوْحِيدِ مِنَ الشِّرْكِ وَمَحَبَّةِ غَيْرِ اللَّهِ وَخَوْفِهِ وَرَجَائِهِ. وَلَا تَرْضَى حَتَّى تُقَدِّمَ مُحَبَّةَ غَيْرِهِ وَخَوْفَهُ وَرَجَاءَهُ عَلَى مَحَبَّتِهِ سُبْحَانَهُ وَخَوْفِهِ وَرَجَائِهِ، فَيَكُونُ مَا لَهُ عِنْدَهَا هُوَ الْمُؤَخَّرُ، وَمَا لِلْخَلْقِ هُوَ الْمُقَدَّمُ، وَهَذَا حَالُ أَكْثَرِ هَذَا الْخَلْقِ.

When the contented soul brings faith and monotheism, the insistent self introduces doubt and hypocrisy to undermine faith, and idolatry and love, fear and hope for others besides Allah to undermine monotheism. It is only satisfied once it elevates the love, fear and hope for others above the love, fear and hope for Allah Himself, taking what belongs to Allah secondary and what belongs to creation primary. This is the condition of the majority of people.

---

136 Al-Ma'idah: 27.

وَإِذَا جَاءَتْ تِلْكَ بِتَجْرِيدِ الْمُتَابَعَةِ لِلرَّسُولِ، جَاءَتْ هَذِهِ بِتَحْكِيمِ آرَاءِ الرِّجَالِ وَأَقْوَالِهِمْ عَلَى الْوَحْيِ، وَأَتَتْ مِنَ الشُّبَهِ الْمُضِلَّةِ بِمَا يَمْنَعُهَا مِنْ كَمَالِ الْمُتَابَعَةِ وَتَحْكِيمِ السُّنَّةِ وَعَدَمِ الِالْتِفَاتِ إِلَى آرَاءِ الرِّجَالِ، فَتَقُومُ الْحَرْبُ بَيْنَ هَاتَيْنِ النَّفْسَيْنِ، وَالْمَنْصُورُ مَنْ نَصَرَهُ اللَّهُ.

When the contented soul seeks to follow the Prophet exclusively, the insistent self subjects human opinions and statements to the divine revelation, presenting misleading doubts to prevent complete adherence to the Sunnah and disregard for human opinions. A battle ensues between these two souls, and the victorious one is the one Allah supports.

وَإِذَا جَاءَتْ تِلْكَ بِالْإِخْلَاصِ وَالصِّدْقِ وَالتَّوَكُّلِ وَالْإِنَابَةِ وَالْمُرَاقَبَةِ، جَاءَتْ هَذِهِ بِأَضْدَادِهَا، وَأَخْرَجَتْهَا فِي عِدَّةِ قَوَالِبَ، وَتُقْسِمُ بِاللَّهِ مَا مُرَادُهَا إِلَّا الْإِحْسَانُ وَالتَّوْفِيقُ. وَاللَّهُ يَعْلَمُ أَنَّهَا كَاذِبَةٌ، وَمَا مُرَادُهَا إِلَّا مُجَرَّدُ حَظِّهَا وَاتِّبَاعُ هَوَاهَا، وَالتَّفَلُّتُ مِنْ سِجْنِ الْمُتَابَعَةِ وَالتَّحْكِيمِ الْمَحْضِ لِلسُّنَّةِ إِلَى فَضَاءِ إِرَادَتِهَا وَشَهْوَتِهَا وَحَظُوظِهَا. وَلَعَمْرُ اللَّهِ مَا تَخَلَّصَتْ إِلَّا مِنْ فَضَاءِ الْمُتَابَعَةِ وَالتَّسْلِيمِ إِلَى سِجْنِ الْهَوَى وَالْإِرَادَةِ وَضِيقِهِ وَظُلْمَتِهِ وَوَحْشَتِهِ. فَهِيَ مَسْجُونَةٌ فِيهِ فِي هَذَا الْعَالَمِ، وَفِي الْبَرْزَخِ فِي أَضْيَقَ مِنْهُ، وَيَوْمَ الْمَعَادِ الثَّانِي فِي أَضْيَقَ مِنْهُمَا.

When the contented soul brings sincerity, truthfulness, reliance on Allah, turning back to Allah and watchfulness, the insistent self counters with their opposites, casting them into various molds, swearing by Allah that its only intention is righteousness and success. But Allah knows that it lies, and its true goal is merely to secure its share and follow its desires, escaping the prison of following the Sunnah and submitting entirely to the Sunnah to indulge its will, desires, and interests. By the life of Allah,[137] it only frees itself from the open space of following and submitting to the prison of desire, will, narrowness, darkness, and

[137] The phrase "لعمر الله" is held by many scholars to be a form of swearing by Allah by swearing by His divine attribute of life.

loneliness. It is imprisoned in this world, in the intermediate state in even narrower confines, and on the Day of Resurrection in the narrowest of all.

وَمِنْ أَعْجَبِ أَمْرِهَا أَنْ تَسْحَرَ الْعَقْلَ وَالْقَلْبَ، فَتَأْتِي إِلَى أَشْرَفِ الْأَشْيَاءِ وَأَفْضَلِهَا وَأَجَلِّهَا، فَتُخْرِجُهُ فِي صُورَةٍ مَذْمُومَةٍ - وَأَكْثَرُ الْخَلْقِ صِبْيَانُ الْعُقُولِ، أَطْفَالُ الْأَحْلَامِ، لَمْ يَصِلُوا إِلَى حَدِّ الْفِطَامِ الْأَوَّلِ عَنِ الْعَوَائِدِ وَالْمَأْلُوفَاتِ، فَضْلًا عَنِ الْبُلُوغِ الَّذِي يُمَيِّزُ بِهِ الْعَاقِلُ الْبَالِغُ بَيْنَ خَيْرِ الْخَيْرَيْنِ فَيُؤْثِرُهُ، وَشَرِّ الشَّرَّيْنِ فَيَجْتَنِبُهُ

One of the most astonishing things is that the insistent self can bewitch the mind and heart, taking the noblest and most exalted of things and presenting them in a reprehensible form. Most people are like children in terms of their intellect and dreams, having not yet reached the first stage of weaning from habits and customs, let alone the maturity that distinguishes the wise adult in choosing between the better of two goods and avoiding the worse of two evils.

- فَتُرِيهِ صُورَةَ تَجْرِيدِ التَّوْحِيدِ، الَّتِي هِيَ أَبْهَى مِنْ صُورَةِ الشَّمْسِ وَالْقَمَرِ، فِي صُورَةِ التَّنَقُّصِ الْمَذْمُومَةِ، وَهَضْمِ الْعُظَمَاءِ مَنَازِلَهُمْ، وَحَطِّهِمْ مِنْهَا إِلَى مَرْتَبَةِ الْعُبُودِيَّةِ الْمَحْضَةِ وَالْمَسْكَنَةِ وَالذُّلِّ وَالْفَقْرِ الْمَحْضِ الَّذِي لَا مَلَكَةَ لَهُمْ مَعَهُ وَلَا إِرَادَةَ وَلَا شَفَاعَةَ إِلَّا مِنْ بَعْدِ إِذْنِ اللَّهِ. فَتُرِيهِمُ النَّفْسُ السَّحَّارَةُ هَذَا الْقَدْرَ غَايَةَ تَنَقُّصِهِمْ وَهَضْمِهِمْ وَنُزُولِ أَقْدَارِهِمْ، وَعَدَمِ تَمَيُّزِهِمْ عَنِ الْمَسَاكِينِ الْفُقَرَاءِ. فَتَنْفِرُ نُفُوسُهُمْ مِنْ تَجْرِيدِ التَّوْحِيدِ أَشَدَّ النِّفَارِ وَيَقُولُونَ: {أَجَعَلَ الْآلِهَةَ إِلَهًا وَاحِدًا إِنَّ هَذَا لَشَيْءٌ عُجَابٌ}.

It shows them the pure concept of monotheism -- which is more radiant than the sun and moon -- in the form of deplorable diminishment, belittling the great ones, reducing them to a state of pure servitude, humiliation, and utter poverty, leaving them without any power, will, or intercession except by Allah's permission. The deceptive soul makes them see this state as the ultimate insult, and their souls repel the idea of pure monotheism with great aversion, saying, "**Has He made the deities into one God? Indeed, this is a strange thing.**"[138]

وَتُرِيهِمُ تَجْرِيدَ الْمُتَابَعَةِ لِلرَّسُولِ وَمَا جَاءَ بِهِ وَتَقْدِيمَهُ عَلَى آرَاءِ الرِّجَالِ فِي صُورَةٍ تَنَقُّصِ الْعُلَمَاءِ وَالرَّغْبَةِ عَنْ أَقْوَالِهِمْ وَمَا فَهِمُوهُ عَنِ اللَّهِ وَرَسُولِهِ، وَأَنَّ هَذَا إِسَاءَةُ أَدَبٍ عَلَيْهِمْ وَتَقَدُّمٌ بَيْنَ أَيْدِيهِمْ، وَهُوَ مُفْضٍ إِلَى إِسَاءَةِ الظَّنِّ بِهِمْ وَأَنَّهُمْ قَدْ فَاتَهُمْ الصَّوَابُ، وَكَيْفَ لَنَا قُوَّةٌ أَنْ نَرُدَّ عَلَيْهِمْ وَنَفُوزَ وَنَحْظَى بِالصَّوَابِ دُونَهُمْ؟ فَتَنْفِرُ مِنْ ذَلِكَ أَشَدَّ النِّفَارِ، وَتَجْعَلُ كَلَامَهُمْ هُوَ الْمُحْكَمُ الْوَاجِبُ الِاتِّبَاعِ، وَكَلَامَ الرَّسُولِ هُوَ الْمُتَشَابِهُ الَّذِي يُعْرَضُ عَلَى أَقْوَالِهِمْ، فَمَا وَافَقَهَا قَبِلْنَاهُ، وَمَا خَالَفَهَا رَدَدْنَاهُ أَوْ أَوَّلْنَاهُ أَوْ فَوَّضْنَاهُ. وَتُقَاسِمُ النَّفْسُ السَّحَّارَةُ بِاللَّهِ إِنْ أَرَدْنَا إِلَّا إِحْسَانًا وَتَوْفِيقًا! أُولَئِكَ الَّذِينَ يَعْلَمُ اللَّهُ مَا فِي قُلُوبِهِمْ.

The insistent self also shows them the idea of following the Prophet and prioritizing his teachings over human opinions as belittling the scholars and disregarding their statements and understanding of Allah and His Messenger. It makes them think this is disrespectful and that they should not question the scholars, implying that they may have missed the truth. They ask themselves how they can have the strength to argue with them and be right without them. This causes a great aversion, making the scholars' words the decisive criterion that must be followed, while the Prophet's words become ambiguous compared to their opinions. They accept what the scholars agree and reject or reinterpret what contradicts them. The deceptive soul swears by Allah that their intentions are only righteousness and success, but Allah knows what is in their hearts.

وَتُرِيهِ صُورَةَ الْإِخْلَاصِ فِي صُورَةٍ يَنْفُرُ مِنْهَا، وَهِيَ الْخُرُوجُ عَنْ حُكْمِ الْعَقْلِ الْمَعِيشِيِّ وَالْمُدَارَاةُ وَالْمُدَاهَنَةُ الَّتِي بِهَا انْدِرَاجُ حَالِ صَاحِبِهَا وَمَشْيُهُ بَيْنَ النَّاسِ. فَمَنْ أَخْلَصَ أَعْمَالَهُ وَلَمْ يَعْمَلْ لِأَحَدٍ شَيْئًا تَجَنَّبَهُمْ وَتَجَنَّبُوهُ، وَأَبْغَضَهُمْ وَأَبْغَضُوهُ،

138 Ṣād (38):5.

وَعَادَاهُمْ وَعَادَوْهُ، وَسَارَ عَلَى جَادَّةٍ وَهُمْ عَلَى جَادَّةٍ؛ فَيَنْفِرُ مِنْ ذَلِكَ أَشَدَّ النِّفَارِ. وَغَايَتُهُ أَنْ يُخْلِصَ فِي الْقَدْرِ الْيَسِيرِ مِنْ أَعْمَالِهِ الَّتِي لَا تَتَعَلَّقُ بِهِمْ، وَسَائِرُ أَعْمَالِهِ لِغَيْرِ اللَّهِ.

It shows them the image of sincerity in a form that repels them: abandoning reasoning, diplomacy and appeasement that allow a person to fit in and move among people. Whoever is sincere in their actions and does nothing for anyone else's sake will be avoided, hated and treated as an enemy by others, walking a different path from them. This causes the greatest aversion, and the person aims to be sincere only in the small portion of their actions that do not involve others, while the rest of their actions are for other than Allah.

وَتُرِيهِ صُورَةَ الصِّدْقِ مَعَ اللَّهِ وَجِهَادِ مَنْ خَرَجَ عَنْ دِينِهِ وَأَمْرِهِ فِي قَالَبِ الِانْتِصَابِ لِعَدَاوَةِ الْخَلْقِ وَأَذَاهُمْ وَحَرْبِهِمْ، وَأَنَّهُ يُعَرِّضُ نَفْسَهُ مِنَ الْبَلَاءِ لِمَا لَا يُطِيقُ، وَأَنَّهُ يَصِيرُ غَرَضًا لِسِهَامِ الطَّاعِنِينَ، وَأَمْثَالَ ذَلِكَ مِنَ الشُّبَهِ الَّتِي تُقِيمُهَا النَّفْسُ السَّحَّارَةُ وَالْخِيَالَاتُ الَّتِي تَخَيَّلُهَا. وَتُرِيهِ حَقِيقَةَ الْجِهَادِ فِي صُورَةٍ تُقْتَلُ فِيهَا النَّفْسُ وَتُنْكَحُ الْمَرْأَةُ، وَيَصِيرُ الْأَوْلَادُ يَتَامَى، وَيُقَسَّمُ الْمَالُ.

It shows them the image of being truthful with Allah and fighting those who have strayed from His religion, depicting it as standing up to create hostility, harming others and waging war. They think they are exposing themselves to trials they cannot bear and will become a target for the slanderers and the like due to the illusions created by the deceptive soul. It shows them the reality of jihad in a form where lives are lost, women are widowed, children become orphans and wealth is divided.

وَتُرِيهِ حَقِيقَةَ الزَّكَاةِ وَالصَّدَقَةِ فِي صُورَةِ مُفَارَقَةِ الْمَالِ وَنَقْصِهِ وَخُلُوِّ الْيَدِ مِنْهُ، وَاحْتِيَاجِهِ إِلَى النَّاسِ، وَمُسَاوَاتِهِ لِلْفَقِيرِ وَعَوْدِهِ بِمَنْزِلَتِهِ.

It presents the reality of zakat and charity as parting with wealth, reducing it, leaving one's hand empty, becoming needy, and being on par with the poor, returning to their status.

وَتُرِيهِ حَقِيقَةَ إِثْبَاتِ صِفَاتِ الْكَمَالِ لِلَّهِ فِي صُورَةِ التَّشْبِيهِ وَالتَّمْثِيلِ، فَيَنْفِرُ مِنَ التَّصْدِيقِ بِهَا وَيُنَفِّرُ غَيْرَهُ. وَتُرِيهِ حَقِيقَةَ التَّعْطِيلِ وَالْإِلْحَادِ فِيهَا فِي صُورَةِ التَّنْزِيهِ وَالتَّعْظِيمِ.

It shows them the reality of attributing the qualities of perfection to Allah in the form of anthropomorphism and similitude, making them repel the idea of affirming these qualities and repelling others as well. It presents the reality of negating and disbelieving in these qualities through exaltation and magnification.

وَأَعْجَبُ مِنْ ذَلِكَ أَنَّهَا تُضَاهِي مَا يُحِبُّهُ اللَّهُ وَرَسُولُهُ مِنَ الصِّفَاتِ وَالْأَخْلَاقِ وَالْأَفْعَالِ بِمَا يُبْغِضُهُ مِنْهَا، وَتُلَبِّسُ عَلَى الْعَبْدِ أَحَدَ الْأَمْرَيْنِ بِالْآخَرِ. وَلَا يُخَلِّصُ هَذَا مِنْ هَذَا إِلَّا أَرْبَابُ الْبَصَائِرِ، فَإِنَّ الْأَفْعَالَ تَصْدُرُ عَنِ الْإِرَادَاتِ وَتَظْهَرُ عَلَى الْأَرْكَانِ مِنَ النَّفْسَيْنِ: الْأَمَّارَةِ وَالْمُطْمَئِنَّةِ، فَيَتَبَايَنُ الْفِعْلَانِ فِي الْبَاطِنِ، وَيَشْتَبِهَانِ فِي الظَّاهِرِ.

Even more astonishing is that the deceptive soul equates what Allah and His Messenger love regarding attributes, morals, and actions with what they dislike. It confuses the servant by mixing one matter with the other. Only those with true insight can differentiate between them, for actions stem from intentions and manifest in two aspects of the soul: the commanding and the tranquil. Thus, the actions differ internally but may appear similar externally.

وَلِذَلِكَ أَمْثِلَةٌ كَثِيرَةٌ. مِنْهَا: الْمُدَارَاةُ وَالْمُدَاهَنَةُ. فَالْأَوَّلُ مِنَ الْمُطْمَئِنَّةِ، وَالثَّانِي مِنَ الْأَمَّارَةِ.

And for that, there are many examples. Among them are flattery and deceit. The former stems from reassurance, while the latter stems from deception.[139]

وَخُشُوعُ الْإِيمَانِ وَخُشُوعُ النِّفَاقِ، وَشَرَفُ النَّفْسِ وَالتِّيهِ، وَالْحَمِيَّةُ وَالْجَفَاءُ، وَالتَّوَاضُعُ وَالْمُهَانَةُ، وَالْقُوَّةُ فِي أَمْرِ اللَّهِ وَالْعُلُوُّ فِي الْأَرْضِ، وَالْحَمِيَّةُ لِلَّهِ وَالْغَضَبُ لَهُ وَالْحَمِيَّةُ لِلنَّفْسِ وَالْغَضَبُ لَهَا، وَالْجُودُ وَالسَّرَفُ، وَالْمَهَابَةُ وَالْكِبْرُ، وَالصِّيَانَةُ وَالتَّكَبُّرُ، وَالشُّجَاعَةُ وَالْجُرَاءَةُ، وَالْحَزْمُ وَالْجُبْنُ، وَالِاقْتِصَادُ وَالشُّحُّ، وَالِاحْتِرَازُ وَسُوءُ الظَّنِّ، وَالْفِرَاسَةُ وَالظَّنُّ، وَالنَّصِيحَةُ وَالْغِيبَةُ، وَالْهَدِيَّةُ وَالرِّشْوَةُ، وَالصَّبْرُ وَالْقَسْوَةُ، وَالْعَفْوُ وَالذُّلُّ، وَسَلَامَةُ الْقَلْبِ وَالْبَلَه وَالْغَفْلَةُ، وَالثِّقَةُ وَالْغِرَّةُ، وَالرَّجَاءُ وَالتَّمَنِّي، وَالتَّحَدُّثُ بِنِعْمَةِ اللَّهِ وَالْفَخْرُ بِهَا، وَفَرَحُ الْقَلْبِ وَفَرَحُ النَّفْسِ، وَرِقَّةُ الْقَلْبِ وَالْجَزَعُ، وَالْمَوْجِدَةُ وَالْحِقْدُ، وَالْمُنَافَسَةُ وَالْحَسَدُ، وَحُبُّ الرِّيَاسَةِ وَحُبُّ الْإِمَامَةِ وَالدَّعْوَةُ إِلَى اللَّهِ، وَالْحُبُّ لِلَّهِ وَالْحُبُّ مَعَ اللَّهِ، وَالتَّوَكُّلُ وَالْعَجْزُ، وَالِاحْتِيَاطُ وَالْوَسْوَسَةُ، وَإِلْهَامُ الْمَلَكِ وَإِلْهَامُ الشَّيْطَانِ، وَالْأَنَاةُ وَالتَّسْوِيفُ، وَالِاقْتِصَادُ وَالتَّقْصِيرُ، وَالِاجْتِهَادُ وَالْغُلُوُّ، وَالنَّصِيحَةُ وَالتَّأْنِيبُ، وَالْمُبَادَرَةُ وَالْعَجَلَةُ، وَالْإِخْبَارُ بِالْحَالِ عِنْدَ الْحَاجَةِ وَالشَّكْوَى.

(The same is the case with the difference between): faith-based humility and disingenuous humility; self-dignity and vanity; protectiveness and coldness; humility and humiliation; strength for Allah's religion and arrogance on Earth; protectiveness (*al ghayrah*) and anger for Allah and protectiveness and anger for the sake of one's self; generosity and wastefulness; awe and pride; being reserved and arrogance; bravery and reckless audacity; firmness and cowardice; frugality and stinginess; cautiousness and suspicion; insight (*firāsah*: being able to read people) and conjecture; advising and backbiting; gifts and bribery; patience and harshness; pardoning and degradation; clean heartedness and naivety and heedlessness; trust and naivety; hopefulness and wishful thinking; speaking of Allah's blessings

---

[139] The following lengthy list of examples are individually explained in detail by Ibn al Qayyim at the end of *Kitāb al-Rūḥ*, in a beautiful section called *al Fūrūq*.

and boasting about them; the joy of the heart and the joy of the self; tender-heartedness and panicking; feeling upset and grudge holding; competitiveness and envy; the love for leadership and inviting to Allah; loving for Allah and loving along with Allah (i.e., polytheistic love); reliance (*al-tawakkul*) and helplessness; taking precaution and being prone to whisperings; the inspiration of the angelic realm and the inspiration of *Shayṭān;* being deliberate and procrastination; being moderate and falling short; striving diligently and extremism; sincere advice and insulting reproach; initiative and hastiness; telling another about one's situation when necessary and complaining.

فَالشَّيْءُ الْوَاحِدُ تَكُونُ صُورَتُهُ وَاحِدَةً، وَهُوَ مُنْقَسِمٌ إِلَى مَحْمُودٍ وَمَذْمُومٍ، كَالْفَرَحِ وَالْحُزْنِ وَالْأَسَفِ وَالْغَضَبِ وَالْغَيْرَةِ وَالْخُيَلَاءِ وَالطَّمَعِ وَالتَّجَمُّلِ وَالْخُشُوعِ وَالْحَسَدِ وَالْغِبْطَةِ وَالْجَرَاءَةِ وَالتَّجَسُّسِ وَالْحِرْصِ وَالتَّنَافُسِ وَإِظْهَارِ النِّعْمَةِ وَالْحَلِفِ وَالْمَسْكَنَةِ وَالصَّمْتِ وَالزُّهْدِ وَالْوَرَعِ وَالتَّخَلِّي وَالْعُزْلَةِ وَالْأَنَفَةِ وَالْحَمِيَّةِ وَالْغِيبَةِ.

For each thing, its image is singular. It is divided into what is praiseworthy and what is blameworthy, such as joy and sadness, regret and anger, jealousy and pompousness, greed and adornment, humility and envy, gloating and audacity, spying and eagerness, displaying blessings and swearing, tranquility and silence, asceticism and piety, detachment and isolation, self-sufficiency and zeal, backbiting and gossip, etc.

وَفِي الْحَدِيثِ: «إِنَّ مِنَ الْغَيْرَةِ مَا يُحِبُّهَا اللَّهُ، وَمِنْهَا مَا يَكْرَهُهُ. فَالْغَيْرَةُ الَّتِي يُحِبُّهَا: الْغَيْرَةُ فِي رِيبَةٍ. وَالَّتِي يَكْرَهُهَا: الْغَيْرَةُ فِي غَيْرِ رِيبَةٍ. وَإِنَّ مِنَ الْخُيَلَاءِ مَا يُحِبُّهُ اللَّهُ، وَمِنْهَا مَا يَكْرَهُهُ. فَالَّتِي يُحِبُّ: الْخُيَلَاءُ فِي الْحَرْبِ».

The hadith is narrated: "Indeed, there is jealousy that Allah loves, and there is jealousy that He dislikes. The jealousy that He loves is jealousy in matters of doubt, while the jealousy that He dislikes is jealousy without any basis. And indeed, there is pride that Allah loves, and there is pride that He dislikes. The one that He loves is pride in battle."

وَفِي الصَّحِيحِ أَيْضًا: «لَا حَسَدَ إِلَّا فِي اثْنَتَيْنِ: رَجُلٌ آتَاهُ اللَّهُ مَالًا فَسَلَّطَهُ عَلَى هَلَكَتِهِ فِي الْحَقِّ، وَرَجُلٌ آتَاهُ الْحِكْمَةَ، فَهُوَ يَقْضِي بِهَا وَيُعَلِّمُهَا».

In another authentic narration: "There is no envy except in two cases: a man whom Allah has given wealth and he uses it in the path of righteousness, and a man whom Allah has given wisdom and he judges and teaches by it."

وَفِي الصَّحِيحِ أَيْضًا: «إِنَّ اللَّهَ رَفِيقٌ يُحِبُّ الرِّفْقَ، وَيُعْطِي عَلَى الرِّفْقِ مَا لَا يُعْطِي عَلَى الْعُنْفِ».

Also, in the authentic narrations: "Indeed, Allah is gentle, and He loves gentleness. He grants through gentleness what He does not grant through harshness."

وَفِيهِ أَيْضًا: «مَنْ أُعْطِيَ حَظَّهُ مِنَ الرِّفْقِ فَقَدْ أُعْطِيَ حَظَّهُ مِنَ الْخَيْرِ»

And it is also mentioned: "Whoever is given a portion of gentleness has been given a portion of good."

فَالرِّفْقُ شَيْءٌ، وَالتَّوَانِي وَالْكَسَلُ شَيْءٌ. فَإِنَّ الْمُتَوَانِيَ يَتَثَاقَلُ عَنْ مَصْلَحَتِهِ بَعْدَ إِمْكَانِهَا، يَتَقَاعَدُ عَنْهَا؛ وَالرَّفِيقُ يَتَلَطَّفُ فِي تَحْصِيلِهَا بِحَسَبِ الْإِمْكَانِ مَعَ الْمُطَاوَلَةِ.

So, gentleness is something praiseworthy, while laziness and sloth are blameworthy. The lazy one neglects their interests despite having the capability, and they withdraw from pursuing them. On the other hand, the one who possesses gentleness is kind and diligent in attaining their interests according to their capacity and perseverance.

وَكَذَلِكَ الْمُدَارَاةُ صِفَةُ مَدْحٍ، وَالْمُدَاهَنَةُ صِفَةُ ذَمٍّ. وَالْفَرْقُ بَيْنَهُمَا: أَنَّ الْمُدَارِي يَتَلَطَّفُ بِصَاحِبِهِ حَتَّى يَسْتَخْرِجَ مِنْهُ الْحَقَّ أَوْ يَرُدَّهُ عَنِ الْبَاطِلِ، وَالْمُدَاهِنُ

يَتَلَطَّفُ بِهِ لِيُقِرَّهُ عَلَى بَاطِلِهِ وَيَتْرُكَهُ عَلَى هَوَاهُ. فَالْمُدَارَاةُ لِأَهْلِ الْإِيمَانِ، وَالْمُدَاهَنَةُ لِأَهْلِ النِّفَاقِ.

Likewise, diplomacy is a praiseworthy quality, while flattery is a blameworthy attribute. The difference between them is that the one who practices moderation is gentle with their companion to extract the truth from them or divert them from falsehood. At the same time, the flatterer is gentle with them to affirm their falsehood and leave them to their desires. Moderation is for the people of faith, while flattery is for the hypocrites.

وَقَدْ ضُرِبَ لِذَلِكَ مَثَلٌ مُطَابِقٌ، وَهُوَ حَالُ رَجُلٍ بِهِ قَرْحَةٌ قَدْ آلَمَتْهُ، فَجَاءَهُ الطَّبِيبُ الْمُدَارِيُّ الرَّفِيقُ، فَتَعَرَّفَ حَالَهَا، ثُمَّ أَخَذَ فِي تَلْيِينِهَا حَتَّى إِذَا نَضِجَتْ أَخَذَ فِي بَطِّهَا بِرِفْقٍ وَسُهُولَةٍ حَتَّى أَخْرَجَ مَا فِيهَا. ثُمَّ وَضَعَ عَلَى مَكَانِهَا مِنَ الدَّوَاءِ وَالْمَرْهَمِ مَا يَمْنَعُ فَسَادَهَا وَيَقْطَعُ مَادَّتَهَا، ثُمَّ تَابَعَ عَلَيْهَا بِالْمَرَاهِمِ الَّتِي تُنْبِتُ اللَّحْمَ، ثُمَّ يَذُرُّ عَلَيْهَا بَعْدَ نَبَاتِ اللَّحْمِ مَا يُنْشِفُ رُطُوبَتَهَا، ثُمَّ يَشُدُّ عَلَيْهَا الرِّبَاطَ، وَلَمْ يَزَلْ يَتَابِعُ ذَلِكَ حَتَّى صَلَحَتْ.

An appropriate analogy for this is that of a person who has a painful sore. The compassionate and gentle doctor comes to him, examines his condition, and softens the sore until it matures. Then, with gentleness and ease, the doctor carefully drains its contents. Afterward, he applies medication and ointment to prevent infection and promote healing. He continues to apply ointments that stimulate tissue growth and then applies a drying agent once the tissue has grown. Finally, he secures it with a bandage and continues monitoring the progress until it is completely healed.

وَالْمُدَاهِنُ قَالَ لِصَاحِبِهَا: لَا بَأْسَ عَلَيْكَ مِنْهَا، وَهَذِهِ لَا شَيْءٌ، فَاسْتُرْهَا عَنِ الْعُيُونِ بِخِرْقَةٍ، ثُمَّ أَلْهُ عَنْهَا. فَلَمْ تَزَلْ مَادَّتُهَا تَقْوَى وَتَسْتَحْكِمُ حَتَّى عَظُمَ فَسَادُهَا.

On the other hand, the flatterer tells the person, "There is nothing wrong with it, it's nothing to worry about," and he covers it with a cloth to conceal it from sight, and he leaves it as it is. Consequently, the sore continues to worsen, and its corruption intensifies.

**وَهَـذَا الْمَثَلُ أَيْضًا مُطَابِقٌ كُلَّ الْمُطَابَقَةِ لِحَالِ النَّفْسِ الْأَمَّارَةِ مَعَ الْمُطْمَئِنَّةِ فَتَأَمَّلْهُ.**

And this analogy also perfectly applies to the state of the soul between the insistent self (the ego) and the reassured self (the soul at peace, )so reflect upon it.

فَإِذَا كَانَتْ هَذِهِ حَالَ قَرْحَةٍ بِقَدْرِ الْحِمْصَةِ، فَكَيْفَ بِسَقَمٍ هَاجَ مِنْ نَفْسٍ أَمَّارَةٍ بِالسُّوءِ، هِيَ مَعْدَنُ الشَّهَوَاتِ وَمَأْوَى كُلِّ فِسْقٍ وَقَدْ قَارَنَهَا شَيْطَانٌ فِي غَايَةِ الْمَكْرِ وَالْخِدَاعِ، يَعِدُهَا وَيُمَنِّيهَا، وَيُسَحِّرُهَا بِجَمِيعِ أَنْوَاعِ السِّحْرِ حَتَّى يُخَيِّلَ إِلَيْهَا النَّافِعَ ضَارًّا، وَالضَّارَّ نَافِعًا، وَالْحَسَنَ قَبِيحًا، وَالْقَبِيحَ جَمِيلًا؟

If this is the state of a sore as small as a chickpea, how about a serious illness that originates from an insistent self inclined towards evil, which is the source of desires and the haven of all wickedness and corruption? Satan has compared it with the utmost cunning and deception, promising it and making it desirable, enchanting it with various forms of magic to make what is beneficial appear harmful and what is harmful appear beneficial, what is beautiful appear ugly, and what is ugly appear beautiful.

وَهَذَا لِعَمْرِو اللَّهِ مِنْ أَعْظَمِ أَنْوَاعِ السِّحْرِ! وَلِهَذَا يَقُولُ سُبْحَانَهُ: {فَأَنَّى تُسْحَرُونَ}.

Indeed, this is one of the greatest forms of magic that Satan employs. Hence, Allah says: "**How can you then be deluded**?"[140]

وَالَّذِي نَسَبُوا إِلَيْهِ الرُّسُلَ مِنْ كَوْنِهِمْ مَسْحُورِينَ هُوَ الَّذِي أَصَابَهُمْ بِعَيْنِهِ، وَهُمْ أَهْلُهُ، لَا رُسُلَ اللَّهِ صَلَوَاتُ اللَّهِ وَسَلَامُهُ عَلَيْهِمْ، كَمَا أَنَّهُمْ نَسَبُوهُمْ إِلَى الضَّلَالِ

140 Al Mu'minūn (23):89.

وَالْفَسَادِ فِي الْأَرْضِ وَالْجُنُونِ وَالسَّفَهِ. وَمَا اسْتَعَاذَتْ الْأَنْبِيَاءُ وَالرُّسُلُ وَأَمَرُوا الْأُمَمَ بِالِاسْتِعَاذَةِ مِنْ شَرِّ النَّفْسِ الْأَمَّارَةِ وَصَاحِبِهَا وَقَرِينِهَا الشَّيْطَانِ إِلَّا لِأَنَّهَا أَصْلُ كُلِّ شَرٍّ وَقَاعِدَتُهُ وَمَنْبَعُهُ، وَهُمَا مُتَسَاعِدَانِ عَلَيْهِ مُتَعَاوِنَانِ.

The attribution of being bewitched that they attributed to the Messengers is the affliction that affected their people, not the messengers of Allah. May Allah's blessings and peace be upon them. Likewise, they attributed misguidance, corruption on Earth, madness, and foolishness to them. The Prophets and Messengers sought refuge in Allah. They commanded their nations to seek refuge from the evil of the insistent self and its companion and associate, *Shayṭān*, because they are the root of all evil, its foundation, and its source. Both of them collaborate and assist each other in perpetrating evil.

رَضِيعَيْ لِبَانٍ ثَدِيَ أُمٍّ تَقَاسَمَا ... بِأَسْحَمَ دَاجٍ عَوَضُ لَا نَتَفَرَّقُ

A breastfeeding baby's suckling the teat of its mother is an
example of their unity; they do not separate.

قَالَ تَعَالَى: {**فَإِذَا قَرَأْتَ الْقُرْآنَ فَاسْتَعِذْ بِاللَّهِ مِنَ الشَّيْطَانِ الرَّجِيمِ**}. وَقَالَ: {**وَإِمَّا يَنْزَغَنَّكَ مِنَ الشَّيْطَانِ نَزْغٌ فَاسْتَعِذْ بِاللَّهِ إِنَّهُ سَمِيعٌ عَلِيمٌ**} وَقَالَ: {وَقُلْ رَبِّ أَعُوذُ بِكَ مِنْ هَمَزَاتِ الشَّيَاطِينِ (97) وَأَعُوذُ بِكَ رَبِّ أَنْ يَحْضُرُونِ} [الْمُؤْمِنُونَ: 97 - 98].

Allah says: "**So when you recite the Qur'an, [first] seek refuge in Allah from Satan, the expelled [from His mercy].**"[141] And He says: "**And if an evil suggestion comes to you from Satan, then seek refuge in Allah. Indeed, He is Hearing and Knowing.**"[142] And He says: "**And say, 'My Lord, I seek refuge in You from the incitements of the devils, and I**

[141] Al-Naḥl (16): 98.

[142] Al 'Arāf (7): 200.

**seek refuge in You, my Lord, lest they be present with me.'"**[143]

وَقَالَ تَعَالَى: {**قُلْ أَعُوذُ بِرَبِّ الْفَلَقِ (1) مِنْ شَرِّ مَا خَلَقَ (2) وَمِنْ شَرِّ غَاسِقٍ إِذَا وَقَبَ (3) وَمِنْ شَرِّ النَّفَّاثَاتِ فِي الْعُقَدِ (4) وَمِنْ شَرِّ حَاسِدٍ إِذَا حَسَدَ**} فَهَذِهِ اسْتِعَاذَةٌ مِنْ شَرِّ النَّفْسِ.

He also says: "**Say, 'I seek refuge in the Lord of daybreak, from the evil of that which He created, and from the evil of darkness when it settles, and from the evil of the blowers in knots, and from the evil of an envier when he envies.'"** This is seeking refuge from the evil of the self.

وَقَالَ: {**قُلْ أَعُوذُ بِرَبِّ النَّاسِ (1) مَلِكِ النَّاسِ (2) إِلَهِ النَّاسِ (3) مِنْ شَرِّ الْوَسْوَاسِ الْخَنَّاسِ (4) الَّذِي يُوَسْوِسُ فِي صُدُورِ النَّاسِ (5) مِنَ الْجِنَّةِ وَالنَّاسِ**}. فَهَذَا اسْتِعَاذَةٌ مِنْ شَرِّ قَرِينِهَا وَصَاحِبِهَا، وَبِئْسَ الْقَرِينُ وَالصَّاحِبُ.

And He says: "**Say, 'I seek refuge in the Lord of mankind, the Sovereign of mankind, the God of mankind, from the evil of the retreating whisperer, who whispers [evil] into the breasts of mankind, from among the jinn and mankind.'"** This is seeking refuge from the evil of its companion and associate. Indeed, what a terrible companion and associate they are!

فَأَمَرَ سُبْحَانَهُ نَبِيَّهُ وَأَتْبَاعَهُ بِالاسْتِعَاذَةِ بِرُبُوبِيَّتِهِ التَّامَّةِ الْكَامِلَةِ مِنْ هَذَيْنِ الْخَلْقَيْنِ الْعَظِيمِ شَأْنُهُمَا فِي الشَّرِّ وَالْفَسَادِ.

So, Allah has commanded His Prophet and his followers to seek refuge in His perfect lordship from these two great adversaries due to their evil and corruption.

[143] Al Mu'minūn (23):97-98.

**وَالْقَلْبُ بَيْنَ هَذَيْنِ الْعَدُوَّيْنِ،** لَا يَزَالُ شَرُّهُمَا يَطْرُقُهُ وَيَنْتَابُهُ. وَأَوَّلُ مَا يَدِبُّ فِيهِ السَقَمُ مِنَ النَّفْسِ الْأَمَّارَةِ مِنَ الشَّهْوَةِ وَمَا يَتْبَعُهَا مِنَ الْحُبِّ وَالْحِرْصِ وَالطَّلَبِ وَالْغَضَبِ، وَمَا يَتْبَعُهُ مِنَ الْكِبْرِ وَالْحَسَدِ وَالظُّلْمِ وَالتَّسَلُّطِ.

The heart is between these two enemies, and their evil continues to assail and attack it. The first thing that affects it is the illness that arises from the insistent self, which includes desires and all that follow, such as love, greed, seeking, anger, arrogance, envy, injustice, and domination.

فَيَعْلَمُ الطَّبِيبُ الْغَاشُّ الْخَائِنُ بِمَرَضِهِ، فَيَعُودُهُ، وَيَصِفُ لَهُ أَنْوَاعَ السُّمُومِ وَالْمُؤْذِيَّاتِ، وَيُخَيِّلُ إِلَيْهِ بِسِحْرِهِ أَنَّ شِفَاءَهُ فِيهَا.

The cunning and treacherous physician is aware of his illness. He visits him and prescribes different toxins and harmful substances, making the patient believe through his enchantment that his healing lies in them.

وَيَتَّفِقَ ضَعْفُ الْقَلْبِ بِالْمَرَضِ، وَقُوَّةُ النَّفْسِ الْأَمَّارَةِ وَالشَّيْطَانِ وَتَتَابُعُ أَمْدَادِهِمَا، وَأَنَّهُ نَقْدٌ حَاضِرٌ وَلَذَّةٌ عَاجِلَةٌ، وَالدَّاعِي إِلَيْهِ يَدْعُو مِنْ كُلِّ نَاحِيَةٍ، وَالْهَوَى يُنَفِّذُ، وَالشُّبْهَةُ تُهَوِّنُ، وَالتَّأَسِّي بِالْأَكْثَرِ، وَالتَّشَبُّهُ بِهِمْ، وَالرِّضَا بِأَنْ يَصِيبَهُ مَا أَصَابَهُمْ.

The weakened state of the heart, arising from its illness, aligns with the powerful influence of the inciting soul and the devil. They continuously reinforce each other, urging one to seek immediate, material gains and instant gratification. The call from within invites that from all directions. Desires execute this, and doubts minimize its seriousness. There is also the habit of emulating and imitating the majority and accepting to befall you whatever befalls them.

فَكَيْفَ يَسْتَجِيبُ مَعَ هَذِهِ الْقَوَاطِعِ وَأَضْعَافِهَا لِدَاعِي الْإِيمَانِ وَمُنَادِي الْجَنَّةِ إِلَّا مَنْ أَمَدَّهُ اللَّهُ بِأَمْدَادِ التَّوْفِيقِ، وَأَيَّدَهُ بِرَحْمَتِهِ، وَتَوَلَّى حِفْظَهُ وَحِمَايَتِهِ، وَفَتَحَ

بَصِيرَةَ قَلْبِهِ، فَرَأَى سُرْعَةَ انْقِطَاعِ الدُّنْيَا وَزَوَالِهَا وَتَقَلُّبَهَا بِأَهْلِهَا، وَفِعْلَهَا بِهِمْ، وَأَنَّهَا فِي الْحَيَاةِ الدَّائِمَةِ الْأَبَدِيَّةِ كَغَمْسِ إِصْبَعٍ فِي الْبَحْرِ بِالنِّسْبَةِ إِلَيْهِ.

Faced with these obstacles and many more, how can one respond to the caller of faith and the invitation to Paradise unless he is one whom Allah guides to success, supports through His mercy, and grants His guardianship and protection? He opens the insight of their heart so they perceive the rapid transience of worldly life, its constant changes with its inhabitants and how it treats them. They realize that compared to eternal life, it is like dipping a finger into the ocean."

**Notes:**

**Notes:**

**Notes:**

Printed in Great Britain
by Amazon

28490582R00126